TIGER WALLAH

Sudha G Pillarisetti

ISBN-13: 9798353083719
ISBN-10:

Cover design by: Sudha G Pillarisetti
Library of Congress Control Number: 2018675309
Printed in the United States of America

*This manuscript is dedicated to
My deceased parents, dad Venu and mom Kamala.*

My grandmother and Chinnamma who brought me up.

Michael D. Wynne for help and support

To all, A-Z I acknowledge for inspiration.

And all those long gone characters of the past.

India, 1960s the good the bad and the ugly seen through the eyes and lives of four youth.

CONTENTS

PREFACE

I lived and went to school and college in the town in which this story of the four – Anand, Vidya, Zahina and Ambika lived and grew up in, is based. After a dozen years of stay in USA, I discovered upon my visit that India changed remarkably and the people I knew, and their personalities have disappeared. This is my attempt at documenting some of those. I suspect the change was also in me having lived in a foreign land and was looking at the current landscape through colored lenses.

At their first meeting rich Anand resents poor Vidya. A series of events strengthen their bonds and they become fast friends. Anand gives Vidya the game wining cricket ball as appreciation of his role in their victory. In college Vidya meets Zahina a Muslim, their friendship leads to love and commitment. They plan their future together, he to become a doctor and she a nurse. Anand moves to USA for specialization. Zahina stays back to support her family.

Vidya gives up on further education after college and becomes a bank teller to support his ailing mom. In the bank he meets Ambika. Ambika's dad a very rich businessman suspects Vidya is wooing his daughter because of her wealth.

The struggles of these four to attain their goals, their experiences, the people they encounter and societal influences on their lives illustrates the good, the bad and the ugly of life in India and elsewhere.

I planned this story, decided on the characters and outcomes to the nth degree. While writing, uninvited characters appeared and ran helter-skelter on my envisioned landscape. The intended characters took a life of their own and changed my planned narration with their voices. I became a transcriber of their actions.

PART ONE - ANAND

CHAPTER 1

Present -The Beginning

The forest road to my village in Southern India was progressively getting narrower and bumpier; darkness and fog were creeping in. Had I known what was about to unfold and turned back, I would have lost my opportunity for redemption.

#

It was mid-afternoon when my driver and I started from my hometown to our village. The first fifty kilometers were on a well-paved multilane highway. The highway ended abruptly, and we turned onto narrowing roads with potholes. About another fifty kilometers later, we were on an uneven dirt track with potholes. The travel was slow, the jeep groaning and squeaking, while the driver mumbled and cursed.

"What happened to the paved road?" I asked.

"It was dug up to make way for a four-lane highway. The diversion is through the forest. We should be there by sunset."

The slow trek came to a standstill. A fallen tree blocked the road. There were about ten men with axes, saws, and ropes working to remove it, branch by branch. The driver turned off the engine, lit a cigarette, and started hauling the cut branches out of the way.

The crew cleared the road in an hour, and the sweaty driver returned. "Only 20 more kilometers Sahib, we will be at your place for dinner."

It was pitch black and the jeep's dim headlights were losing the battle against darkness. One moment we were crawling along, and the next there was a bright light and a violent lurch. The vehicle teetered and almost rolled over. The force of the explosion threw me out of the jeep. I felt my head hit something hard and everything went dark.

I do not know how much later, a bright light assaulted my eye. The voices of a man and a woman broke through my semiconsciousness. I shut my eyes tightly and mumbled. A hand forced one of my eyelids open. The light came closer. The same happened with the other eye.

"His pupils are reacting to light." A voice in the distance.

The words and voice soothed my troubled soul. I felt I was in safe hands.

USA

Two weeks earlier, my sister Durga called while I was busy working in the hospital pathology department. I told her I will call that evening. It was 9PM when I got home, showered, poured a single malt Scotch, and stretched out on the recliner to channel surf when I remembered my promise to call Durga. I called Durga next.

"Hello Durga, you called me at a busy time in my hospital and I could not return the call sooner. How did you track me down?"

"Mom, gave me your number and the message for you. Did you get your ticket? When are you landing in India? What is your flight number? This can't wait. You must handle this immediately."

Nothing had changed in a dozen years. She was still the same intense, take no nonsense from anybody she was during college, an honor's student pursuing her masters in abstract math. One of her class fellows who later moved to New York, said, "Your sister is one of a kind even her professors feared her."

Durga, aptly named after a Hindu goddess who rides a tiger and slays demons, is self-assured and fearless. Unlike her, I am laid back and have no reason to be intense. I felt an inner sense of dread; this would shatter my calm and controlled life. I mumbled something about work, leave, my expired visa to explain that this may not happen soon.

"Anand, act grown up and be the man of the house and stop mumbling. I expect you here by the end of the week. Let me know when and where you will land. I will arrange a car to take you to Mom. She will fill you on the details. And do not come to see me. I have not forgotten or forgiven you, Anand, and I never will."

"But..."

Durga hung up.

#

Our ancestral lands were in a village about 100KM from my hometown in India. Our two story home with a terrace on the top floor was in the officers' colony in the town. My mom was a retired surgical nurse supervisor who ruled over her OR and all that worked in it. She had a strong personality. My dad, a major in the Indian army assigned to the UN Peacekeeping Force, was mostly overseas.

I called my mom that evening.

"We have a big problem," she said.

"Is your health okay?"

"I am fine," she reassured me. "There is agitation in our village and the surrounding areas. Our farmworkers are demanding ownership rights and a group against timber harvesting moved into the forest land we own. I am too old to travel. You must come here and make our farm workers see reason. Then we will discuss how to proceed."

What? I have not been to India or the village in twelve years. What do I know about how to deal with this? I never took an interest in the farm or its management.

Mom noticed my hesitation and said, "You are the man of the house. Your sister is busy with her children and her job. It is your duty and responsibility to handle such affairs."

I knew I couldn't get out of this.

#

A week later, I was in business class on a flight to Delhi, then to Hyderabad, and a five-hour drive to my hometown. Altogether, over 40 hours of travel with a time difference of eleven hours. *My circadian clock would be out of sync when I reached my hometown. But for now, enjoy the business class travel.* The Scotch was smooth, and I felt relaxed after the hectic arrangements for international travel and handing over my duties to associates. Halfway through my drink, as I relaxed, thoughts of my boyhood came rushing back.

CHAPTER 2

Past – The Boy Who Came For Lunch

The summer of 1960 was a hot one in my hometown. School was closed, and I was relaxing in my room reading 'The Man Eaters of Kumaon'.

"Your lunch is ready. Come down."

I ate alone after Durga moved to college, but today there were two place settings.

"Who is coming for lunch, Amma?"

"I came across this lady with a son your age. I asked them to join us for lunch. His mom is working today and asked if he could come alone."

"I don't like to meet strangers."

"Hush! He is here. Behave."

The boy who walked in was thin, broad shouldered, and tall. He had a fair complexion and bright eyes, but he appeared nervous and only gave me a side glance with a hint of a smile.

"Vidya, this is Anand, my son."

I nodded from my seat at the table. He sat opposite me as Mom served food. To my chagrin, there was neither chicken nor fish curry, just dal and potato fry. I looked at my mom curiously, but she just shook her head. After eating, Vidya washed his hands and whispered to my mom.

"Sit for just a minute with Anand and get acquainted. I will be back."

We sat without saying a word.

"Did you both talk?" Mom said as she walked in with containers of food.

We nodded as she handed the containers to Vidya. He bowed and left.

"Why no meat or fish today?"

"Vidya comes from a strict vegetarian family."

"He could have just eaten the other dishes!"

"Son, we do not offend our guests' beliefs or sensibilities. I wanted Vidya to feel comfortable during his visit."

"What did he say to you, and why did you give him food?"

"Not now." My attitude displeased Mom.

The encounter with Vidya left me in a foul mood. I did not want him as my friend. *Why do I have to give up favorite meat dishes? Why is my mom so considerate toward him? Is he pretending to be friendly toward me to seek attention from my mom?*

#

One evening, about a week later, the doorbell rang. I opened the gate and saw Vidya with a nervous look on his face.

"Hi, is your mom home? I have a message for her."

I asked him to step in and went in to call mom, as a dark shape blurred by. Oh no! Pluto, my German Shepherd, was out of its pen. Scared of what it would do to Vidya, I ran back to the porch. Vidya was smiling and Pluto was wagging its tail and sniffing his hand. Pluto never reacted gently to strangers.

Vidya smiled. "Dogs attack those who are afraid. I am not."

"Hello Vidya! How are you and your mom?" Amma came in.

Vidya bowed and folded his hands in Namaste and said, "We are doing well. Thank you. My mom asked if..." and his voice dropped.

Amma turned around and went inside, leaving us both with Pluto.

"Do you play cricket?" I was always looking to bolster my team.

"No, I don't play any games. "

"What do you do during these vacations?"

"Chores around the house and work in a shop."

"What kind of work do you do in the shop?"

"I sweep the floor and help the owner unload and put away merchandise."

"How much does he pay you?"

"Anand, stop. It is not polite." Mom walked in with a bulging sac. Vidya bowed his said namaste, took the sac and walked out.

During these visits Vidya and I discovered that when school starts, he and I would be in the same class, I planned to recruit Vidya to my cricket team, The Gunners.

#

The German Shepherd was barking signaling the postman's arrival. He handed me the mail and a note. "Padma, the lady on my route, gave this for your mom."

I took the mail in and picked up my favorite magazine and began reading a story of Jim Corbett, the famous hunter of man-eating tigers. I was lost in the drama of Corbett's tracking and hunting man-eaters when my mom walked in and interrupted my journey into the forest with Mr. Corbett. She read the note laying on the table.

"Why didn't you give this to me immediately?" Amma was displeased. "Shower and get ready in ten minutes. We must go soon."

I got ready, came down, and saw three bulging brown paper bags on the dining table.

"Our driver is off today, so we will walk. You carry these two."

"Where are we going? Is it far away? These look heavy."

"Don't whine. You are a big boy. Learn a few things from Vidya. He works so hard."

What is with this Vidya thing? Why is Mom talking about Vidya now? I hefted the sacks, one in each hand.

We walked through our neighborhood to the adjoining poorer section and stopped at a brick house. The front yard had two rose bushes and a small lemon tree.

Mom knocked on the front door. "Padma! Anand and I are here."

We stepped into a one room structure. There were two low cots lying on either side of the room and two curtains hung on wires extending from one wall dividing it into three sections. On one bed, a woman's pale face and sweaty brow were visible from under a blanket. *This must be Padma who sent the note.* Amma placed her hand on Padma's forehead, checked the woman's temperature and announced, "Padma, you have high fever."

Mom instructed me to take the bags into the kitchen on the other side of the curtain.

In the kitchen, I saw a boy with his back toward me, picking at a plate. He turned around and I came face to face with Vidya. I was confused, until I realized Padma was his mom.

"I am picking rice for cooking. Can I make some for you too?"

Isn't anybody else here to cook rice? Do kids cook rice? "You got me there with your joke. Ha."

"It is not a joke. I am about to make rice."

Amma walked in, handed me a prescription and a rupee and said, "Go to the pharmacy and get me these tablets. Pick up two bananas and two oranges before returning. Don't wander around. Come back soon."

I was happy to escape my embarrassment about the rice and went to the pharmacy. "Who are these for, kid?" the pharmacist asked.

"My mom asked me to get these for Padma."

"Oh my! Does she have a fever? I will give you six tablets and I won't charge that poor woman."

"My mom is paying. Why do you keep calling Padma poor?"

"You don't know? Her husband was killed about six months ago, fighting in the war. The army gives her twelve rupees per month. If it was in my authority, I would give her one hundred rupees. What is the world coming to? The man gives his life for the nation, and we let his widow and child starve."

10

He handed me two packets of tablets. "Your mom has cared for many. Son, you come from a well-to-do family. Don't be selfish; help the poor and downtrodden."

Padma was sitting and sipping water when I returned. Mom gave her two tablets and put a wet cloth on her forehead. I walked into the kitchen and saw the rice soaking and Vidya lighting up the chulla. He put a few twigs and charcoal over a crumpled sheet of newspaper and lit the paper. He picked up a length of metal pipe and blew into the fire.

"Let me try that."

He passed me the contraption. I took a deep breath and blew hard into the flickering flame, blowing ashes all over.

"Just blow gently, that's all it needs." Vidya cleaned the ashes and got the fire going.

"For each measure of rice, you add two measures of water."

"I learned something today."

"What, you don't know how to make rice?"

"Our cook does all that. I never go in the kitchen."

"I will teach you to cook so you don't have to rely on anybody to eat."

"Okay, I'll watch, but I don't think I will ever need to cook for myself."

Amma walked in. "I bought you some dal and vegetable curry and supplies to last you a few days. If you need anything, just come by. I will visit tomorrow in the morning to check on your mom. Are you coming with me?"

"No, I will stay. We are cooking rice."

Amma looked surprised, a smile appeared on her lips. "Okay. Look after your aunt Padma," she said and left.

"How do you know when the rice is done?"

"You take one rice grain and if it is soft, the rice is done. My grandmother told me that if one grain is done, all are done."

Later we sat on the floor to eat rice with dal and a vegetable dish. Never for a moment did I think of the meat curry waiting for me at home. This was the start of a friendship that would last for years. I did not know then I would break it by my act later.

CHAPTER 3

Friendship

Vidya came once or twice a week and would leave with a sack full of food. Amma never said why she did this. One evening while eating dinner I broached it again. "Why are we supporting Vidya's family?"

"We are fortunate to have enough to eat and more to spare. Vidya and his mom are facing hard times. Helping them is the right thing to do. We have many sources of income besides my salary, we should share some of our blessings."

"How many can we help?"

"Son, the people who work our farms are illiterate. I pay for their children to get educated. I insist that all my workers send their boys and girls to school. I want them to get suitable jobs and not be laborers. You must treat people who work for you as family. Not all of them are perfect. When they make a mistake, you must give them another chance. If you don't, you destroy what little they have and that is a bigger mistake."

#

On the first day of school, I went to Vidya's house and we both walked together.

"My mom says she cannot repay your family for all that your mom does for us. She asked that I should help you in any way I can. I've decided to carry your book bag from school to your home every day," said Vidya.

"Okay, I will run home after school. You can bring it."

After school, I handed my bag to Vidya and ran home. Mom was waiting for me at the gate. "Where is your bag?" she said.

"Vidya is carrying it for me." I did not see the stinging slap that rocked me.

"How dare you let that poor child carry your stuff! Have you not learned anything from all our conversations? Never do I want you to do something so demeaning to anybody, let alone Vidya." Mom was furious, like I'd never seen before. "I want you to go to his place and apologize."

"But he is coming here ...." I realized it would not be in my best interest to complete the sentence.

"You heard me."

I ran out before it got any worse, caught up with Vidya.

He looked at me and asked, "Why are you crying and why is your cheek so red?"

"I want to apologize for letting you carry my stuff. Amma said that was a terrible thing to do. I am sorry, I will never do that again."

"But it was my idea. I will talk to your mom and explain it to her."

"If you want to see me unharmed, never bring this topic up with my mom or your mom. *Please.*"

#

The first weekend after school was a relief, it was a day of freedom earned. I headed to Vidya's place. Vidya was standing in shorts, bare chested, in his backyard doing strange moves.

"You are early," he said.

"I get up early on Sunday to enjoy the holiday to the fullest. What are you doing?"

"I do yoga every morning and evening. When my dad was alive, we used to do this together. Would you like to join me?"

"I will pass, I came to ask you to join us to go out."

"I have to be at the store for work."

"What? On a Sunday?" I was incredulous someone my age was working.

"Sunday is the best day because I can work the entire day and make almost two rupees. In a month, it will cover my tuition and supplies for school."

14

"Wow, doesn't your mom pay for that?"

"Anand, my mom works six days a week and makes twenty rupees. This is *her* day off. She can rest. I am now the man of the house and have to do whatever it takes to do my share."

"Guess you are not coming to play cricket this afternoon?"

Vidya had a wistful smile on his face. I left looking for friends to share my Sunday with.

#

The following Sunday morning Vidya invited me to his place.

"I will, only if you join us for a game of cricket."

"Yes, but I will be a nuisance, I never played cricket before."

"I saw you making all those moves during yoga the other day. I am sure you are nimble and strong enough, to put us to shame." I encouraged him. "What happened to your job?"

"I was fired. I dropped a box of glassware and broke the contents. The owner was furious and abusive and did not pay me for the work I did the week."

"Did you complain and demand the money he owed you?"

"It was my mistake, and I deserved the punishment."

"Not paying your earned money is same as stealing. I will tell my mom and she will make it right."

"Your mom always does so much for my family, please do not bother her."

I did not answer, and we both ran to his house.

"My Mom's gone to visit my uncle. We will make anapakaya pappu and eat it with rice. Come with me." We went into his backyard with the anapakaya vine.

"We must be careful not to hurt the plant." He looked, selected a gourd and pressed the nail of his forefinger on its skin. It made a slight indentation. "It is ready for cooking."

"Why?"

"That's why I poked it with the nail. If the skin is tough, the nail will not indent it, and then I must skin it. You make the right choice, less problems later."

Ok, wise ass now you are showing off.

15

"Anand, I wish we had a few tomatoes to add here since you are used to excellent food."

"I will run home and get a few."

"No. That's not what I meant. I was just thinking about your taste. Any way we must find satisfaction with what we have."

Why do I get this impression that Vidya is always telling me something more than the literal meaning of his words?

Once the gourd cooked he said, "Now we mix the dal into this and bring it to a simmer we temper it," Vidya said.

"Temper! What temper?" I inquired.

"I will show how to make this bland dal and gourd into a fragrant dish fit for a Maharaja, Your Highness!"

"How do you know that?"

"My grandmother told me."

This is the second reference to his grandmother in the recent weeks.

"Where is your grandmother? I have not seen her."

"She lives in her village." He told me the name of the village.

"Oh! That's close to our village, where we have farms and our other house."

We were ready to eat, the dal with the gourd and rice; knew this is one of the best meals I had; impressed he turned these raw ingredients into a nourishing and tasty meal.

#

Next day I said, "Vidya Amma wants your help. We are to meet her at your store, after school. She needs help carrying the stuff home."

He agreed reluctantly. We got to the market and stood outside side the store, Amma went in.

"We wait here until my mom is ready, then we go in get the packages and go home."

Vidya noticed something was fishy. "Why isn't your mom in her car?"

"The driver is sick, and she had to get these today."

A few minutes later we saw Amma approaching the counter with packages.

"Time for us to go in." I dragged Vidya with me into the crowded and busy store.

"Amma we are here."

"Just in time, give me a minute, how are you Vidya?" She turned to the manager, "Are your prices fair, they seem high?"

"Our prices are the lowest in town. I am an honest merchant," the owner whined.

"He hasn't paid Vidya, for the work he has done, when he fired him." My loud voice turned a few heads in our direction.

"Is that so?" Amma's steely voice and looks had their chosen effect.

"No madam, Vidya must have misunderstood me, I wanted him to come back for his wages, I did not have cash that day," said the flustered owner.

The shoppers gathered around us to watch the spectacle.

"Son, how much do I owe you?" The owner voice was shaky voice.

"Five rupees, sir."

"Is that for a single day's work?" Amma wouldn't let the owner escape.

"It is for five days of work." Vidya found his voice.

"It is a shame. A rupee a day?" Amma glared at the owner.

"No madam, the kid is confused. It is 25 rupees for five days."

"What are you waiting for? Pay him now," demanded Amma.

"Pay, pay," the crowd chanted.

The owner dipped into his cash drawer and counted twenty-five one-rupee notes and handed them to Vidya with a shaky hand. Vidya pocketed the money.

CHAPTER 4

Gunners

Cricket was a passion and sport of choice for most kids in India. A few friends and I formed our own team 'Gunners'. After a few weeks of practice, we started playing matches with other teams in the town. In the beginning we lost most, but persevered and started to win matches.

Six months later I announced to my team, "I challenged the Prabhus for a match. We will play them in four weeks."

Everybody's eyes were wide open. "Prabhus! Are you crazy, they are the best team in the district? We are certain to lose."

I looked around at the faces looking at me, Thomas, Venkat, Mohammed, Rao and others not as a friend but a demanding captain. The named four are my best players. A group of kids from four different faiths and the foundation Gunners. *I will make this group to be the best junior cricket team in the town. The path for attaining my goal is through Prabhus, the unbeaten town team, that I challenged for a match. There is no backing out now, I must convince, cajole, or coerce my team to fulfill my ambition and this team's destiny.*

"Thomas, Mohammed, you both are excellent batsmen. I will send you one and two down. Between the opening pair and you two, we will break the back of the Prabhus' bowlers. Venkat, you are the pace bowler. I will bowl from the other end. Later we will unleash Rao's spin attack on them. We have talent, just need to practice. Agree?"

Nobody replied.

One day Vidya came to play. We showed him the basics and asked him to bat. Vidya had good reflexes and focus which he attributed to Yoga and hit the ball with a lot of force. I realized we have a player with potential on our hands and Vidya would help us in our matches. *Maybe I should do some yoga too.*

Vidya attended practice occasionally. He turned out to be a good batsman especially, against pace bowlers. On the match day I planned to unleash Vidya as the opening batsman, on their pace bowlers. Best laid plans .... On Sunday morning the opposing captain and I inspected the pitch before the coin toss a tradition of cricket.

"You have a new player on the team. He was not on your team when we agreed to play. It is fair that that you drop him for this match," the opposing captain raised his concern.

"He is a part of my team. I will not drop him."

"We refuse to play if you insist on Vidya playing."

"Okay, I will have him as a twelfth man, so he can't bat or bowl," I conceded.

Maybe I was too hasty in challenging the Prabhus.

I went to bat with our score at 26, scored ten runs and got run out when I slipped, fell and twisted my ankle. By lunch time, we were all out for a score of 91, a respectable score for a junior team. *Would that be enough to beat the unbeaten Prabhus?*

The Prabhus went to bat. My opening bowlers gave away only one run in four overs. The batsmen were getting restless and anxious. I was ready to lay my trap. I went to bowl next, delivered two easy balls that did not break and gave away six runs. The next ball was like the previous one, the batsman got cocky took a mighty swing; but the ball did not go straight as he expected but turned sharply towards the wickets and uprooted the middle wicket. He looked disgusted with himself for falling into the trap. I gave away six runs in that over but got rid of their opener. Another tactical victory netted. *My confidence was surging.*

My ankle was hurting, and I sent Vidya to field in my place after notifying the Prabhus captain.

The match went on Prabhus score reached 88 with the last batsmen on the field. If we get one of their batsmen out before they scored 92 runs we will be winners. I knew the victory was slipping away. One boundary shot would give Prabhus' victory.

I sent Vidya to cover the field near the boundary. Rao came into bowl, all depended on him. Tense, I clenched my fists, and could not breathe. The next ball was the best Rao ever delivered, aiming at a spot that makes most batsmen play a defensive shot. But the batsman, not defensive, stepped back, raised himself on his toes and smacked the ball in an off drive. The ball was flying to the off-side boundary line, and the batsmen ran. Vidya, about 30 yards from the ball, moved with lightning speed. Vidya slid on the ground scraping his knees and elbows, grabbed the ball before it crossed the boundary line, as the batsman completed their second run and were going for the third. Vidya stood up facing the wickets closest to him, and swung back and threw the ball in a classic over the shoulder throw. The ball hit the ground in front of the wickets, bounced knocking two of the wickets with the runners caught in the middle. We broke in loud cheer, hoisted Vidya on our shoulders and congratulated him.

I presented Vidya the ball as a token of our appreciation. Vidya held the once shiny red ball close to his heart and with tears in his eyes said, "Anand, you don't know how much this means to me. I will keep this with me always."

CHAPTER 5

College

During the next year, our friendship grew stronger. We would meet whenever Vidya was not working or doing household chores. Once a week at least he came alone to eat with us. I never got him to play cricket again. Vidya used to say, "I have more important things to do than chase or hit a ball on the cricket field."

Summer 1962 was special. We graduated from high school, were free until colleges opened. It was doubly exciting realizing that we were young adults with the associated freedoms. Vidya and I met whenever he had time; walking around or sometimes going to a temple nearby, to hear the priest recite prayers, and hit the bronze gong with a wooden mallet, the sound so loud and reverberating into ones' bones.

Vidya was working more hours during the summer and was preoccupied. He talked about his desire to attend college but he was convinced he would not get admission.

When the admission list was posted we both got selected, I for pre-med courses and Vidya accounting. We rode bicycles together to college. After classes, I rode home alone while Vidya went to his evening jobs. I was happy with my books and playing cricket, trying to get into the college team.

I spent time between classes in the college library. The librarian noticed my reading habits, introduced me to the larger regional library and got me access to the restricted sections there. It was a gift I cherished. I gave up all my other activities including cricket and spent my time reading books on science, literature, philosophy, religion, and anything I could get my hands on.

One day I walked to the market get a Masala Dosa for lunch. Finished eating, satiated, walking back, I saw a billboard, 'USIS - United States Information Service Library'. I went in and an American lady at the counter asked, "How can I help you?"

I wasn't sure if I was welcome or if this was a trick question to boot me out. "I wanted to have a look. Do I need to pay to get in?"

The lady smiled. "Please come, look around, it is free. If you want to borrow books, or to be on our mailing list, fill out this form." She handed me a form.

Having read about CIA doing some clandestine operations in North-East India, I suspected this generous gesture. "Why do you want my address? Are you with the CIA?"

She burst out laughing. "I am not CIA. I am a middle-aged woman from Nebraska who wanted to get away from the cold. Moved from a freezer to a furnace. No, the address is to mail informational items and magazines."

Relieved, I filled up the form and entered the library room with enormous glass windows, carpeting, cool air that smelled pleasant. It was full of American magazines and books. I became a frequent visitor, to learn about America, its people, culture, and literature. The desire to go to America took root in my soul.

CHAPTER 6

Quiz Bowl

Second year of my college life revolved around libraries, books, and conversations with Vidya. I did not make any new friends the previous year.

"You book worm if you read so much why don't you show us what you got. Enter a team and compete in the college quiz bowl. It will expose your knowledge or lack of." Mahajan's voice was loud as I entered the classroom.

Every eye turned to stare at me. I felt my face turn hot. He was the class bully and an obnoxious human being, always ridiculing friends and foes alike. He was tall and dark with a round fleshy face and eyes of a pig. *Is the student body waiting for me to respond to this bully?*

"Sure! My team and I will bring the championship to this class," I answered.

"The last five championships have gone to the senior class teams. You and your team will be sorry losers. Mark my words."

I sat through the class fuming and angry. At the end, I decided that the only way to put this guy in his place is not a verbal duel but by putting a team together and winning the quiz bowl.

I spent the next day to figure out who, where and when of the quiz bowl. I found out most of the teams had already registered and have been in practice for the last few weeks; each team of five students must contain at least one girl. The quiz bowl was ten days away; this year's focus was science, technology, and foreign affairs. I cajoled three of my classmates to join the team. The bigger problem was finding a girl to join our team.

In those days, though we were in a co-ed college, interaction with the opposite sex was minimal to nonexistent. There were about twenty girls in our class of sixty. The only girl I knew by name, but never talked to, was Zahina. She was very fair and beautiful. *How can I approach her? What would I say? Would I get tongue tied and mumble, like I do when I am tense? What if she says no? Do I have to ask her privately, or in front of the entire class?* My mind was in turmoil with doubts and wondered why I fell into Mahajan's trap. That day I wasted with thoughts I could not control, and questions for which I had no answers. That night I during a call to Durga I told her about my dilemma.

Next day, I was deep in my own thoughts and never realized that the last class was over and most of the students left for the day. I picked my books and stepped out to see Zahina, standing in the corridor. She had a red rose tucked in her hair over the right ear. She took my breath away. However, much I told myself, this is the time to ask her to join our team, and get it over with, my legs would not change direction and my eyes would not leave the floor.

As I passed her, she said, "My dad says I should pursue my dreams with confidence. I want to join your team for the quiz bowl if your team is not full."

"No, I mean yes. No. No. my team is not full. Yes, please be on my team," I was fascinated by the red nail polish on her toenails.

She laughed at my awkwardness and said, "I am just asking to be on your team, not to marry me. You can look up, there is nothing interesting on the floor."

I looked up and my jaw dropped as I saw a face with badly squinted eyes and a markedly lopsided grin.

"Sorry!" she laughed as her the squint and the lopsided grin disappeared, "That is my habit since I was a kid, I give my squinty look if anyone pays me too little or too much attention."

As I gazed into the most beautiful brown eyes with a touch of gold, a chill went up my body.

"Do you like what you see?"

"Uh uh, yes."

"If you have trouble speaking, you shouldn't be competing in the quiz bowl."

I continued looking into her eyes lost in their beauty and Zahina, suddenly lowered her eyes, and said, "Okay we will meet the next few days for team practice. We will quiz each other and see what our strong and weak points are. Is that all right with you?"

"Yes, my name is Anand."

"I know. We have been in the same class for over a year."

In an instant, she left, and I stood there awestruck. This was my first interaction with a girl who was not a cousin or one of my sister's friends, impressed by her self-confidence and the ease with which she insinuated herself into our team. Having read about the women's liberation movement in USA, I was surprised a girl in my town could be so assertive.

#

We registered our team; were official, the seventh and the last team. The rules were—each team will have a team leader; two quiz masters, would ask questions; teams may consult among themselves, the team leader will answer; if the answer is incorrect another team can answer; if no one answers in thirty seconds a new question will be announced. The contestants may not question the decision of the professors, but the audience may.

The first order of business was to elect a team leader. I proposed Zahina since she was outspoken and fearless.

"It is your battle with Mahajan, that bought this on. I will not let you chicken out," said Zahina,

and settled the issue. We split up the topics; one team member to focus on chemistry; another biology; the third foreign policy and Zahina physics. I volunteered to browse through stuff and catch stray questions that may face us. Zahina's raised eyebrows her suspicions. I planned to study a dictionary of science and technology, I checked out from the USIS library.

Every evening we met to discuss our progress. When my turn came, I would just blurt out the letter I was on E or K or another letter while others looked at me with disbelief. On the third day after the team practice Zahina remained behind. "Let us go get something to drink Anand. Maybe a cup of coffee in the cafeteria."

Zahina had a smug look on her face when I returned with the coffee.

"I knew you were up to something. Reciting the alphabet when asked about your progress. I couldn't figure that out. My apologies, I peeked in your book bag. It is astonishing that you would study a dictionary. Only an idiot would have thought of that," she paused; "or an absolute genius."

Why haven't I met this girl on the first day of college?

We drank coffee and chatted about movies and songs and books.

"I love to read. I am reading a book by Leon Uris until you dragged me away from my book and into this quiz team," she complained.

"If I remember, you barged in."

"Don't be so sure, I wouldn't be here if you did not think of asking me." She had a mysterious look on her face.

How can she know? Am I that transparent? I did not think I said to anybody about this in the class.

"I have spies everywhere," the mysterious smile was back on her face, "Some details best remain a mystery."

It was getting late, she left. I got on my bicycle and pedaled home.

"What happened to you? You are glowing." Mom was waiting for me.

"Things are going well mom, really well."

#

On the day of the Quiz Bowl, we were as ready as we would be. I was nervous being on stage, with hundreds watching us. Zahina squeezed my hand under the table and said, "Once it starts you will be just fine."

The touch of her hand sent a shock wave through me. After explaining the rules, the competition started with the first question "What is epiglottis and what does it do?"

There was absolute silence. Nobody raised their hand to answer. The clock was ticking, and I looked at my team if anybody had an answer. The timer passed 15 seconds. My mind was whirling. I knew something but could not vocalize it. Epi meaning something on the top. I raised my hand. "It is a structure that sits on top of the glottis. It protects the glottis," I said as the buzzer went off.

"Nice try. You are wrong. It is the structure that sits on the larynx. It prevents food from entering the windpipe." The professor was ready to punch the timer again.

There was a commotion in the audience. I saw the lady doctor sitting with mom came forward. "He is right, that student who answered the question. The upper part of the larynx is the glottis, the epiglottis protects the glottis from injury by keeping the food and water from entering it. You should give him the points."

"How would you know all this, madam?" The quiz master challenged.

"Because I am a medical doctor."

The audience broke into applause, and my team got the first points. I relaxed. It went on until we reached the end with one question remaining. Zahina was keeping score said we were in a tie with the senior team. If we get the next one correct, we win.

"Who is the American Secretary of State during President John F ..."

I raised my hand, "David Dean Rusk." I answered even before the question was completed. My visits to USIS were not a waste.

"Disqualified for premature answering." The quiz master announced. The audience broke into a pandemonium.

The senior team repeated my answer and ended with victory. I was unfazed by the turn of events or the yet to come pronouncements and taunts from Mahajan, ecstatic that Zahina was squeezing my hand under the table as we looked into each other's eyes.

CHAPTER 7

Zahina & Vidya

Zahina and I met most evenings for coffee or a snack in the cafeteria, chatting and discovering each other. We both had a common interest in books and reading. One day Zahina pulled out a copy of Leon Uris Mila 18, and we discussed the story and its impact on our thoughts and feelings. Our topics for discussion varied, persecution and perseverance, love and hate, success and failure, religion and atheism, etc. We talked about our studies and friends, about our plans and ambitions. We agreed on some, disagreed on others, sometimes leading to fiery discussions and anger, because we could not convince the other of firmly held beliefs. Some days we walked away, mad at the other, but after a sleepless night would get back to our evening meetings, all forgiven and forgotten.

One day, I told her about my best friend Vidya.

"If he is your best friend, why haven't I met him?"

"With my studies and spending time with you, Vidya and I haven't been seeing each other except during our morning ride together."

"What is wrong with you? If he is your best friend, you must make time for him."

Zahina hit a nerve. I knew what was wrong with me. My attention span was for who was with me. Once I or they move, I rarely thought of them, like my ex-teammates Gunners who I never met once college started. It was like a door closing on that chapter of my life. *Will I do the same to Zahina if we go our different ways after college?* The thought sent me into a state of mind I cannot describe. The thought of losing Zahina terrified me.

"One must try to make connections and hold on to those, otherwise you will be like a driftwood. All of us need anchors to sustain us." Zahina looked at me with a serious look on her face. I was scared if Zahina figuring out my weakness and my inability to hold on to relationships, left me.

I laid my hand on hers, "Zahina I will never forget or leave you."

I noticed a sadness and angst in Zahina's eyes. *When I just promised her, I would never let go of her why sadness? What does she foresee that causes her this gloom? Only much later I realized that she knew more about me than I did.*

"Ask Vidya to come and join us one day. I would like to meet him." Zahina changed the subject and the somber mood of that evening.

"It is difficult to get to Vidya these days because he is working two jobs every evening. Let me find an occasion that he would not refuse." I failed to mention to Zahina I never told him about her.

#

"You changed a lot, Anand! Is it because of that girl?"

"You are the one who is always busy with work after classes. Don't blame me."

"I am not complaining just wanted to let you know. I saw you with that girl many times."

"We have a lot in common and we talk about books and other things."

"Is it friendship or...?" He had a smile on his face.

"We are just friends. Zahina wants to meet you."

"Is she a Muslim?"

"Yes, what does it matter? She wants to meet you," I was irritated.

"I would love to meet her. Tell me the time and I will be there."

"What about your work?"

"Leave that to me. Anything for you and your girl."

"Zahina is not my girl. We are just friends."

"You may be blind, but I am not." He had with a serious look on his face and a moment later burst out laughing "Should I announce this to your mom?"

"If you value our friendship, you will say nothing about this to my mom or anybody. Promise me." I did not want this spread like wildfire in my family circles.

"I promise you nothing."

#

Zahina chose a park to meet Vidya. After introductions, Vidya and Zahina talked to each other non-stop, comfortable with each other, they were joking and laughing.

Zahina said to me, "Why don't you get us something to drink?"

"Where? There is nothing in this park, not even tap for drinking water."

"Get on your bike and get Fanta," Zahina can be forceful.

While walking towards the cycle stand, I turned around to see them chatting away without a glance in my direction. My brain loves to kick in to top gear at the slightest provocation and this was as good as any. *Why did Zahina send me away? What were they talking about?* Thoughts kept coming and going with such intensity, I was not conscious of getting the Fanta and cycling back. My arrival halted their conversation.

"What! Were you flying? You came back so soon?"

"I was dying to quench your thirst for Fanta Zahina! Sorry to interrupt your conversation. What were you discussing?"

"Not for you to know. Thanks for the Fanta".

Each grabbed a Fanta and resumed their conversation. Left out, I sat sulking.

Vidya stood up. "I need to get to work. Please finish your drinks and I will drop the bottles with the shopkeeper."

"He is holding twenty-five paisa for each bottle. Make sure you collect it."

31

Before leaving, he turned to Zahina, "We must talk more. Okay?"

Zahina nodded her head, and I was itching to smack Vidya on the head with one of the bottles he was carrying.

"What are you fretting about? You look like you are ready to have a stroke."

"Not stroke. Strike. Strike Vidya on the head, with a bottle."

"My! My! I have not seen that side of your personality, your temper."

"What were you both talking about? Why did you send me away?"

"Is that what was bothering you? Your friend Vidya wanted to tell me stories about you. I thought he would be more forthright if you were not around. Don't tell me you were jealous? You don't know with how much high respect and friendship Vidya holds you, Anand. He told of how you resented him when you first met; you both sat and ate a simple meal in his home he cooked; how you blew the ashes all over the kitchen; your mom's help. It was all about you. He would give his life for you. You have a loyal friend in Vidya. I wish I had a friend like that."

"I am sorry if I behaved like an ass."

"There is no if." Zahina laughed.

#

Vidya joined us once every few weeks; I ran errands; Zahina and Vidya talked.

"You are always so engrossed in your own thoughts; you never express yourself, or talk about your experiences, so I have to depend on Vidya to learn about you."

We were in our senior year, apprehensive but optimistic about what the future holds. My goal was to become a doctor and then do specialization in America. Zahina's family circumstances made her to change to nursing. Her father was in poor health and Zahina decided to opt for nursing and not medicine, to have a job by the time her dad retires.

I ignore issues likely to cause anguish or confrontation, lock it in the deepest recesses of my mind. This singular trait of mine was the driving force of my existence. I hoped to overcome this trait in my relationship with Zahina.

CHAPTER 8

Trouble in Paradise

One evening while Zahina and I were drinking coffee my mind drifted away. When my focus returned, I noticed Zahina somber and irritated. I tried to lighten the mood by to telling a few jokes.

"Anand! Stop fooling around. When will you grow up and be a man?"

What in the heaven is she talking about? I was just trying to cheer her.

"If you let me know what is bothering you, maybe I can do something about it?"

"What is bothering me? It is you, Anand, you are bothering me! Can you do something about it? Yes, you can if you open your eyes and look; open your ears and listen. But no, you cannot perceive what is in front of you. You are worse than a blind and deaf person. You are so in your own world." Zahina grabbed her bag, and stormed out.

Her rage dumbfounded me. *What did I do to inflame her? Did I tell her a bad or inappropriate joke? Is she having a bad day and taking it out on me?*

The following week Zahina never showed for our evening meetings. *I was desperate to talk to her. I was restless and unable to focus. The world I knew ceased to exist. I realized and accepted what I refused to acknowledge. I love this girl and I would like to spend the rest of my life with her. I wanted us to resume our relationship. Alas, she walked out on me.* I sought Vidya's help.

"You are on your own? I have no experience with women."

"You know her well. What does she want?"

"I can't help. Talk to Amma or should I?"

"No. Amma shouldn't get involved."

"At least talk to your sister. She may help you."

A ray of hope. *Why did I not think of Durga, who knows Zahina's sister, inside help. Groveling in front of my sister would get me out of this mess.*

#

Mom went out that evening to a religious event. I called Durga.

"I was planning on calling you." Durga sounded unusually jovial.

"Why?"

"Mom said for the last ten days you were moping around. She asked me if I knew. I told her I knew nothing of your affairs."

Was she giggling in the background? What is this with women? Upbeat Zahina is breathing fire, and serious Durga is giggling? I was ready to hang up.

"What's up little brother you called me for something?"

"Yes, Durga, I need to find out ..."

"Yes, yes. Tell me all about it."

Was she giggling again?

"Well, I have a problem..."

"My genius brother has a problem he cannot solve. I wonder what it is?"

She would not let me finish what I want to say, and this was turning out to be more harrowing than I expected.

"Durga please give me a break. This is serious, very serious."

"Don't tell me, you were having a lovers' spat."

"We are not lovers, just friends."

"Oh really! Tell me all about it."

Was there someone laughing in the background? People don't know when to be serious and when to be jovial. This is not a time to laugh at my misery.

"Ok, let me tell you what happened last week. Zahina, and I

met ..."

"Don't tell me anything I shouldn't hear. What were you two doing?" more giggles.

"If you don't stop giggling, I will hang up," I was angry and frustrated. "Is there someone with you in the room?"

"You know your girlfriend's sister Shabnam and I share a room."

"She is just a friend, not my girlfriend. Maybe I should call later when you are alone."

"She says she is sorry and will not giggle anymore. Go ahead. We won't interrupt, promise!"

With that assurance, I told Durga what happened that evening when Zahina stormed out. All the while I heard strange sounds, squeaks and squeals. It was humiliating.

"What does she want?"

"I wouldn't be calling you if I knew what she wanted from me."

"Maybe she doesn't want to be a friend anymore."

"But ... but, we have been friends for two years now. How can she ...," I choked.

Giggling became uncontrolled laughter.

"Are you going to help or are you both going to just laugh and squeal?"

"Anand, we are here to help you. We don't know what Zahina wants. Yes, we got it. Shabnam will talk to Zahina tonight. We will find out and let you know tomorrow." I heard more squealing in the background.

Beggars can't be choosers. "Okay. Please call me tomorrow"

"Yes, little brother good night and sweet dreams." Loud laughter.

#

After a sleepless night and inattentive classroom stay, I got home and sat next to the phone waiting. When it rang, I almost fell out of the chair. My hands were sweaty, and my heart was thumping.

"Hi" I croaked.

"Anand! Is that you? What is wrong with your voice?"

"I am catching a cold or something."

"Ok get well. We have great news. Are you ready?"

"Yes."

"Zahina wants a rose, not any red rose, a long-stemmed red rose with two green leaves."

"Ok, I am sure I can find one."

"Now do what you should have done long ago. Give her the rose as a token of love and tell her you love her. I know what you are capable of Anand. If I ever find out you wronged this girl, I will skin you alive."

Durga hung up before I could say thanks,

#

I bought the best looking long stemmed red rose with two green leaves from a Phool Wallah on the roadside which he wrapped in a piece of newspaper handed it, winked and wished me, "Good luck, Sahib."

The sisters told me to be at the park by 4:30 PM and wait for Zahina. It was a scorching hot day, and the ground was radiating heat like hot coals. 4:45 No sign of Zahina. 5:00 No Zahina. The rose in my hand was wilting and lost its luster and beauty. I looked around for water to revive it, saw a lily pond, ran there and sprinkled water on the rose. I turned around and saw Zahina looking around. In my eagerness to get to her before she left, I stepped into mud, which held on to my shoe. I pulled and my foot came out sans shoe. I saw Zahina leaving and ran shouting "Zahina! Zahina! Wait. Don't leave Zahina".

People in the park gawked at the crazy fellow with one shoe on and a sock on the other foot chasing after a girl waving something in his hand. Zahina turned around her eyes opened wide staring, a hand covering her mouth. Two men who thought I was about to assault her, stepped in front of her.

Zahina burst out laughing, "What are you trying to prove Anand? What is all this drama? Is this your idea or your evil sister's?"

I was breathless with emotion and exertion, "Zahina, please

don't leave. I brought you the best rose I could find."

A small crowd has gathered around us, expecting more drama. A loud voice said, "This must be a movie shoot."

"No, no, this is not a movie we are rehearsing a scene, for a college drama. Please come and see it during our College Anniversary celebration. Thank you, we must go now." Zahina's quick thinking got us out of the gawkers.

"Sorry I saw the rose wilting, went to sprinkle water on it and you know the rest."

"That's the best rose anyone ever gave me. I will keep it with me always."

"Are we ok now?"

"Okay with what? What do you want to say? Say it!"

"I love you and always will."

"I knew it a long time ago, just wanted you to say it and own up to it. Anand, I know our destinies are entwined, until death do us apart. When you know something, express it and own it. That's what my Abbu taught me."

"What do you say Zahina?"

"What do you want me to say?"

"Say what is in your heart"

"I love you too, Promise me that if we lose each other, you will search and comeback for me. I want to be with you until I die Anand. I want to die with you holding me in your arms."

"I will always love you and never forget you. I promise. Anything else?"

"I am going home, you should too, it is getting late. See you tomorrow."

"Yes, Madam!" I was on cloud nine and headed home.

That day Zahina and I have embarked on a journey into uncharted territory. We were young in our late teens, naïve, with the exuberance of youth and raging hormones, committed to each other. Whether our dreams come true or break under the onslaught of societal pressures and the turbulence time doles out, was unknown. We were like two uprooted saplings fallen into a swift flowing river, with their branches tangled and journeyed together until the strong currents forced them apart.

CHAPTER 9

Reality

By the final year of college, most of the student body knew of our love, between a Muslim and a Hindu. The Muslim invasions and the centuries of conflicts between Hindus and Muslims led to distrust and animosity between the two major Indian religions, exacerbated by the partition of the nation at the time of independence in 1947, when boundaries were drawn to carve out two Muslim dominant countries from the Hindu dominant India. Zahina and I knew this would be a major hinderance to our union, not unsurmountable because we both believed our families were open minded and not influenced by religious dogma.

I wondered if her dad a devout Muslim accept me. What would we do if her dad opposes her marrying a non-Muslim? Will Zahina disobey her dad? What about the society we live in?. Will we be ostracized or accepted? I knew Amma would welcome Zahina with open arms. We knew of the many hurdles to cross before we could talk about marriage and the insurmountable problems, being of two different faiths pose. I believed all religions preach the same message but with a different name or language. Religion molded humanity into the current society, instead of being collection of hairless apes. Religious teachings established the concepts of community, family, responsibility, and the distinction between good and evil. My friends were from all major religions in India, and I celebrated all religious holidays with them. I went to temples with Hindu, churches with Christian and mosques with Muslim friends. I hoped Zahina and her family would accept me, a pantheist.

The time to merge our plans and act on our future studies was hanging heavily on us. We spent most of the time together to sort out the intricacies of staying together without compromising our future goals. After weeks of discussions Zahina decided she would apply for the Nursing school and I for Medical college, in a neighboring city.

The college days were over, I got admission to the medical school and Zahina to nursing as planned. The summer vacations, normally a time of joy, were a major hindrance to us. Lack of classes meant no simple way to meet. Our families were unaware of our love except for the sisters who pledged silence.

Durga was home for the summer holidays as was Shabnam and this provided an opportunity for Zahina and I. Durga was busy most of the day with tennis practice and her thesis work on some crazy math stuff. In the evenings Shabnam would come to visit and Zahina tagged along. Zahina and I would sneak up on to the terrace. Occasionally Vidya came along. Sunset was a sign that the tryst must end; it was time for the sisters to head home.

Durga teased me at every opportunity.

"What are you both whispering about?" Mom heard us.

"I am finding out if he is making any progress."

"What progress?"

"I am not at liberty to say Amma. Anand will tell you when he is ready."

Mom looked at me and raised her eyebrows questioning.

"Durga is full of nonsense mom. I am going out to meet Vidya," I gave Durga a dirty look and escaped the teasing and went off to Vidya's.

#

We chatted about college and my plans. Noticing that his mom was looking tired, Vidya told his mom to get some rest, and we stepped out into the front yard.

"Have you applied for advanced accounting, that would help you in a banking career?" I asked.

"No, I have given up on additional degrees. It is time for me to find a job. Mom's sick for this week and hasn't gone to work. She is worried of losing her job. I do not know what to do. If she doesn't get paid, we may have to vacate our home."

"Let me ask Amma if she can help?"

"Do not involve your mom, Anand. It is time for me to take responsibility for my family. Your mom has done a lot for us over these years, and I am deeply indebted. I cannot accept any more."

I was so involved with Zahina I ignored my best friend all these months. Unlike before, where we would meet every morning and some evenings, during the last year I was going early to college to meet Zahina. I was ashamed of my neglect of Vidya and decided to help him without his knowledge.

That evening I talked to mom about Vidya.

I asked her, "Why can't Aunt Padma an educated lady find a better job?"

"In a perfect world, yes, it should not be a problem. That she is a woman and a widow, makes it very difficult to find a suitable job. Jobs are a commodity which the powerful exploit for money and power. Many jobs require a bribe to be selected."

"Maybe you can pay someone and get her a job, to let Vidya continue his studies."

Mom looked at me intensely for a few moments. "I never paid a bribe nor intend to. You should not either. It is immoral and self-destructive. I know what is going on but did not realize that Vidya's mom is that sick, on the verge of losing her job. I will inquire at our bank."

#

Two days later I asked Vidya to accompany me to the market. On the way, we passed a bank.

I said, "Vidya, why don't you go in there and ask the manger if there are any job openings?"

"I don't think he will even talk. How can I go barge in there, asking for a job?"

"If you are looking for one you must seek it. It will not fall into your lap. If you don't, I will ask."

"No, I will."

Vidya walked nervously, into the bank; I waited outside. Half an hour later he walked out beaming and said, "The manger was very nice. He said they are expecting a vacancy soon and I should put in an application."

"Are you going to put in the application?"

"I already did. They will let me know."

#

When we returned to his home, Vidya's mom was crying. Vidya went hugged her and asked what the matter was.

"The landlord asked us to vacate these premises by weekend because of unpaid rent. What are we going to do?"

"I applied for a job in the bank and will know in two weeks if I got the job."

"We don't have two weeks. We must do something in the next three days, or we will not have a roof over our heads."

"I will find a cheaper place to rent and leave by the deadline. I will pay the landlord what we owe once I get paid."

CHAPTER 10

Promise

Zahina and I moved to the city pursuing our chosen studies staying in the respective hostels. We met some evenings and most weekends. Two years later Zahina graduated from nursing and started internship in the hospital associated with the medical school. Six months later she took the job of staff nurse at the same hospital. The last year of medical college, I took the test for ECFMG certification. Six weeks later a letter of successful completion arrived from Philadelphia. I was thrilled and could not wait to tell Zahina.

"I have great news."

The ever-present smile disappeared from Zahina's face. I saw tears in her downcast eyes. When she looked up there was sadness and anger in Zahina's eyes, a look that scorched my psyche and branded my heart. *What have I done to my love?*

"Congratulations on your success. I wish you all the best."

"How did you know what it's about?"

"Anand, for me you are an open book. I see you beaming with happiness that only ECFMG success would elicit."

We sat there looking at each other and after a few minutes Zahina bade farewell and headed to her quarters, with drooped shoulders and bowed head. I watched with a heavy heart until she turned a corner.

We reached a turning point in our relationship. *My lifelong desire to go to America and Zahina's to be there for her family. We both can fulfill our dreams. But to be together alas, one of us must give in. The turbulence of time has shaken our relationship. Will*

44

this pass or break the bonds we so lovingly nurtured for the last few years? I sat there my brain frozen, a weightlessness crept into my being, no thoughts in my overactive brain. The world around me came to a standstill.

We continued to meet, but there was a chasm between us. Outgoing Zahina was subdued and quiet. *I should give in and for once take the initiative and break the impasse, a solution, which I was not ready to accept and say, 'Zahina I love you, I want to be with you forever, my place is by your side, not in America.' I was a slave to my ambitions, my aspirations, and my own inadequacies.*

This continued for two months. During this time Durga called repeatedly to convince me that I was on the wrong path, a path that would destroy Zahina and me.

"Remember that day you called me years ago seeking help because Zahina was angry. I warned if you wrong Zahina I would skin you alive. I meant every one of those words, Anand!"

#

"Anand, I need a break to spend time with my sister. She is getting married this summer," Zahina announced one evening.

"The university she is at, is on the beautiful Bay of Bengal beaches. Enjoy! Say hello to Durga and your Shabnam."

#

We met the evening Zahina returned. Gone was the subdued and quiet Zahina of the last two months. Her eyes were sparkling, and the smile and radiance were back. *What happened? Why is she so happy while I am depressed and unhappy? Has she found a new love and given up on me in a week? Who caused this change?*

"Anand what is the matter with you? Are you not happy to see me?"

"I am very happy to see you. Just unable to sort out all that's happening with us."

"Listen Anand, we have a few months before you leave for America. We should be happy and enjoy our days together instead of behaving like zombies. Let us go walk by the river.

45

We haven't done that in ages."

"I will bring my camera and take some pictures."

It was once again Zahina that had the initiative to change the existing situation. I knew inside she was as perturbed as I was or more, but the courage to hide it and her effort to get me out of my depression revealed the strength of her love.

We walked on the dry riverbed, with isolated pools of water. I took many photos, one of which turned out well, we standing together shoulder to shoulder with our footprints visible in the sand. I got two prints made of the photo, one for Zahina and one for my collection. On the back of one I wrote, 'Remember Our Good Times' and signed my name.

We went on without an outward show of torment. We both lost weight, stopped mingling with other others. We stopped talking about books, work or family. We only talked about each other and sometimes sat there gazing into the other's eyes; our souls communicating without words; I my apologies and regrets; Zahina her love and optimism.

#

It was Friday, two days before I was to leave on my long journey to America.

"Come this evening to my room; I have a present for you, Anand."

"Won't your roommates mind?"

"They are going to a movie."

"What time?"

"Come by 5PM."

#

I went shopping and found a sandalwood frame to place the photograph of us on the riverbed. At the nurses' quarters I waited clutching the photo as all my life depended on it, while the attendant went to fetch Zahina. She came out wearing a white cotton churidar and kurta with blue embroidery and a red dupatta covering her head. Her eyes were bright and there was a radiant smile on her face. My heart ached with longing to embrace and hold her.

"I made coffee, let's go in before it gets cold."

We went up to her room on the second floor. I noticed all the nooks and crannies filled with books. It was a large airy room with three beds and a table in one corner on which was a coffee pot. Zahina poured two cups.

"Is this the end of the road for us, Anand?"

"I will be back Zahina. I will be back soon."

"Don't leave me Anand, please do not leave me!" Zahina clung to me. Her body racked with sobs Her tears soaked through my shirt. I held Zahina trying to soothe her.

"Zahina I will come back for you."

"You don't know yourself that well Anand, when you leave here, your world will change and what you believe now will no longer be true. Please don't do this Anand. I cannot live without you."

I ran my hand through her hair trying to soothe her. Zahina buried her face in my chest and I felt her heart thumping and her muscles tightening with her sobs. We stood there holding each other. I was angry with myself for all the trouble I have caused her. Her sobs lessened; the tension in her body slowly dissipated.

I could feel the warmth and softness of her body, a new experience. Her hair smelled of jasmine and I felt their silky softness. I pulled my hand kerchief, to clean her face of tears. I gently turned her face towards me and noticed her eyes were red with emotion and crying. Zahina grabbed the back of my head and pulled it down towards her. I tasted the saltiness of her tears. She pulled my lips to hers, we were lip locked a conscious effort for the first few seconds, changing into a crescendo of passion and desire, as repressed biological urges took over our conscious actions. Our hands moved over each other exciting and uncontrolled. We tugged at each other's clothes; forgotten were the moral and societal boundaries; we moved lip locked together towards her bed, like a four-legged creature; not willing to let go of each other even for a moment, oblivious of surroundings.

Thump! Thump! The door amplified the sound and interrupted our progress toward the bed.

"Zahina are you in there? Are you sleeping? Why is the door locked from inside?" Her roommates were hollering outside. Zahina and I were back into reality. We quickly adjusted our clothes.

"Anand and I are discussing our plans for the future. Can we have privacy please? He is leaving for USA in two days. We have a lot to talk about.".

"All right you two love birds, we couldn't get tickets for the movie. Don't do anything naughty. We will be back in an hour."

Zahina and I looked at each other relieved. We both were emotionally and physically drained and had no intention of continuing what got interrupted. I gave her the present and she gave me a chaste kiss on the cheek.

"I will write to you from America. I love you, Zahina." I exited without waiting for her response.

I slept fitfully that night waking up and wondered if fate hadn't intervened that evening, if we had ended making love, would I have changed my decision and done the honorable thing. *A question I cannot answer.*

But that night I knew in my heart I would come back for her. The date was December 10. My flight was on Dec 12. On the day before Christmas Eve, Dec 23 I would break my commitment to Zahina and betray her love.

CHAPTER 11

USA

I arrived in New York JFK airport on December 12th, with five dollars in my pocket. I got to my miwest destination after midnight. The person I was to meet was not there and I decided to stay in the airport and get to the hotel early morning. I found a seat in one corner, stretched out and dozed off.

"Hey, buddy get up. You cannot stay here. No more flights are coming in tonight. I have to lock this place up." I looked up to see an enormous African American policeman.

"I am waiting for transportation sir."

"Transportation is outside, waiting here will do you no good."

"My transportation is not coming until six in the morning. I have been traveling for almost 48 hours and I am tired, so please let me stay inside. It is cold outside."

"You think this is cold wait till late January and February, this will feel balmy. Anyway, I cannot let you stay here. It is against regulations. Where are you going?"

I gave him the name of the hotel on Euclid Avenue.

"You must be brave to go there this time of the night. Tell you what. Once I lock up, I go home. Where you want to go is a small detour from my way. Wait for me here, I will drop you at your hotel."

Sticklers for rules but generous in heart these Americans.

#

After orientation I joined the group of physicians who were

starting their residencies. Mine was in Pathology, a subject I loved from the third year of medical school. My room in the residents' quarters had a window overlooking the street 7 floors below. A few days later I bought a few 'Aerogrammes'. My first letter was to Zahina that evening while looking out the window, I saw snowflakes gently falling to the ground. I have never seen snow before and wrote to Zahina how peaceful and heavenly it looked form my warm and cozy room. How much I missed her and how much I loved her. I did not know then; this would be the last letter I write to Zahina.

#

On December 20th I met Leslie, a technologist who worked in the lab. She was in her twenties, blue eyed with blond hair cut short. My lab manager introduced us; she was the one to go to for supplies. I left India with a suitcase full of clothes and nothing else, had a long list of items I needed for work. Leslie showed me the new automated system for ordering office supplies, lab reagents, dissecting instruments etc.

"Oh wow." I was impressed.

"Stay around me and you will have many oh wow moments." She smiled, "Are you going to the Lab Christmas party?"

"I was not invited."

"There is no formal invitation, everybody is welcome."

"I don't know where it is. I have no transportation."

"Be ready by 6 o'clock December 23, evening, at the main entrance, I will pick you up. We have a date. Don't forget a present. All the presents will end up in a pile and everyone picks one. It is a lot of fun."

I have a date, my first. *I am lucky there is always somebody to drive me around.* At the party there was a lighted Christmas tree with multicolored ornaments. A table was covered with food brought in by the guests and a large bowl, with a pink effervescent fluid. This is a potluck dinner explained Leslie and in that bowl is punch. I got some, it tasted like cough medicine on ice. I drank it, slowly mingling with other guests. I noticed most of the guests were women and only a few men around. I felt relaxed talking and joking, not my usual mode of behavior. The second glass of punch tasted better than the first and went in much faster.

I was getting into my third Leslie cautioned, "Take it easy. It is potent. I want you to be awake and not dozing off, rest of the evening."

We both picked up food found a table when I noticed that my glass was empty.

"I will get another. Can I get one for you?" I asked Leslie.

"No thanks. One glass of that stuff is enough to give me a buzz and I have to get you home safe."

After finishing our meal Leslie said, "How about we get out now? This party is boring, I will drive and show you the town."

I felt lightheaded as I walked out with Leslie. She drove around, pointed the landmarks and interesting places for about half an hour. We stopped in front of a multistory building. "This is where I live. Do you want to come up, the view from my apartment is spectacular at night?"

We entered a corner apartment which was spacious and open.

"This is the great room with the kitchen." One wall was all glass, she held my hand and pulled me towards it. I saw the lights of the city glowing spectacularly.

"Is this safe?" I tapped the pane of glass separating us from a fall to the ground thirteen floors below. "Will it break?"

"This is triple paned armored glass, guaranteed not to break even if you ran into it full speed. Can I get you a bourbon? I am getting a glass of wine."

She brought both our drinks and we stood by the window appreciating the view.

"If you think this view is spectacular let me show you the other room. You can see the entire lake drive form there."

The room we entered was her bedroom with a similar glass wall. The view was breath taking. It was a clear night, and the stars were twinkling in the clear sky. I realized that I was drunk with all the punch and now the whiskey which was almost gone.

"Be a gentleman and don't look as I change into something more comfortable, just look out and finish your drink."

I did not or need not look back because there was her reflection in the glass as clear as in a mirror, her disrobing and pulling a dress over her head.

"Did you enjoy the view?" Leslie laughed at my discomfort, put her arms around me pressing her body into my back. "Come on lover boy, let us get in bed."

I woke up with a splitting headache. Leslie was lying next to me clothes in disarray. I was wearing only shorts and nothing else. I had a vague recollection of what transpired that night and wondered if I was in full control of my senses. I was about to get out of bed when Leslie pulled me down and rolled over me. This time I was in full control of my senses and obliged her desires and demands.

"I had a good time. Don't worry I am on the pill and am clean."

"You are the best," I said not knowing what to say and what the etiquette demands, in such instances.

The pleasures of sin and sins of pleasure seized and held me like an insect in a cocoon. It was Christmas Eve, a holiday. I was not on call that day or the next day, I stayed with Leslie those two days and nights, going out once that afternoon to pick up a change of clothes from my quarters.

Our hectic affair continued for about three months. After the first week, I moved in with her. I cook chicken curry and rice. We eat and get in bed for the night. Our relationship had no commitments, or love, just physical gratification. We fell into a routine until Leslie announced, it was over, and I had to move out. What started at the Christmas party was over before the snows melted and spring arrived.

I was back in my assigned quarters confused about the way it started and ended. There were two letters from Zahina unopened in my mailbox. I did not have the courage to open them let alone, read and respond. I hoped she would get over me and go on with her life. I made a terrible mistake and the honorable thing to do would be to let Zahina know what I did, not to ask for forgiveness but let her know what a cur I was and break any affection she had for me. As true to my nature, I did nothing. A few months later another sealed envelope arrived, with a Z as the sender and all corners of the envelope stained yellow with turmeric. I knew what the envelope contained without opening it. It was a wedding announcement. Zahina was getting married. Wedding announcements were sent in envelopes with yellow corners, a custom in my native state. I wished her all happiness and closed that chapter of my life. I put all the unopened envelopes with my papers. I was not yet ready to discard them.

It was a bitter period in my life having realized, once again of my inability to do right, if it meant turmoil and stress. I am like water, always going downhill, taking the path of least resistance. However, much I rationalize and theorize on the correct path when I act it will always be the easy way out. Arguments and confrontation with those close, I avoid at all costs. In most instances, such decision's affected me, but with this one I broke my promise to the love of my life. I decided not to develop deep relationships, because I might destroy that person. I thought of the promise Vidya made to take care of Zahina and Druga's promise to skin me alive if I hurt this girl. How could I ever face them again? It is best they forget me. I cannot go to my native land without facing them, I decided that I would not return to India.

PART TWO - VIDYA

CHAPTER 12

Leaky Roof

Vidya woke up with a start as rainwater dripped on his face in the rented shack, a mud and bamboo dwelling with a leaky tin roof. I must find a better place to live once I get settled in the new job. He thought of his chores—check on mom; make her a cup of warm sweet tea; bathe; pack a bowl of rice and butter milk with a pickle; get on his bike and go to his job as a bank teller.

His grandmother was up, fixing tea for his mom, and the smoke from the wood burning chulla stung his eye. "Bring a kg of rice and some vegetables on your return. Say a prayer to Lord Ganesh before you step out. If a black cat crosses your path, come back, wash your hands and feet and go out praying."

"Yes, granny."

The sewer and rotting refuse smell assaulted his nose as he pedaled to work.

#

Every day before the bank opened for customers, the bank manager opened the safe and gave each teller cash to dispense. The tellers counted the money and signed the register and made appropriate entries in their ledgers. If they dispensed all the money in their till, the process was repeated.

At the end of the day, the manager tallied their ledgers to the last paisa. "If you make an error, you will be held accountable. You must pay for any short fall, or I will report to police, and you will face the consequences. So be careful!"

Vidya was very careful, did not want to be in prison for theft. *Who would take care of mom?*

#

It thrilled both mom and granny when he went home with sweets for them on getting his first pay.

"Do not do that again. We can do without sweets. Next month, buy yourself a set of new clothes. You have outgrown your old ones."

Vidya's efficiency was liked by the customers and the bank manager made other tellers dislike him. There was a talk of Vidya becoming a supervisor. Vidya for his part remained aloof, not getting involved in friendships with coworkers, the office politics or the gossip. His quiet life changed when Ambika arrived.

#

One morning at the opening he saw a smart young woman with dark flawless skin and large bright eyes with the manager. He noticed her sharp nose, pearly white teeth when she smiled and the dark curly tresses extending below her waist.

"Everybody! I want you to meet Ambika, our new assistant bank manager. Please introduce yourselves."

As Vidya introduced himself, she turned and looked at him. Her head tilted in acknowledgment. After introductions, the manager asked Vidya to wait while other went to their stations.

"Ambika, Vidya is our best teller. His performance is flawless. Please follow him for the next two weeks to learn. He is the best. Is it ok Vidya?"

"Yes sir, I will show of Ms. Ambika all my work."

The thought of this lady shadowing for two weeks him made him nervous. *If I mess up her training, I may be fired.*

"Ms. Ambika, madam, please come with me. I will take you through my routine."

"You can call me Ambika or Ambi. No, Ms. or madam needed.".

"You are the assistant manager, I have to respect your position, madam."

"Please don't call me madam, makes me feel middle aged."

"I which case I will stick with Ms. Ambika."

"What if, as assistant manager, I asked you to call me Ambika? Will you obey me?"

"Ms. Ambika, excuse me, I decline to maintain the decorum of the workplace. Let us go to work. The customers will be in, the moment we open."

He talked to Ambika as he worked explaining each step, how and why. Every15 minutes an attendant gathered the checks from the tellers and took them to the manager's office. The manger put his initials on the checks. Once the approved checks were back, the tellers doled out the money and updated their ledgers. It was a long-drawn process with manual calculations which Vidya did at least twice for each customer.

He handled ten or more customers in an hour, but with training Ambika, the workflow slowed his pace down. The line of customers grew longer. The other tellers grumbled when the waiting customers moved to their windows.

Kumar, the senior most teller, walked over, "Vidya, just because you have a pretty lady by your side doesn't mean you can shunt your work to others. You are lazy and inefficient."

"Sorry, I will hurry."

"Sorry does not cut it. Speed up or I will ...."

"What will you Mr. ...?" Ambika went to Vidya's defense.

"Kumar, I am a senior teller. It is my responsibility, to see that there is an equal distribution of work."

"Mr. Kumar, I am the new assistant manager. You are not in charge of distribution of labor. The manager and I decide that. Please go back to your window and take care of the customers who are waiting. I will be watching you."

Kumar gave Vidya a venomous look, turned to Ambika, "Yes, Madam."

"Mr. Vidya don't let people bully you. You are a good worker."

"Anand says the same. He says I have no self-confidence."

"Who is Anand?"

"He is my only and best friend."

Ambika looked at Vidya, a tall well-built handsome young man. *He is efficient but naïve.* She asked him to show how he reconciled the books and soon they were immersed in the nitty gritty of account keeping from the teller's perspective.

After the day's work was over, on the way out Ambika asked, "Vidya would you like to go for coffee?"

"I am sorry, I must go home and attend to my family."

Ambika thought this good-looking young man has a family. What a bummer!

#

Her training completed Ambika moved into her office. She depended on Vidya for help with problems. *Vidya was never confrontational with coworkers. If he develops leadership skills, he can become a good supervisor.* Ambika tested him with difficult scenarios. He successfully handled those with no complaints or claimed credit.

One day when the work was light, she invited him to her office and offered him a cup of coffee. "I want to discuss future opportunities. You are a very hardworking and loyal to this bank. I like to see you succeed and move up. Mr. Desai is retiring in a few months. I will be stepping into his position. My current job will be open. You should apply for it. This will double your current salary with benefits such as housing allowance and schooling subsidies."

"I appreciate your kind offer. It will make my mom happy."

"Won't your wife be happy to know of the promotion?"

"I am not married. I live with my mother and grandmother."

"Oh! I thought, you had a wife."

"Why? I never told you about being married. Did I?"

"Never mind."

Most days at the end of work she and Vidya used to chat. Though reluctant at first, Vidya opened to her and talked about his ambition of working in the bank and taking care of his mother. He enjoyed her company. She talked about her family and her dad, whom she respected and revered.

These evening meetings did not go unnoticed. The bank's rumor mill was going full blast. The staff frequently cornered the attendant who would be the last to leave for juicy tidbits, became the center of their attraction, kept track of these meetings between Ambika and Vidya.

#

"Vidya, I want to ask you a favor? Can you promise me, you will honor it?"

"If it is legal I will, I promise."

"Please call me Ambi, not Ms. Ambika; we have known each other now for over six months and I would like us to be friends."

"Yes, but only when we are by ourselves. I will not address you Ambi, when others are present."

"Agreed," Ambika and got out of her chair and gave Vidya a hug. They separated, but not before the attendant noticed, and broadcasted what he saw. This scandalized the coworkers, none more so than Kumar. He wanted to use this information and get his revenge and destroy both these with one stroke.

#

Vidya was reluctant to accept her invitation to join Ambika's family celebrating her birthday. Ambika gave him a three-month notice and refused to take no for an answer and threatened, to end up at his place on her birthday to celebrate. The idea that Ambika, the daughter of a wealthy businessman visiting his shack, mortified Vidya. *I must find a better house soon. Then Ambika*
can visit my mom and granny.

#

Vidya arrived at Ambika's palatial home with a walled off compound and an ornate iron gate guarded by a uniformed watchman.

"I am here for Ms. Ambika's birthday party," said Vidya nervously

"Please write your name and time, In the visitor's logbook and go in Sir. Leave your bike by the gate. Ring the bell at the door and someone will get you." said the watchman.

Vidya walked through the well-maintained garden, admiring the flower beds and trimmed lawn. The front door opened, Ambika gave him a hug and pulled him inside. He looked around nervously and disengaged from her embrace.

"Happy Birthday! A small present Ambi. I hope you like it." Vidya handed a small package.

"What is it? Can I open it now?"

"My granny made it for you."

"I am honored, she would take the time and effort make something. I absolutely love it."

Ambika was about to tear open the paper wrapping.

"Aren't you introducing your friend?" said the booming voice of a man who just entered the room. Vidya realized he was Ambika's dad.

"Vidya, meet my dad, Sri. Srinivas."

"Sir, my name is Vidya. I work in the same bank as your daughter."

"Ah a coworker. That's how you met my daughter. How do you like the bank?"

"Yes, sir, I like the bank. This is my first job. When your daughter joined the bank, I trained her in the teller's job."

"Oh! You are a teller. They can't be paying a teller much."

"Dad, we are not here to discuss bank jobs and salaries. Time to celebrate."

"Aren't any more of your friends coming?" Srinivas was surprised.

"On this birthday, Vidya is my only guest."

Vidya saw Srinivas frown and his face darkening. *This family is way above my head.*

Ambika led all of them into the dining room. A cake, frosted in white and a pink rose on the top was on the table. She introduced Vidya to her mother and her aunt. Srinivas lit a single candle, Ambika blew the candle and cut the cake. The small gathering sang Happy Birthday. All were eating and appreciating the cake except Vidya, who was looking at the cake with a dreaded look.

"Vidya take a bite, it won't kill you." Ambika encouraged.

"I cannot eat cake. I am vegetarian."

Srinivas was aghast. "WHAT?"

"Dad Vidya is my guest!! If he doesn't want to eat cake, that's ok. Don't mind him, Vidya. He thinks everybody is like him. We have other things to eat besides cake; laddu, pakora and other goodies."

"I am not hungry but wouldn't mind taking a few home for my mom and granny."

It was time to open the presents. The present I brought is so simple compared to all the expensive gifts from her family. His brown paper wrapped present was the last one unwrapped. Ambika opened the wrapping without tearing it and squealed with joy as she pulled out the white linen handkerchief with finely embroidered pink roses all along the edges and 'Ambika 1968' in one corner.

"Thank you Vidya for such a precious gift. Please thank your grandma for all the time and effort she put into this. This is the best gift I ever had."

Ambika's dad angry with his daughter's proclamation left the room with his dark complexion turning a shade of purple. I must talk to my daughter before this goes any further. *This teller from my bank is wooing my daughter, no doubt for her wealth. Srinivas thought of his friend an industrialist told him how his only daughter fell in love with a new young recruit at work, got married and divorced a year later with the husband owning one half his business.*

#

"Who is this Vidya guy and why was he in my house?" Srinivas said after the party. *If I let this continue without nipping it in the bud, dad would take my silence as a surrender. It will be very difficult to convince him later.*

"He is a friend and a good person. This is my house too and

62

I will invite my friends here," Srinivas was surprised by her assertiveness.

"How good is a good friend? Where is this headed?"

"We like each other."

"Like each other like love, like marriage?" Srinivas' blood pressure was rising.

"Vidya and I, haven't talked about love or marriage, we like each other, spend a lot of time together and will commit to each other soon." Ambika tried to ease her dad into what she has to say.

Srinivas's face turned purple with anger and his eyes bloodshot. "What is this commitment? Does it mean marriage? Does it mean live in sin and be an outcast of the society? What about my standing in this community?"

"Dad, please relax. I am not saying anything like that, when we both are ready, we will ask for your blessings?"

"Blessing? What blessing? Like to get married?"

"Yes, dad, when we decide to marry, we will ask for your and his mom's blessing."

"You think he loves you and wants your happiness? People like him, all they want is your wealth. You think he would even look at you if you were poor. He knows you are a rich father's only child. By telling a few sweet words, he deceived you. I will not allow this bank teller to steal my hard earned wealth."

"Dad, you said what you want to say. Now listen when we get married, which may be sooner than you think, we will get married with or without your blessing."

"I will throw you out of my house, what will you do then?"

"We both have jobs. We will find a place to live, we can support ourselves."

"No! You won't be working in any of my banks."

"You are not the only banker in town, dad. Your competitors would love to have your daughter and son in law work in their banks. What would that do to your status, Dad?" Ambika's was ready for a fight, her face flushed, and nostrils flared.

"All right! Can we have a rational talk about this? No need to fight. Let us think through this and deal with it later." Srinivas realized this has gone far enough, time to retreat now, and win the war, with a different approach.

"Don't think you or mom can sweet talk me out of this."

"What are you both shouting about? That is all you both do? Can we have peace like normal families?" Ambika's mom walked in.

"Normal families don't have a dictator as dad." *I love my dad, but it is time he let me decide these matters. I am not a child anymore.*

"Look at all your friends, Janaki and Anjali, they let their dad's pick a suitable man to marry." Mom rose in defense of her husband.

"I am not Janaki, or Anjali I am Ambika, and I will decide who I marry. Is that clear to both of you? My decision will not change."

Srinivas whispered into his wife's ear. She nodded, and both left the room to let Ambika cool down.

CHAPTER 13

Problem

Returning from Ambika's party, Vidya stopped at home and dropped the laddus and pakoras for mom and granny and headed to Anand's since he heard of Anand was visiting his mom.

"Vidya what calamity brings you here, you look as if you have seen a ghost," said Anand

"You look no better," said Vidya.

"Let us go up. Amma is in the adjoining room. We don't want to disturb her."

Both grabbed a banana each and headed to the terrace.

Vidya told him everything that happened from the moment he reached the gates of Ambika's home to the moment he exited. "I created a conflict between Ambika and her dad. He was not too pleased. Every turn I seem to run into an insurmountable obstacle. I want to back or break it off to let Ambika patch up with her dad."

"Vidya, Ambika has an equal say. You cannot break up now. You will break her heart and no telling what she will do, she has a fiery temper, that girl. If you both are serious, decide together how to handle your relationship."

"Okay. I will. Anand, you tell me why the look of despair I saw on your face earlier."

"My story is almost the same as yours. Zahina's dad is a devout Muslim. We are not sure how to handle it. Any ideas?"

"No."

"You think we should go ahead with marriage, when the

time is ready?"

"Yes."

"Can't you elaborate?"

"No."

"I give up Vidya, I don't know why you always answer yes, no or maybe."

No answer.

"So be it, you are what you are. Here is my problem in a nutshell, Zahina is not ready to go against her father's wishes and it scares me, she never will. We are best friends for many years now, more like brothers. I want you to promise, you will be there for Zahina, if I am not around and she needs help."

"Yes, but why are you saying this now? Where are you planning to go? You are not dying, are you? What are you hiding from me? Is anybody threatening you because of your relationship with Zahina?"

"No, silly. I wanted you to be a big brother to Zahina, whatever happens between Zahina and I. Promise me Vidya"

"You don't have to ask, I will," Vidya promised.

#

Two days later Vidya and Ambika met after work and went for a walk. "Your dad was not happy with my visit, and he seemed upset about our friendship."

"Do not mind him Vidya, he gets upset for minor things and cools down as fast. We are okay."

"Maybe we should dial back."

"What are you saying, Vidya? This is not a clock you can dial back. It is our lives and future. I will deal with my family and get them on the right track. Don't let my dad intimidate you."

"Anand said we should discuss our relationship and that it should be a mutual decision if it should continue or slow it down?"

"It is customary in our tradition for the man to take the initiative. I expect no less from you." Ambika was peeved that Anand has taken upon himself to advise Vidya about their relationship.

Story of My Life, Vidya thought as he finally built up his courage, concerned that she would refuse and he would lose her said, "Ambi I am deeply in love with you and want you to be my life's partner. Ambi will you marry me?"

Surprised and delighted Ambika let out a loud joyful sound. Ambika recovered, flung her arms around him, hugging him and said, "I love you too. I had a crush on you since I laid my eyes on you. Vidya, if my parents disagree to our marriage, I will disown them. I will be the master of my life."

"You must come and meet my mom, Ambika. Excuse our current home, really a shack. Soon I am planning on moving into a better house and then I will invite you home."

"It will be a momentous occasion for me to meet your mom, let us do it soon."

#

Kumar, the senior teller in the bank, though middle aged and married, infatuated by Ambika, viewed Vidya as an interference. *He must be eliminated from the scene, to seduce Ambika.* Many evenings working late in his cubicle, he waited to catch them in a compromising situation. If Vidya went into Ambika's office and the door closed, Kumar would try to eavesdrop on their conversation. He heard no compromising conversation or sounds; ordinary conversations about family and the bank affairs until one day he heard Ambika talking in a loud voice with the word marriage and angry dad, repeated many times. He surmised that her dad was angry with her affair. He decided to find more about her dad to do something about it.

On the pretext of a work-related question, he entered manager Desai's office; during their conversation, "I am surprised at such a young age how Ambika became an assistant manager?"

"When your dad owns the bank and all its branches, it is easy."

Kumar came out of the office, thrilled with the information. He decided to meet Ambika's dad and inform him of the affair between Ambika and Vidya at an opportune time.

#

Srinivas after his retreat from the battle with Ambika likewise was thinking of getting rid of Vidya. He couldn't accomplish that with Ambika present. He must get rid of Vidya when Ambika was away. Firing Vidya will not be enough. He had to drive this guy, who is trying to get his hand on his wealth through marriage, out of town for good. He had a plan in mind and wanted to put it into action as soon as possible.

Srinivas told his wife, "You and Ambika visit Tirupati to pray to Lord Venkateshwara. I reserved a cottage on the hilltop for a week. I am convinced the Lord would take care of our problem." Srinivas never told her his plan.

Once Ambika and her mom got on the train to Tirupati, he called Desai. "Send me the last month's accounts statement in a sealed envelope. I need it right away, send it with Vidya."

"I can bring it myself, sir."

"The manager should be in the bank. Just send Vidya with that report."

"Yes sir, you will have it in an hour."

"Desai send me five thousand rupees from my personal account, in a separate sealed envelope."

"Yes sir."

#

Within the hour, Vidya was standing in Srinivas' home office. He knew Ambika's dad was a wealthy businessman but not as the owner of the bank. Srinivas took the envelope from Vidya and opened the report and read it. He took a pen and made notations, circled numbers humming and ignoring Vidya. Vidya's palms were sweaty, and his mouth was dry. He wished he was somewhere else, and that this was just an unpleasant dream.

After fifteen minutes, Srinivas looked at him. "I know you thought you can sweet talk my daughter into love and marriage and become wealthy. I started young and worked hard, made many sacrifices to get rich. I will not let you get away with it. I forbid you to marry my daughter. Being a kind-hearted man, I will give you a thousand rupees. That's a lot of money for someone like you. Use that to start a business or buy a piece of land or whatever you wish. Work hard and you can be successful. The road to riches for you will not be through Ambika. I want you to leave town today, never to return."

Srinivas counted and pulled out money from the envelope and pushed it toward Vidya.

Vidya took a step back, looked Srinivas straight in the eye and replied, "You are mistaken. I never knew Ambika was your daughter until I came to your home on her birthday. I did not know you owned the bank until a few minutes ago. Ambika and I like each other, and we are committed to each other."

What is this committed to each other nonsense with these young people? In my days, the only commitment we knew was to obey our parents or bosses. Srinivas said, "I am impressed by your courage but not with your commitment. Take this generous offer and leave town."

"Sorry sir, I cannot accept the money and I am not leaving town."

"If you believe this amount is not enough, say what you want? How about five thousand? That is five years' salary for you. Buy land and live off the land. This is my last and final offer. Leave town by the end of day tomorrow. Nobody will know. I will never say a word about this to anyone."

"I will not accept the money and I am not leaving town."

Srinivas was flabbergasted on hearing those words. He was about to explode in anger but realized that temper tantrums do not work with this younger generation and said, "Look Vidya, I have a lot of life's experiences and being a generous person, I will leave this offer open until 12 noon tomorrow. Go home and talk to your mom tonight and let me know tomorrow. Better yet, take this money today and show it to your mom. This will stay secret."

"Sir, I respect you. I am not here for your money. And I will not take it. Even if you offer me ten thousand or a lakh I will not. Fire me if you must. I may be poor, but I am not for sale. Namaste." Vidya left Srinivas open mouthed and apoplectic.

That evening as the bank was closing Kumar asked Vidya for help with accounting. Vidya obliged and found the error Kumar knowingly made and corrected it.

Kumar thanked Vidya profusely and asked, "Can I buy you a coffee or a cool drink?"

Vidya agreed, and they went to a coffee shop. Kumar made conversation about the bank and the people and asked, "What did Sri. Srinivas want? You spent a lot of time with him."

"Oh, nothing much. Just bank affairs."

"Everybody in the bank thinks it is because of your relationship with Ambika. I am sure he is thrilled. Are congratulations in order?"

"Nothing of that sort. Sri. Srinivasan tried to buy me off," blurted Vidya and immediately regretted his words.

"What a shame. Buy you off! How could he? That is evil my friend."

"It is getting late, thank you for the coffee." Vidya got up to leave.

Best twenty-five paisa, I ever spent thought Kumar heading to Sri. Srinivas' home.

CHAPTER 14

The Black Cat

It was a miserable, restless night for Vidya. With Ambika gone for a week and Anand getting ready for USA, he had no one to talk to about the hard times. Rainwater was dripping from the leaky roof. Vidya looked at his wristwatch and noticed it was an hour past the usual wake up time, he dressed hastily.

"It is getting late. I have to hurry or I will be late grandma."

Grandma said the usual about the black cat.

He stepped outside and saw the sewage culvert was overflowing on to the already filthy pathway leading to the road. *Lord, let me get through this day.* Pedaling his bike, he saw a black cat streak across his path chased by a dog. He did not have the time to follow his grandmother's instructions. He pedaled fast and arrived at the bank in time.

The rest of the day went well and Vidya felt relieved nothing bad happened. An hour before the money transactions closed for the day, Desai came rushing to Vidya handed him an envelope.

"You must take this to Sri. Srinivas. He is waiting for it. You must leave now, or there will be big trouble."

"I will leave as soon as I tally my accounts it won't take but 15 minutes."

"Vidya, Sri. Srinivas is wants this now; he will not wait. On your return we tally your books. I will even pay you overtime. Please go now."

Reluctantly Vidya took the envelope and biked to Sri.

Srinivas' home, hoping this encounter will be different from the last. He was ushered straight to the Srinivas' office. With trepidation, he entered the office. Sri. Srinivas was smiling. "How are you doing, Vidya? Please sit down."

"I need to go Sri. Srinivas, and tally my ledgers."

"Sit. Sit. Let me look at these papers before you go. If you get late, I will allow overtime pay. Don't worry, sit." Srinivas rang a bell and ordered coffee for Vidya.

Why I am I getting this royal treatment? It cannot be because of a change of heart. Is he going to poison me? This does not make any sense.

The attendant brought two glasses of coffee, one for the master and the other for Vidya.

"Take one. Let me finish this so you won't get late."

Fifteen minutes later the phone rang, and Srinivas picked up the phone, listened for less than a minute and hung up without saying a word.

"You may go now." Srinivas laid the papers he was reading on the table.

Vidya glanced at the papers. They were blank.

Why did they send me in a hurry to deliver blank papers? He figured; Desai sent me on this errand to get me out of the bank. For what purpose? He felt an impending doom. Maybe he will find the bank closed for the day and a note asking him not to return. I will not even go to collect the money they owe me, he promised himself.

When he got back, his station was as he left it. Vidya tallied his ledger and found it was short by a thousand rupees. *I must have made a mistake in tallying.* He repeated the process with the same result. I am too agitated, let me calm down. He did yoga to control his breathing and heart. After the third time, he was still one thousand rupees short and figured the missing thousand was a message from Sri. Srinivas. His heart was beating so fast, Vidya felt faint. *What does Sri. Srinivas want? Ask for mercy? Ask for the expired offer? Was Desai on this too? He must be because he sent me off before closing my books.*

Vidya walked into Desai's office and said, "My tally shows, I am a thousand rupees short."

Desai looked stricken, went pale and placed his hand over his heart, with great difficulty muttered, "Did you say a thousand rupees short? How can that be?"

"Sir, I want you to check the books and tally once again, using the calculator."

The manger was the only one with a mechanical calculator. They did the tally again with the same results. Kumar was watching all this unfolding with a smug expression on his face. He joined them in the tally for the fifth time and the result remained unchanged.

"I must inform Sri. Srinivas. If it is a few rupees, we can put money in and close the books." said Desai.

Srinivas arrived soon and said, "Report this to the police immediately. Vidya you must stay here until the police arrive. They will decide what to do with you. I have an important errand to run and be back before the police leave. The police will want to talk to all of you."

Srinivas got in his car and departed. Desai went to make a police report. Kumar retreated into his cubicle whistling. Vidya trapped, in his own world, was paralyzed by fear of police and thoughts of prison. He remembered telling Anand, 'I fail at everything I do; however hard I try, I always fail.' *This may be the biggest failure of all.* He knew he lost his job, his future with Ambika and most likely his freedom. *This will kill my mom--the thought of her only son behind bars. I see no way out, knew this was a setup. I never made a mistake before. I did not steal the money. How can I prove it? Can I explain to the police about his relationship with Ambika and her dad's opposition? Would anybody believe or corroborate my statements?*

An hour later a police inspector and two police constables arrived in a jeep.

"I am Inspector Cholu Das. I am investigating this crime.'

The interviews started with Desai, then Kumar, each lasting a meager ten minutes. Vidya's interview lasted more than an hour.

"Confess and return the money, I will cut down your jail time to two years, otherwise you will rot in jail for 10-15 years. Bank fraud is a serious crime."

"I cannot confess?"

"Why not?"

"Because if I confess, it will be a lie and my lie will make your lie the truth. I did not steal the money."

He repeatedly asked, "Where did you hide the money?" and "Confess now."

Cholu Das was not interested in hearing the background or Vidya's allegation of Srinivas's involvement.

Vidya asked, "Why don't you fingerprint the cash tray?".

"We do all that stuff when we can't identify the perpetrator, in this case I know who did it."

Vidya was resigned to his fate. There was no one to hear his side of the story. *Is justice so blind? Is truth only a belief in one's own mind? Is there a different truth for each person?* He had no answers; no way to prove his innocence and no way to avoid prison. He was concerned about the effect on his sick mom and old granny. Vidya did not know what Ambika's reaction will be. He desperately wanted to see her again.

#

"Handcuff this thief." The portly, rotund inspector was beaming with pride, fingering his mustache; happy this would be a feather in his cap for solving the crime against a famous bank in one evening and apprehending the criminal. Confident that before the end of the week, he would recover the missing funds. Another chance to get this name in the newspaper and on the radio. He desired to be the next superintendent of police before he was 35. Great day! He lit a cigarette, drew a deep long puff of smoke, as a constable handcuffed Vidya and put him in the jeep. The inspector decided to wait for Sri. Srinivas. A cash gift for his service was likely.

Sitting in the jeep, Vidya was desolate. He saw the car of Sri Srinivas arrive. Srinivas got out of the car, looked at Vidya, "Don't worry, I will take care of this."

Vidya saw Srinivas huddle with Cholu Das. An envelope changed hands. The inspector stuffed it in his pocket, bowed to Srinivas, walked to the jeep and released Vidya's handcuffs "I have a change of heart. You are free to go home. I want you and your family out of this town by tomorrow evening. If I find you are still in town, I will arrest you and throw you in jail. Get out and do not comeback, ever again."

Vidya got on his bike and left before the inspector changed his mind. Entering his small hut, he saw his mom and granny packing up their meager belongings. His mom hugged him and cried. His granny looked at him with a stern look. He was close to tears himself.

He eased his mom to a chair and asked, "Do you know what happened?"

"Yes, that nice man who owns your bank came in his car, to our house and told us, you lost a thousand rupees. The police were about to arrest you and take you to jail. Being a man of honor and a father himself, he felt pity for you. To secure your release he asked us to come up with the money and leave town to keep you safe if the police inspector changed his mind."

"We don't have that amount of money. What did you give him mom?"

"The only help we could think of was Anand's mom. Your nice bank owner took us in his car to Anand's house. Anand's mom 'the angel of mercy' gave us the money without hesitation. Sri. Srinivas brought us home and left to get you released. He is such a kind and honorable man. Before we leave town, you must offer your thanks and gratitude to him."

Vidya was thunderstruck by the diabolical and cunning plan that Srinivas put in to destroy him and his relationship with Ambika. Vidya decided not to tell his mom and granny the truth—the evil banker Srinivas and Desai set this in motion where the only outcome was their victory.

Next morning Vidya rode his bike to Anand's house and thanked Amma for her generosity and that he would remember her help for all the crises in his life.

"I can never repay your debt, the financial help, the timing of your help, and the care you provided for my family all these years, I do not know when I will see you again, because the police will arrest me if I return."

"You were a good friend and companion to my son; were like a brother to him. I will miss you. I told Anand many times, Vidya needs a spark to find his potential. I still believe, one day you will find your true destiny. Tell your mom and granny I will miss you and your family. Goodbye and good luck."

CHAPTER 15

Ambika's Fury

Vidya with his mom, grandmother and their meagre belongings on Bandi Wallah's ox drawn cart headed to the bus stand. The state bus ticket fare five rupees was more than eighteen rupees they had. A by passer said, "Ravi Bus is much cheaper, and sometimes let poor people travel free." They waited by the stop for Ravi bus on the side of the road. An hour later a policeman arrived and said, "Why are you still in town? Did you not know there is an arrest warrant for you? Inspector Sahib wants you to leave immediately, or I will arrest you."

"Sir, we are waiting for the bus. My family and I will leave on the Ravi Bus."

"Give me thirty rupees and I will let you stay until your bus arrives."

"All we have is 18 rupees. Please let us stay," pleaded Vidya

The policeman lowered his voice, "Did you say eighteen rupees. Give me the money, and I will let you stay." The policeman took the money and left.

The Ravi bus came an hour later. Vidya told the conductor of their inability to pay. The middle-aged conductor accepted and made a notation in his pocket ledger the names of the three passengers and that they had no money.

"Ravi Ji the owner is very generous and lets people with no money like your family, travel for free. Let the ladies sit, but you stand until all the paying passengers get a seat."

#

Ambika returned to work after her trip to Tirupati and did not find Vidya at his counter. *Perhaps he or his mom is sick she thought. I am sure he will be in tomorrow.* That evening she noticed nothing unusual in her parents. Next day Vidya was not at work again. Concerned, Ambika decided to find out why. She got Vidya's address from his personnel file and headed to Vidya's home after work, stopped a few times to ask for directions. She entered the poorer areas of the town with narrow crumbling roads, open sewers, roaming dogs, and stray animals. Even with the windows closed there was no escaping the stench of rotting garbage and sewage. When the pathway was too narrow to drive, she parked and locked the car.

After a few more inquiries, she located the one room bamboo and mud dwelling with a tin roof. She jumped over a sewer and reached the door, pushed it open and stepped inside. It was empty, no furniture, no signs of any human habitation. Ambika was at her wits' end. *Oh! Vidya, where are you? What happened? Has your mother fallen sick and in the hospital? What happened to all your belongings?* Waves of fear and despair rolled over her, she suspected a dreadful event. *Must be they moved to a nicer place like he said. Vidya must be busy settling in the new house. He will return in a day or two.*

Next morning Vidya was not at work. Before going home Ambika walked into Desai's office. "I viewed Vidya's personnel file. It was missing a lot of stuff."

The moment he heard the word Vidya, Desai's face became pale with the look of a frightened and cornered animal. Ambika flew into a rage, suspecting foul play by Desai. She leaned across Desai's table, grabbed him by his shirt and yanked him out of the chair. Desai looked at her furious face and rage filled eyes and muttered, "Please, please..."

"What have you done, you miserable human being? Where is Vidya? Tell me now or I will squeeze the life out of your scrawny neck!"

Fearing for his life Desai told her all that happened that

afternoon

"You are the bloody bank manager. What do you mean you don't know what happened to Vidya? Who put you up to this? Answer me now!"

"I swear I know nothing more. Vidya's till was short by one thousand rupees when he returned."

"Where did he go?"

"Sri. Srinivas asked me to send Vidya with some papers for his review. He went to your home."

Ambika figured the mastermind of this act and stormed out of the bank.

"Madam. Madam! Please. Don't act in haste. He is your father."

The tidal wave of fury and anguish, ready to disrupt and destroy any being or thing in its path, engulfed Ambika. She stormed right into Srinivas's office. He was sitting in a comfortable chair, with a bottle of whiskey and a half full glass next to it on a table. With a loud crash, the bottle and the glass went flying as she shoved the table away.

"What have you done? Why? Why? Why?" she screamed at him eyes glaring, face flushed with anger and fists tightly clenched.

Hearing the commotion, her mom came running into the room. Srinivas stood up and faced his daughter. "I had to do what any dad in my position would do. I got rid of the leech that stuck to you, forever and never to return. I understand your anger and frustration. Let time pass and you will thank me for what I have done. Vidya was after your money, not for love."

"You destroyed your own daughter's life. I am leaving this house, never to return. I disown you and your cruel ways."

Ambika's mom intervened, "How can you speak like that to your father? He gave you everything you have. You are our only child."

Ambika turned her fury on her mother. "Stay out of this mom. This so-called loving dad conspired and hurt an innocent man I love. He claims he got rid of Vidya, never to return. What he doesn't realize, is that with the same action, he also lost his daughter. I am not coming back ever again. I hate you! You heartless monster."

Srinivas said, "Ambika do you realize that everything I do and earn is for you. You are my only child. You will inherit all my wealth. I am even willing to give all this to you now. Forget Vidya."

"It is not happening. I do not want your wealth or your sweet talk. You have done irreparable damage to me and my love Vidya. I cannot live under the same roof with you."

"You can't be serious. Why does this guy mean that much more than your parents?" Mom stepped in.

"If you leave what will I do with all my wealth and money?," said Srinivas.

"Take it with you. Maybe light your funeral pyre with your money." Ambika grabbed her clothes and some of her belongings and walked out never to return. She got in the car went to her friend Janaki's house to stay there for a few days and plan on finding Vidya.

Next morning Ambika closed her bank accounts, drew all her money out and emptied the locker with her papers and her grandmother's jewelry. She knew her dad would try to lock her out of her accounts and safe deposit boxes to make her come to him for money. She was a step ahead of his treacherous reach.

Next mission was to find what happened to Vidya and who else took part, in the plot that her dad hatched. She also needed to find Vidya's whereabouts and unite with her love. *Vidya was naïve and had no chance against someone like her dad. I must protect him. My dad manipulated mom, to accomplish his dastardly deed. Whether her mom was complicit in the entire affair or was an unwitting participant was of no consequence and not my focus. I must find who in the bank, helped dad, and give them their due.*

Ambika spent about 30 minutes with Desai and learned of all that transpired that fateful afternoon and Desai did not know the destination of Vidya and his family. When asked the reason why Vidya was sent to her father's house he replied "Sri. Srinivas asked to send accounting papers Kumar prepared immediately with Vidya."

"Did Vidya tally his accounts before he left?"

"No madam, the call came just a few minutes before the windows closed. Vidya was reluctant to go without tallying."

"Was Kumar on any special accounting projects?"

"No. Kumar doesn't know enough about accounting to do any important work."

"Did Kumar get any calls from my dad, or did he call my dad?"

"Yes, he called Sri. Srinivas about 30 minutes after Vidya left."

"Who else was in the bank?"

"Only Kumar and me."

"Where were you and Kumar?"

"I was in my office, finishing paperwork and Kumar in his cubicle."

"Thank you, Mr. Desai. I apologize for my outburst yesterday; thought you were hiding something from me. Please do me a favor, call my father's home and talk to the cook or the maid and find out if Kumar went to the house and met with my dad recently. Do this without alerting my parents."

Desai got on the phone and talked for a while and said, "Yes. Kumar went to see Sri. Srinivas a few days ago. The watchman keeps a log who comes and goes to the house. I can find the exact date and time if you wish."

"No need. This is not a police investigation. I got enough information to connect the dots."

CHAPTER 16

Woman Scorned

Ambika entered Kumar's cubicle, who was bent down, looking under his desk for a pen that rolled down.

"KUMAR!" Ambika's voice was so loud, it startled Kumar, who jumped up, bumped his head into the table collapsed on the floor stunned.

"Get up, you swine, face me, you pathetic human being, look at me when I am talking to you."

Kumar, dazed, his head hurting, crawled from under the table, lest Ambika stomp him like Lord Shiva on the evil demon Apasmara. He stood up facing Ambika to see her anger and worried she might kill him.

"Madam calm down. Please tell me how I can help. I was just looking for my pen, not hiding or ignoring you."

"Ok, grab a pen and a paper and write your confession. And do it now!"

"Confession? I have done nothing wrong."

"Kumar, I know what you did to Vidya. I am giving you a chance. Give me your written confession, or I am going straight to the Police Superintendent. Take the easy way out, give me what I want, and I will let you go."

"Madam please don't do this. I have a wife and three children. Please don't involve the police. I did what your dad ordered me."

"Put it on paper and sign your name, write everything down that happened. I will show no mercy if you fail to document the whole truth. This is also a test of your honesty. I will know if you lie to me. Get to it NOW!"

With shaky hands and sweaty brow, Kumar wrote his confession signed and gave it to Ambika.

"Now I am letting you go, meaning you are fired. Get your belongings and get out of here. If see your face or hear your voice, I will deliver this to the police. I give you five minutes to leave. Let me not find you anywhere here." Ambika walked out on bewildered Kumar.

She trip to Vidya's home in the slums to make enquiries about Vidya was in vain. Dejected Ambika was walking back to her car when an old man stopped her and said, "I heard you are asking about the family in that house, I took them and their belongings to the bus stand in my bullock cart. Come here tomorrow during the day. You can give me a ride in your car to the bus stand. You can make inquiries there."

"Yes, thanks for the information. What is your name, Chacha Ji?"

"People call me Bandi Wallah. I will see you tomorrow where you parked the car. No need to walk all the way into this slum."

"Namaste."

"Namaste."

#

Ambika drove Bandi Wallah to the bus stand next morning. He said, "I first took them to the main bus stand, and they didn't have enough money to get on the bus. A passerby told them told them about a cheaper bus. I unloaded their belongings and waited to get hired. I saw a policeman came, threatened the young man and took all their money."

Hearing it got Ambika's blood boiling again. How could an educated, wealthy person like her dad cause such misery to Vidya? Her turned eyes red, and fists were clenched.

"Memsahib please control yourself. People might mistake you for Goddess Kali, the slayer of evil."

Yes, I must control my emotions if I want to succeed in my quest. I cannot help Vidya if I have a stroke. "Thank you, Chacha

Ji. I will now take you back to your place and I will return before the Ravi Bus gets here. Hopefully, I will get some useful information."

"Bless you, my child. I hope you find that family you are searching for. Thank you for the car ride. I can tell my grandchildren I rode in a car. I will also tell them that if they study hard and work hard, they can own a car and take their grandpa for rides. May Lord Ganesh grant you success."

#

Ambika arrived at the bus stand an hour before the Ravi Bus arrived. *The trail is getting hot. In the next day or two my quest will be complete.* She sought the conductor when the bus arrived and told him about trying to find this family that took the same bus a week ago, hoping the conductor would remember Vidya and his family.

"Sorry madam. I am the regular conductor on this route, I was away for the last ten days because of a marriage in the family."

"Please find out who was the conductor that time and contact him for me. I will pay you for your time and effort."

"Madam our bus service covers almost the entire nation. We have traveling conductors who cover, when the regular one is on leave. These folks travel all over the country to fill vacancies. Even if I find who filled my shift, there is no way for me to contact him or her. They may be a thousand miles from here. Sorry madam, I would do this for free, if I could."

The words dashed Ambika's hopes of finding Vidya. *Am I going the wrong way to tackle this? Should I start over again?* Ambika thought what she must do; difficult, but doable with determination and perseverance.

"What is the final destination of this bus?"

"The last stop is Poonam Nagar, two hundred twenty kilometers away. Why do you ask?"

"I will tell you in a minute. How many scheduled stops are on the way?"

"There are twelve scheduled stops, but sometimes if

a passenger wants off closer to their village, we make an unscheduled stop. Bus Wallah the owner wants to accommodate as any people as possible."

"How many villages are there between here and the last stop?"

"People walk 5 to 8 kilometers to get a bus in rural areas. If you add that distance on both sides of the stop, there are at least a hundred villages."

"Thank you very much Bhai Saab for your help. Please take this money for your time." Ambika handed him a ten rupee note.

"No, madam, I am helping you because you needed help. I cannot accept any money. My mom always told me to do at least one good deed every day. And this is my good deed of the day. We are ready to leave, I must go. Good luck, madam."

Within a month I can cover all villages on the route. This is the best way and take thoughts of revenge out of my mind.

#

After a lengthy journey, Vidya and the two ladies disembarked on the road next to the village an hour after midnight. His granny's house was about a mile from there. The two women headed home and let Vidya stay with their belongings until daybreak. Vidya piled their possessions upon the roadside leaned against the pile and dozed off. Every few minutes a noisy truck passed and woke him. After a few rounds of sleep and waking, he decided to stay up. *My life has turned from bad to worse and I am in an uncontrollable slide with no end in sight. My best moments were those I spent with Ambika where the future seemed rosy. This maybe the time to leave everything and go away. Granny has a modest house where mom and granny could live their remaining years. Will leaving all behind, make me more content, knowing I left my old grandmother to look after ailing mom? Can I leave Ambika without her ever knowing what happened to me or why? I owe her a goodbye. I should have fought the charges, for the truth was on my side. I let everybody roll over me due to lack of self-confidence and this will be with me until my last breath. I must contact Ambi and let her know. I cannot write to her home because of her dad; and not to the bank because Desai was part of the plot. My only option is to write a letter to Anand's mom and ask her to contact Ambika. I will work in the fields to earn money and support myself. I cannot and will not be a burden on grandma and mom.* His thoughts turned to Ambika and quenched the fire in his bosom. He fell asleep as the dawn was breaking.

He woke up to a sudden shaking of his shoulder by an elderly man asking, "Are you Vidya?"

"Yes, chacha Ji."

"Come on, load up we have to go, your grandma is waiting." The man pointing to his bullock cart. They loaded the belongings.

"You go ahead chacha ji. I will walk. I know the way."

CHAPTER 17

Granny's Village

Vidya woke up to a bright sunny morning in his own room, to the smell of fresh cut hay drifting through the windows and the sounds of the bustling cowherds and bleating goats on their way to feeding grounds. As was routine all his life, Vidya washed, did yoga for half an hour.

His granny leased a few acres of inherited land after husband's death, to supplement the pension money. Though meager, they had a better life than in the town.

"Your mom is not doing well today. Go sit with her while I bathe and prepare lunch."

His mom was in bed, pale with a sweaty brow. He put his hand on her forehead, but it did not feel like she had any fever. Her breathing was rapid, and she was restless.

"Mom, tell me what is wrong. I will get medicine from the doctor."

"I feel very weak, Vidya. My heart is beating fast and my chest hurts."

"Is it on the left side?"

"No, on the right side. It feels like I cannot get enough air when I breathe."

"I will go into town and talk to a doctor. Don't get up by yourself, call granny. I will bring you water and a banana before I leave."

"Grandma, I am going to town to get medicine for mom."

"Take ten rupees from my money box for the medicine.

Bring a packet of glucose biscuits for your mom, she is not eating much."

"Ok, grandma, I will be back soon."

He pedaled to town about five miles away, located and got to a doctor's clinic. Five people were ahead of him. At his turn he met the elderly doctor with a kind face to whom he explained his mother's illness.

"This sounds like pneumonia, but I have to examine her to be certain. Can you bring her here?"

"No sir, she is not well, and we live in the village, with no mode of travel except my bike. Please give me the medicine for her illness."

"Okay, but you must bring her here if she does not get better in five days or earlier if she gets worse. Check her breathing rate and temperature every six hours and write them down. Come in two days with your recordings. I will give antibiotic tablets for five days from my samples. She must take two tablets to start and one every six hours thereafter. She must take these with food and a glass of water. Is that clear or do I have to write it down?"

"Clear Doctor Saab. I will follow your instructions. I will be back in two days with my recordings. What is your charge for this Doctor Saab?"

"Young man, we will talk about all that when your mom recovers. For now, there is no charge. In my old age, I am trying to do a few good deeds, for the Lord to grant mercy on my soul."

"Thank you, Doctor Saab. You are an angel."

Vidya picked up the medicine, bought biscuits and headed home. On the way out he stopped at a post office and mailed a postcard to Amma asking to contact and inform Ambika of his location.

#

Vidya took care of his mom day and night, sleeping on the floor next to her bed, dispensing the tablets at designated times and maintaining a record of her breathing rate and temperature every six hours as the doctor ordered. The third day he went to see the doctor and gave him the recordings.

"If she does not improve in by tomorrow, you must bring her to the municipal hospital in town. Tell them 'Dr. Narayan said to admit her, to put her on oxygen and to call me'."

"What is wrong with my mom, Doctor Saab? Please tell me. I am worried."

"I see no improvement in her condition. If she doesn't get enough oxygen, she may have complications. That's why I am asking to go to hospital to get oxygen treatment."

"I will bring her to the hospital as you suggested Dr. Narayan. Thank you, sir, I do not know how I can repay your help."

"Son, you don't have to repay me anything. I can see you are facing tough times. Remember this day, and when you can, help a poor soul, and ask him to do the same. Humanity would be much better if we take care of the needy. Go and look after your mom."

When Vidya got home, his mom was sleeping. He woke her gave her a glucose biscuit to eat and the tablet, after drinking a full glass of water, she lay down. The thought of losing her terrified him. After his dad's death, mom and he were inseparable, leaning on each other for support and survival. Lord, let her get better soon, he prayed. After about an hour his mom woke up and asked for something to eat. He brought her a banana, but she wanted rice and yogurt.

She sat up and asked, "What really happened that day?"

Vidya knew which day his mom was referring to. The pent-up frustration and hurt, he was suppressing until then burst out and he hugged his mom. With tears flowing down his eyes and said, "I let you down, mom. Let you down. I am so sorry."

"You have not let me down. You are my son and I love you. I know you did nothing to be ashamed of. Unfortunate things happen, and I am glad that Sri. Srinivas stepped into save us. You must repay the man for all he did for you"

"Yes mom I will, when I get a chance, with a lot more of what he gave. That is a promise mom."

"Who do you think took the money that day from your till?"

"I don't know mom, whoever it is will pay, if not now when he faces the almighty."

"I am very proud of you I want you to think about your future and act on it. You must pursue what your heart wants. Make good decisions and proceed."

"Yes mom, rest now. Don't exert yourself too much. Get better!" said Vidya relieved, mom appears to be getting better.

He got his bed sheet spread it on the floor and lay down. Vidya was fast asleep a few moments later. A few minutes before mom's medicine was due, he woke up to loud snores from his mom. *She is sleeping; I hate to wake her, but I must he thought getting up and turning on the kerosene lamp by the bedside.* When he looked at his mom, his heart skipped a beat, it was not snoring he heard; she was gasping for breath. He rushed to her side and tried to wake her up and she did not respond. He called loudly for granny.

She came out of her room and asked, "What is the matter, Vidya?"

"Mom, she is gasping and unresponsive. We must take her to the hospital immediately."

"You watch over her. I will get help." Grandma walked out. Ten minutes later, she returned with a neighbor's car. With mom on the back seat with her head in granny's lap, Vidya in front, they rushed to the hospital.

Granny returned home and Vidya stayed by his mom's bedside. The next few days were a blur of activity, chest x-rays, blood tests, IV fluids and drugs, oxygen treatment and round the clock nursing attention, all thanks to Dr. Narayan who spent many hours at her bedside, adjusting oxygen, fluids and medications. On the third day, Dr. Narayan examined her. "Your mom is out of the woods and on the road to recovery. Vidya go home and rest now. You have been here for the last three days."

"I am too tired now to ride my bike to my village and back. I will take a break, get something to eat and be back in an hour."

Vidya washed, changed his clothes and headed into town to get breakfast and coffee. The aroma of frying dosa from a dhaba enticed him. *This is as good as any because there was a crowd hanging around the shack, including a few expensive cars.* He waited in line and went in, only one table was open. He sat down and ordered a masala dosa and coffee.

"Good choice we are famous for our masala dosa and yard coffee. I have not seen you here before, are you new in town?" asked the waiter.

"My mom is sick and in the hospital. We live in a village nearby."

Vidya was waiting when he heard, "Excuse us, can we share this table?"

Vidya turned and saw a teenage girl and a gentleman who he assumed was her father standing by his table, said "Yes, please sit."

"Sorry to bother you, we were in a hurry, and Rani, my daughter was hungry. I am Hari. You sound educated. Where did you go to college? What are you doing here?"

"I went to college and have BA degree in accounting and math. I live in a village, five miles from here. My Mom is in the hospital." Vidya noticed the sudden interest on Rani's face, as she turned and whispered in her dad's ears.

Hari thought for a moment "Rani wants to be an engineer and needs math coaching. Can you coach her?"

"I would love to but have no time to come to your village."

"I will send my daughter to yours every morning I will pay you 50 rupees for each session."

"Yes, Hari Ji, thank you."

Vidya finished eating, bade them goodbye and headed back to the hospital with a renewed sense of optimism.

CHAPTER 18

Search

Some villages were easy to get to, just by the side of the road, others miles from the road forcing Ambika to walk. Seven days since I started. My search is going much slower than expected; covered only thirty kilometers in six days. It will take two months or more to visit all the villages along the bus route. At each village, she showed the photo of Vidya and asked if anybody saw or know him. She got no positive leads, only advice.

"Go see an astrologist and he will know."

"You should not be on such a journey alone. It is not a woman's job."

"You should have married him before he ran away."

"Forget him. My son is looking for a bride. I am sure he will accept you."

"Go to Tirupati and pray to the Lord Venkateshwara. The Lord will send him back." *That's how I lost him.*

One day a woman said, "I saw this man with his mother and grandmother, about two weeks ago on the bus I was in. I got down here and they continued on the bus to where to I don't know."

This is my first positive lead. I am on the right track. I must continue and find Vidya, however long it takes. I am coming Vidya, please stay strong, my love. Words cannot express my sorrow for what my father did to you. No words and apologies can quench the despair and agony you are suffering. Once I find you, I will not leave your side and will shield you from the cruel world around. Be patient, Vidya. I am on my way.

#

Anand's mom was on a different mission, searching for Ambika in response to the postcard from Vidya. She went to Ambika's workplace. Nobody there had seen her in a week.

She sent her driver to Ambika's home. He returned said, "The talk is that she left town looking for Vidya."

If this letter was a few days earlier, I could have given her Vidya's location. I wonder where that poor child is wandering.

#

A day after his encounter with Hari and Rani, Vidya's mom was discharged. She was very weak and rarely spoke. He waited on her day and night.

Monday Rani arrived in a shiny black car. The driver unloaded fresh vegetables, milk and butter from Hari's farm. Vidya spread two reed mats, on the verandah's slate floor. Rani settled on one and was attentive throughout the hour. He asked her questions probing her knowledge. The last fifteen minutes were spent on background theory on her homework problems.

At the end of the class, she bowed to him and said, "Namaste, I am eager to solve those problems. Until now I thought math is beyond my capabilities. I will work hard. Thank you, Vidya Ji."

"Glad to hear that. Please convey my thanks to Hari Ji for all the food."

"Yes, I will here at nine tomorrow."

The driver came in, handed an envelope. He took it to show mom. She was asleep. He showed granny the money. "Once mom gets better, we all will go to the town and I will buy new saris for you both."

Two weeks passed with the daily coaching, receiving farm fresh grains and vegetables and the envelope with fifty rupees. Vidya was glad he was contributing to the family's income and rations. However, he knew this would end soon; Rani was a fast learner.

"I never had a teacher like you. You made math interesting."

I must find another job to keep earning. He was also happy for his mom's slow but continuous recovery. Still weak, she would sit up on her own, take a few steps to the bathroom and was eating a little more every day. That night after supper he sat with his mom. She talked about his dad. "We met in the bank where I worked, had a whirlwind romance and got married six months later. His parents were against our marriage because he was Brahmin and I was not. His parents' opposition did not dissuade your dad. I want you to know and remember, your dad was a wonderful human being, ignored caste or status. He considered all were God's children and we should love and respect each other."

"I remember joining him every morning for yoga."

"You were just five years old when he joined the army."

"I love you very much. Your dad would be proud of you. I better go to sleep now. I am very tired."

#

The next morning his mother did not get up at her usual time. Vidya tried to wake her and discovered she died in her sleep. The death of his mom was like a hammer blow. He stood there holding his mother's hand, unable to move or think. He wasn't sure how long he stood there until granny came in to announce that Rani arrived. He looked at his granny, teary eyed, and managed a whisper. "Mom is no more."

It took grandma a few seconds for his words to register. Granny moved to his side, hugged him and both put their arms around the dead woman and cried.

Granny stood up, wiped her tears and said, "Send Rani home. You go to the priest's house and bring him for prayers. I will gather woman folks to help me prepare my daughter for cremation. We have a lot of work to do."

Vidya looked at his mom's body once again, kissed her on the cheek and said, "Goodbye mom, go, be with dad."

Before sunset, the body must be cremated, the funeral pyre lit by the eldest son by tradition. Lighting a funeral pyre and see the body consumed by flames signified the finality of death; releasing the elements of the body into the universe of which it was born; from which there is no return; life must go on, and the living must endure. For Vidya, it was gut wrenching experience to see his mom's body consumed by flames. Even the tears stopped flowing. He was numb and drained, thinking the only person with him since dawn of time until today was no longer there. He wasn't sure how he would survive without his mom, his anchor, who brought him up. He thought of the sacrifices she made to get him educated. In his heart, he believed he failed her miserably.

#

He told granny, "Grandma, I decided. I am leaving."

"I would hate to see you go, but if that is what you decide I will not try to dissuade you. Where are you going?"

"I don't know."

"What are you going to do?"

"I don't know."

"When are you leaving?"

"Tomorrow."

"Vidya you cannot leave tomorrow. You must be present for the ninth- and thirtieth-day religious ceremonies for your mom."

"Grandma I cannot stay in this house any longer, it will drive me mad."

"Vidya I understand your feelings. I have similar thoughts, losing my only daughter. But we must go on because that's what life is all about. Your mom would want that. You must stay strong and continue with your life."

"Grandma, I fail at everything I attempt or do. I never succeeded. Didn't take proper care of mom. Failed at the bank job and failed Ambika."

"Who is she and how have you failed her?"

"She is the one you made the handkerchief for, remember grandma?"

"Yes, what about her? What happened?"

Vidya poured his heart out.

"Did your mom know? She thought Srinivas was a savior and prevented you from going to prison."

"No grandma, I haven't talked to anybody about this until now, you are the only person who knows. Never told mom. Didn't want to upset her."

"Your mom was always sensitive and kindhearted. She loved you very much. This would have broken her heart." Grandma thought for a moment. "Vidya, I want you to go to the store and bring me some jaggery, a handful of raisins, cashews and half a kg of milk. There is a person I want you to meet and tell him all you told me today."

CHAPTER 19

Pandit Ji

Grandma made 'Paramannam' a rice dish cooked with milk, nuts, raisins and sweetened with jaggery. She packed the warm dish in a clay bowl and walked with Vidya in tow. They crossed through narrow paths between fields and houses and reached a thatched hut, with a patch of vegetable plants in the front yard and a clay planter with a Tulsi plant. Vidya waited outside while grandma went in. Minutes later she stepped out and beckoned Vidya in. An old man with flowing white hair, beard and bright intense eyes was sitting on a bamboo cot.

"Pandit Ji, this is my grandson Vidya. His mom passed away yesterday. He wants to leave the village and go away."

"Vidya, what a name. Means knowledge, learning. Please come sit by my side son," Pandit Ji said showing the place next to him on the cot, and turned to grandma, "Every bird must leave the nest. Only it knows when the right time is. If Vidya says he wants to leave, means he knows the right time is now. That is the way of nature and life," while his piercing bright eyes locked on to Vidya's. *He is looking into my soul and what he will find is not something I am proud of.*

"Let him stay with me for the next few weeks. I am a lonely old man he can help me with my chores. I will be a mentor and talk to him about his plans."

He showed Vidya the room with a cot that will be his until he is ready to leave.

"I expect you to get up in the morning, bathe and get me

my breakfast of milk and fruit. Then we will do yoga together, after which you will clean the kitchen and make my lunch of rice and lentils. The food I eat is unseasoned, no salt, pepper or spices and no chilies. Just boiled. We will eat together and talk. I will not tell you what to do with your life. That is for you to decide. You, however, can tell me what you are planning. If I think you are on the right path, I will let you know, if not I will ask you to rethink it. Once you decide, I will try to help you in achieving your goal."

"Pandit Ji, can I go to my grandma's house to get my belongings?"

"Son, you don't need my permission. Just tell me where you are going. Learn to express yourself forcefully. That's today's lesson."

Vidya returned an hour later with a bag containing his earthly possessions, clothes, a framed picture of his mom dad and him and another one of Ambika and him. Held in his hand was the cricket ball. Pandit Ji asked him, "Do you play cricket?"

Vidya told him about Anand and Gunners and his role in their victory over Prabhus.

"How did it feel when it happened?"

"I was proud of myself for my role, but soon I realized that it was a fluke."

"Did you not play in the championships?"

"No, I had to take care of my mom; work in the evenings to earn money to support our household."

"You think, Anand who built a team and won the championship is a leader and admirable, and you, who stuck to your responsibilities and contributed to the welfare of your mom, any less admirable?" Pandit Ji's bright eyes were probing.

Vidya mumbled, "I never thought on those lines."

"Societal and cultural beliefs define success and failure. By those standards one may consider you to be a failure, however if you look at your life so far, the commitment to your family and welfare of your mom, are so much more admirable. I consider that a success. Follow your heart, persevere in causes you believe in or those that beckon you because of their value to humanity, society or nature. Just do not equate success with how many prizes you win or how much money you make or how big a house you build."

"Yes, Pandit Ji."

"What I hear is during those moments your focus was intense and without thought, completed the task, giving your team the greatest win in their early days. You remind me of Arjun, the elite warrior and archer of the Pandavas. When Drona was teaching Pandavas archery, he asked each one of the five brothers aiming their arrows at a small target 'what do you see?' all brothers except Arjun said, 'we see the target, the tree, the forest, and you master'. Arjun said, 'I see the target and nothing else'."

#

One day Vidya asked, "Pandit Ji, I would like to continue coaching Rani for the next two weeks. I would like to prepare her for exams."

"Is that the daughter of Hari Ji who lives in the village the other side of the town?"

"Yes."

"I will send a message to Hari Ji, to send his daughter here, after lunch around 2 o'clock. You can coach Rani in the hallway."

Vidya continued coaching Rani, earning money, most of which he planned to leave for his granny and some for himself and rest to Pandit Ji. When he gave money to Pandit Ji, he refused. "I have no need for any money. I have enough to sustain me through whatever time I have of left on this earth."

#

After breakfast and in the evenings, Pandit Ji talked to him about his life and his views on life, honor and responsibilities. They discussed—good and evil and the grey zone in between. Most of us move between the two; we must try to stay on the good side; tolerate people who unknowingly wander to the dark side; deal with those that have willfully gone there; and it is everyone's duty to fight those on the dark side, explained Pandit Ji.

"If you do not fight evil it will propagate, encircle the good and destroy it."

"I faced evil, did not recognize it and lost the only girl I loved."

"Is that the girl in the photograph next to your bed?"

"Yes, Pandit Ji that is Ambika." Vidya told his story.

"If you knew the nature of her dad, anticipated his devious move, you could have avoided this entire affair."

"Yes Pandit Ji, we did not know how far her father would go."

"You both were young and naïve. You were expecting a happy ending, but that did not have a chance, with one so cunning and resourceful. I am very sorry it has happened to you. If I were in your position, and if I came across my love again, I wouldn't waste any time, and formalize the relationship through marriage. No dad would disrupt the sanctity of marriage, we strongly believe in."

"Yes, Pandit Ji, that is where we were wrong. We should have gotten married at the first sign of trouble, instead we tried to change the person to our thinking and failed."

One day the conversation turned to how to fight unjust acts. "Before you start a fight to correct an unjust action, you must be able to discern what is just and unjust, the transition between one and the other is gradual like between night and day. If you are fighting for your life, then any action you take is just. You may not take a life to protect your material goods. In certain situations, you must act without thinking because you may not have enough time; act on instinct; like the day you won the game for your team. When time is of the essence and you must act on instinct, sometimes you succeed other times fail. If you do not act, the outcome is always failure. Remember that."

"Pandit Ji, when the person being unjust is too rich or

powerful how can fighting help?"

"Fighting unjust does not just mean picking up a weapon and going into a physical fight. Resistance is another way of fighting; like Gandhi fought the British. Another way of fighting unjust is by exposing their actions to the public or governing bodies. As a last resort, one may fight the powerful by letting them believe they have won, and when the time is right, trap them or expose them."

Another day the conversation turned to the fateful day and the black cat incident.

"Grandma always told me that if a black cat ran across the street on which I was going, to come back wash up, say prayers to Lord Ganesh before heading back out again. I did not follow grandma's advice and headed straight out to work on the day I lost my job and Ambika."

"What you are saying is a classic example of 'post hoc ergo propter hoc' the Latin saying this happened so that happened. Vidya you are tying up two unrelated incidents in a causal relationship. Whether the cat crossed your path, or you followed or failed to follow your granny's instructions, had no bearing on the outcome. The plan set in motion to entrap you had a predetermined outcome."

"If I had returned home and followed her instructions, maybe this would not have happened."

"You cannot let superstitions rule your life. Stop blaming yourself for every misfortune that comes your way. Pursue your destiny with no reservation. Positive attitude gets you farther ahead; negative thoughts always hinder."

"What can I do to gain a positive attitude?"

"We all have inner demons that try to destroy us from within, learn to control those. You must find your own way to identify and deal with the ones that are bothering you.

"Ravana kidnapped Rama's wife Sita and took her to Sri Lanka. Rama and his brother Lakshman went to rescue Sita, sought help from Hanuman and his monkey army. After a great battle, Rama slayed Ravana. On the return journey to their kingdom, the thought, Sita is not pure, being a captive of Ravana, plagued Rama. That was Rama's inner demon, he killed the real demon Ravana, but could not conquer his inner demon. It is not a simple task, if you don't, those insecurities will consume and destroy you."

"What is the best way to fight insecurities, Pandit Ji?"

"There is no general rule, if heights frighten you, go up a high mountain and look down into the valley, if water, find a large lake and swim across it. The insecurity dictates the way to fight it."

"I understand Pandit Ji, thank you."

#

That night Vidya slept thinking of his talk with Pandit Ji. When he awoke, knew what his inner demon was and how to slay it. After the morning ritual of Yoga and breakfast, he sat down with Pandit Ji.

"Your talk about inner demons made me realize what I have known for a long time. Thank you for enlightening me on this subject, now I know what it is, how to face it, fight it and destroy it."

"Vidya I am glad you have decided. If you wish, share it with me."

"My inner demon is that cat crossing my path, I have to face a cat not any cat, the biggest of them all, a tiger. When I come face to face with a tiger, I am sure that will slay my inner demon."

Pandit Ji was aghast. *What have I done? How does this young fellow's brain work? Facing a tiger because of a superstition about a cat? Does he know what a tiger is capable of? What do I tell his granny who sought my help and as a result her grandson is going to his death by a tiger? What should I say to him now?*

"If you want to face a tiger Vidya, why don't you go to a zoo?"

"That is cheating, and it would not destroy my inner demon."

"I think it is a terrible idea, going to face a wild tiger in the forest. Some are man eaters!"

"My decision is final. Tomorrow is my mother's thirtieth day ceremony. I will leave tomorrow afternoon. I will see Hari Ji this afternoon after I finish coaching Rani. I will ask him to talk to Ravi Ji, the Bus Wallah, to help me get to a tiger preserve. I will walk the forest until I come across a tiger."

"What in heaven's name are you going to do when you come across a tiger? You think it will let you walk away. It will attack and maul you. Lucky if you came out alive. Why don't we talk more and do something less drastic?"

"Pandit Ji, you lifted the fog that's been clouding my mind. My destination begins with my encounter with a tiger but does not end there. I know what I am getting into. I will be back within two months, a changed person."

"Is there anything I can do for you?"

"Look after my grandmother and If you know anybody who has faced a tiger before, please let me know. I need help to find a tiger."

"I know of a fellow Narula, in a village in Madhya Pradesh. People say some days he lives in a cave with a wild tiger. I do not know if it is true, but I can give you a letter for him. He is eccentric and may not help."

Next day Vidya met with Hari Ji and asked him if he would help him get to the tiger preserve in Madhya Pradesh.

Hari asked, "Why do you want to go to the forest? Are you not happy here? Do you need a job? I have many businesses and properties and need someone like you to be my accountant."

"I am going there to face a tiger and erase my inner demons. No, I am not happy. I must follow my destiny. When I return, we can talk about the job."

"I know the right person to help, in Bombay, the one who saved my daughter's life. I will call him now and see what he says."

CHAPTER 20

Tiger Here I Come

Four days of bus journey from the village to the megacity of Bombay with multiple bus changes, a tired Vidya arrived in Mumbai and waited for Ravi at the MSRTC bus stand. He was being drawn to a tiger like a moth to a flame. *Maybe this will be the last thing I do, and the tiger will end my pathetic life. No regrets there. Mom's gone, Ambika was lost. My desire to tell her at least once, I love her, and look at her beautiful face, seemed impossible now. May Lord Ganesh bless her with a happy life.*

"You must be Vidya, welcome to Bombay, I am Ravi" said the nondescript smiling man in his forties disrupting his thoughts. Ravi, bald, of medium build not deserving a second glance was the owner of the largest bus service in the country.

"Namaste, Ravi Ji. it is nice of you to take time out of your busy schedule to pick me up."

"Hari Ji asked me for a favor and I cannot refuse. What he has done for me is beyond belief. I owe all this to him. Come on let us go home, where you can rest and relax. After dinner, we will talk of your plans."

Ravi took Vidya to his modest four-bedroom home, where he met the rest of the family. That evening after a simple meal of rice, roti, dal and green beans he sat down with Ravi.

"Hari Ji told me you want to face a tiger in the wild. There is a reason it is the king of the jungle. It does not react well to intruders. Please reconsider your decision."

"Ravi Ji, all my life I listened to reason and everybody's

advice. It got me nowhere. No disrespect to you, my decision is final. If I lose my life, it is no loss to anybody except my grandma."

"If I have not promised Hari Ji, I would refuse to help in your foolish decision. I will arrange your transportation to the village adjoining the tiger preserve in Madhya Pradesh. If you do not return in 2 months, I will consider you to be a victim of the tiger and send word to Hari Ji and inform your grandmother. Do you understand?"

"Yes, Ravi Ji. I cannot thank you enough for your help. I will return, if not please send this money to my grandma," Vidya handed his money to Ravi.

#

Forty eight hours of bus journey and a night in the town later, Vidya found himself on the pillion of Prakash Khan's Royal Enfield motor bike. They stopped at a dhaba to get hot tea and a breakfast of aloo poori.

"I am a mixed breed," Prakash explained, "My mother is a Hindu and my father is a Muslim, that's how I got this weird name, the Hindus avoid me because they think I am a Muslim and the Muslims because they think I am a Hindu. There is no family in the town to accept me as their son in law, so there is no marriage for me in my future."

"I am sorry to hear that. I have a friend Anand a Hindu, in love with a Muslim girl. I wonder how they and their children will fare. He left for USA to pursue his dreams and I haven't heard from him or his girl. But Prakash, don't give up, the country is changing, and you will meet a girl who doesn't care about these differences."

"Inshah Allah. Let us get going. It is a rough ride to our destination. I like to get there in time for me to return home safe. Part of the track is through the forest and dangerous to travel after sunset."

#

Once out of the town, the road narrowed between fields and soon turned into a dirt track. They quickly passed the fields and entered the fringes of the forest home to a variety of wildlife.

"I lived in the village we are going to when I was a forest ranger. My partner and I tracked all the tigers in this preserve and have given them names or numbers. The most ferocious one, we named 'Rudra' the angry one. He is the largest of the tigers in this preserve and very protective of his territory, which includes all the areas you will be in. Rudra charges anyone who enters his territory."

"Also tell me about the man who lives with a tiger, I would like to meet and talk to him."

"He is a holy man living in the village. People have seen him enter a cave, sometimes followed by a tiger. The first time it happened everybody thought he became food for the tiger. He stepped out of the cave a few hours after the tiger departed, without a scratch. People in the village believe the tiger will not attack him because Lord Shiva protects him."

"Maybe he will take me with him to the cave to see the tiger and face it."

"Just because the tiger won't attack him doesn't mean it won't attack you. Why would Lord Shiva try to protect you? You are not a holy man."

"When we get to the village, please take me to him."

"Where will you be staying in the village?"

"I don't know yet. I will find somebody to let me sleep on their verandah."

"When I lived in the village, the only person who did not shun me was Kalu. He lives with his mother. They have a covered area for their goats with an attic. I will ask them to let you stay in the attic if you like."

"Thanks."

They were halfway through their journey and Vidya noticed the jungle getting dense. Multiple small pathways extended into the forest from the track they were traveling on.

"We are at the lake the animals drinking spot and Rudra's favorite hunting ground. Do not worry, the sound of the motorbike will keep them away. We have another ten kilometers to go, skirting the lake and reaching the other bank. There is shortcut closer to the lake, but it is passable only by foot," said Prakash pointing a path. "Nobody ventures on that during early hours of the morning or the late evenings, that's when Rudra hunts around the lake."

Soon they arrived at the village composed of thatched huts with mud walls and a few brick-and-mortar homes. There was a small store with a metal roof and a thatched hut with a crude sign 'Fresh Fish Cooked to Your Taste' the only restaurant in the village. Another hut, a little larger than the others with knee high walls, proclaimed 'The School' painted on a tin sheet. Scattered haphazardly were the rest of the buildings, with no defined roads or planning. Most of these dwellings had a fence made of bamboo or rough timber that housed the humans and livestock. Stray dogs roamed and scavenged the garbage.

"We have arrived at the village I call Rudra Pura, home of Rudra the tiger, though it has an official name. First we will go to Kalu's and ask if they can accommodate you. After lunch at the restaurant, I will show you the sadhu's hut and depart."

At Kalu's place, Vidya waited outside while Prakash talked, came out and said, "They have no objection to you staying in the attic over the goat shed. You can bathe at the communal well in the village or in the lake. They agreed to share their rations with you. I promised to bring rice, flour, lentils and butter on Saturdays. Ravi Ji will reimburse me. Now let us get food, I am starving."

The restaurant Vidya noticed was a small one room hut, a curtain separated the kitchen from the dining area with a few chairs and a long wooden bench.

Vidya said, "I am a vegetarian. I do not eat fish or meat."

"Even if you eat fish, do not order fish here unless you have a few hours to spend. The first time I came here I ordered the fish. I sat here for twenty minutes. The owner's wife came out with a glass of hot tea, which I accepted. Every half hour she would walk in, fill my glass with more tea. When she came out the fifth time to fill my cup, I asked her 'Where is the fish?' 'Bhai Saab, my husband has gone to catch fish. We serve fresh fish only,' replied the wife. Here you order rice and dal unless you have the rest of the day to wait."

#

After lunch, Prakash pointed to a hut almost at the edge of the village. "That's where the sadhu lives. Good luck!"

Vidya got to the hut, nobody was in. He waited under a shade tree, noticed the edge of the lake about half a mile away and beyond that the thick forest. He saw a few deer, monkeys and a large antelope come to the water's edge but no tiger appeared. The weariness of travel and the stress caught up with him and he fell asleep. He woke up and saw a man on a cot outside the hut. The man was old, thin as a rail with a long flowing beard and a bald head.

As Vidya approached, the man opened his eyes, "If you wander in the forest, be silent or you will scare the animals or attract the notice of the killers."

"Namaste, I have a letter for you from Pandit Ji." Vidya handed the man the letter.

Narula read the letter. "I have lost touch with this fellow many years ago. I am glad he is alive. He has asked me to help Vidya. Are you Vidya?"

"Yes, Narula Ji, my name is Vidya. I need your help."

"Vidya! I am not in the habit of helping. I came here to be one with the nature, having denounced all earthly connections. Helping you or trying to help you will rekindle lost connections and stray me from my pursuit of moksha. I cannot help you."

"Narula Ji, all I want is an encounter with a tiger. They say you shared a cave with a tiger. Let me know how I can cross paths with this tiger?"

"In seeking moksha, one has to abandon hurting or killing any being. By telling you how to face the tiger I will cause you harm."

"Please tell me where this tiger's cave is, Narula Ji."

"No."

Disappointed, Vidya went back to the attic in Kalu's compound. He carried dry hay into the attic and spread it on the bamboo floor, into a makeshift bed and spread the cloth he carried his belongings in on top and lay down.

A strange buzzing sound woke him. It was pitch dark and he had no lamp to find out where the noise was coming from. The incessant buzzing made it difficult to sleep. He tossed around in the hay bed. When it was light, he looked around and found a large beehive in one corner. He was glad he did not blunder around in the dark and bump into the beehive.

Vidya got down the rickety ladder to the bleating goats. He joined Kalu and his mother for tea, settling in and letting the rich, creamy drink warm him."

"My name is Kalu. Sorry I did not meet you yesterday to tell you about the beehive up there, I gather honey every month. I just got back from my trip to watch the tiger."

Hearing the word tiger, Vidya forgot all about the bees and asked Kalu, "Did you see the tiger? Can I go with you next time? I want to see the tiger face to face."

"You don't want to see the tiger face to face. It is evil. It tried to kill me instead of eating the antelope it killed."

"Tell me all about it," begged Vidya.

CHAPTER 21

Kalu

Holding the rusty spear with a wooden shaft in his arms Kalu was thinking of the owner of the spear. Grandpa Nannu the only man in this and the surrounding villages, who killed a tiger in his youth. Nannu tending goats saw the tiger attacking one of his goats. He charged the tiger with the spear and got mauled but managed to drive the spear into the tiger's side. After recovering from the mauling Nannu found the tiger dead and retrieved his spear from its carcass. Kalu hefted the spear in his grip and thought of his grandfather's bravery.

He sought the advice of Balanna, the village potter who was always ready to offer advice. The potter was spinning the wheel and transforming a lump of grayish black clay into a pot. Once a month he loaded his bullock cart with the pots and sold them in the town.

Balanna noticed the nineteen-year-old Kalu observing him and asked,

"What are you doing here? Don't you have anything to do? If you have nothing to do, you can spin the pottery wheel. I will give you a clay pot."

"I am delighted to help you, Chacha Ji. Can we talk about tiger hunting while we do the pottery?"

Balanna looked at this young man who he knew was not very bright said, "Okay. What tiger hunt were you talking about?"

"Balanna, you know my grandfather was a great hunter and

killed a tiger with his spear; I want to use the same spear and go on a tiger hunt. I will prove myself a great hunter and shut up the kids up who laugh at me."

"Kalu does your mother know about this? After your father's death, you are the only one left for her?"

"My mother worries too much about me. If I tell her, it will upset her. Will you tell me how to hunt a tiger?"

"I am just a potter who works with clay and mud; what do I know about tiger hunting?" Balanna tried to sidestep the issue.

"Everybody in this town comes to you with their problems and you help them. Why wouldn't you do the same for me?"

"I know nothing about hunting a tiger."

"Okay. If you are not willing to help, I will grab the spear and enter the forest this evening. I will take a piglet with me; cut its ear off and put salt on the cut ear. The squealing will bring the tiger to where I am and then I will kill it with the spear."

"I will tell your mom. She knows how to stop you."

"You can't; she has gone for a week to see her brother."

"Listen Kalu, you are like my son. Hunting a tiger with a spear will get you hurt or killed." Balanna decided to delay him until his mother came back. "Okay, before you go hunting a tiger you must know the habits of the tiger, when and where it hunts. I suggest you go into the forest two hours before sunset, climb a tall tree with a view of the lake and stay there until daybreak, watching for the tiger. Take food and water with you along with a thick blanket. Do it for a week. Then we talk about hunting."

#

Rudra is a full grown Royal Bengal Tiger weighing 230kg with pug marks the size of dinner plates, commanding a territory of about 150 square kilometers. At the far end of the Rudra's territory a lake separated the forest from the village. Rudra charges with a mighty roar, when anyone enter its territory, sometimes panicking even the most experienced forest rangers. It would stop a hundred feet from the intruders, bare his long canines and snarl. The rangers backed out or fired their guns into the air a sign for it to retreat.

Recently a juvenile male tiger encroached on his territory, and Rudra severely mauled it and was extra vigilant, patrolled and marked its territory with urine, deep claw marks on the trunks of trees and rubbing its glistening coat against rough trees leaving a few strands of his orange and black hairs.

#

Kalu spent the last three nights in a tall tree waiting for a glimpse of the tiger. He decided that if he did not see the tiger tonight, he might change his location to a fresh vantage point. It was dusk and Kalu was staring into the jungle adjacent the lake. Nothing moved except the leaves and small branches in the wind. He dozed and suddenly his eyes jerked open, not knowing what woke him. A slight rustling sound reached his ears and looking in that direction and saw an imperceptible movement wide in the tall grass. Is it the tiger? A chill ran up his body, and the hairs on his forearms stood up. *Even if the tiger is here, I am beyond its reach, safe, high on the tree.* He heard heavy snorting, branches scraping and dry leaves crackling. Kalu saw a huge Nilgai ambling toward the lake, its muscles rippling under its grayish blue skin, the head with two sharp horns moving from side to side looking for predators. Seeing none, the animal reached the edge of the lake and dipped its head down to the water.

#

Rudra let out a heart stopping snarl and leaped out of the grass. The sudden explosive move of the tiger startled Kalu. He almost fell off his perch. The roar of the tiger panicked the nilgai. It waded into the lake. Rudra had the beast where he had the advantage. Rudra leaped to land on the bull's back, but the nilgai twisted to one side, Rudra missed, landed in the lake with a big splash and let out a bloodcurdling snarl. The massive bull realized its best chance for survival was to face the tiger; not expose the hind legs to the tiger's attack. It turned around to face the tiger with its head down, protecting the underside of the neck and his horns pointing at the tiger.

Rudra went and swam under water and clamped his powerful jaws on the snout of the nilgai. With a powerful heave, the nilgai lifted the tiger out of water and flung it sideways. Rudra landed a few feet away in the water and charged the bull again. The bite of the tiger badly damaged the snout and upper airways of the bull. It tottered and collapsed. Rudra clamped its teeth on the underside of the bull's neck and his mighty forelegs with razor sharp claws encircled the sides of the antelope's neck. Rudra held this position until death released the nilgai from further suffering.

Scared Kalu watched the fight, was shivering and had an incredible urge to urinate. He tried to hold it for a few minutes and as he noticed the tiger tear into his recent kill; he let loose a stream of urine that splattered the forest floor. The sound of the urine falling on the dried leaves interrupted tiger's meal. Sensing an intruder and protective of its kill, Rudra snarled and moved towards the sound.

Kalu held on to the branch as the tiger approached and hoped it would go back to the kill. But to his dismay the tiger looked up, and he was staring into the orange yellow eyes of the tiger. Rudra, sat on its haunches watching him. Kalu stayed silent hoping it would go away. In a blink the tiger leaped, its blood-stained face coming closer and closer. It seemed like an eternity but lasted just a fraction of a second. The tiger's open mouth was just a few feet away from him. Paralyzed with fear and hypnotized by the tiger's eyes, Kalu could not move. The tiger tried to reach for Kalu with one of its forelegs. The momentum of the leap slowed, and it fell away. Kalu woke up from the trance and saw the tiger crouching below. *The next jump, the tiger will grab me.* He looked around hoping to scramble up but could not find a branch strong enough to support him. Kalu held the rusted spear tip facing the tiger in his right hand, his left wrapped around a branch and readied for the fight of his life. He saw the muscles of the tiger's hind legs and back bunching; it was now or never. He raised his arm above his head with the spear still pointed down, to thrust at the tiger. In a blur of motion, Rudra leaped. Kalu leaned back to be out of its reach and as the front leg was extending toward him, he thrust the spear down. His arm jarred as the spear impacted the tiger's paw and almost caused him to lose balance, but his arm around the branch held. The tiger disappeared from view with a loud snarl. It was nowhere to be seen, but the shaft of the spear was on the ground.

Kalu waited until the sun was shining brightly, looked around and slithered down the tree gathered the broken half of the spear and ran home.

Though the encounter with Rudra frightened Kalu, he continued to watch for the tiger many evenings, perched on a much higher tree with a very sturdy branch and thick foliage to hide him. He noticed the tiger was limping. It hunted around the lake for about a week and then retreated into the jungle and left the area for three to four weeks; it was near the lake a few days before and after full moon night.

CHAPTER 22

Success

Ambika was in her eighth week of searching for Vidya. Realized she was overly optimistic to complete the search in a month. There were too many villages on this stretch of the road, she showed the Vidya' photo around and asked if anybody seen or heard of him. Except for the one person who saw him on the Ravi Bus, a month ago, no other sightings came to light. Vidya disappeared into thin air with his mom and grandma. I wish I knew which village his grandma came from. Is this search all in vain? Have I lost track of him, never to find him again? I cannot survive if these negative thoughts take root in my soul. I must and will find him. He cannot be too far because I can feel his thoughts about me. I am on the right track. I must go on. In all the villages adjoining the road the word spread about this young woman with wavy black hair and large bright eyes looking for a man named Vidya.

The long walks to villages and the toll of travel showed their effect on Ambika. Her dark skin turned darker, whatever fat she had on her lanky body melted away and her muscles showed on her firm body like that of a finely tuned athlete. At the end of the day when she settled herself in some dharmsala, would sometime sink into depression, let her tears flow. By morning, Ambika put her sorrows away and resumed her quest, got to her car checked the fuel, oil level, and the tires before the journey to the next village. She worried Vidya would not take the stress, well. One day she stopped at a temple for Lord Ganesh by the roadside and prayed for the Lord's blessings. The presence of a temple so close to the road surprised her. As she did most days, she showed Vidya's photo and asked if anybody had seen him. And as always, she got the answer "No we have not seen this young man."

Before leaving the temple, she prayed again to Lord Ganesh for success in her search. By noon she reached a town and stopped at a roadside dhaba. She ordered a dosa and coffee. Coffee arrived, and Ambika took a few sips of steaming coffee, felt better and looked around. Thinking this may be a good place went from table to table making inquiries, made a full circle back to her table disappointed. She was close to tears when the waiter brought her food.

"Madam are you ok? Is anybody bothering you here?"

"Nobody is bothering me. Bhai Saab can you look at this photo and tell me if you have seen this person?"

He looked at the photo for a while, "I saw him about six weeks ago. He came here ordered a dosa and coffee like you and said his mother was in the hospital here."

Ambika jumped out of her chair and said, "Where is the hospital? I am going there right now."

"Madam please finish your food and coffee. The hospital is not going anywhere. You look starved and ready to faint."

She wolfed the food and rushed to the hospital. *Lord you have answered my prayers.* It was a small hospital with about sixty beds. She went to every ward showing the photo and asking.

A nurse looked at the photo said. "I saw this man tending to his mom, sometime ago. I don't know his name or where he went." Noticing Ambika's disappointment, she said, "Please wait here, let me look up something in my ward register. Don't leave until we talk again."

She returned 10 minutes later, "The patient Padma was discharged after recovery from pneumonia with this man her son, tending. I do not have further information or their address. I am sorry. You might ask Dr. Narayan who was close to the young man."

"Where can I find Dr. Narayan? I must see him."

Ambika followed the nurse's directions, arrived at Dr. Narayan's office and found patients waiting. She was told to wait for her turn.

"I am not a patient. I need to see him on a personal matter, would you tell him Vidya's ..."

The door behind her opened and she heard a soft voice, "Did somebody say Vidya?"

Ambika turned towards the voice and saw an elderly doctor. "Yes, Doctors Saab, for the last two months I was searching for Vidya. Can you please help me?"

"Beti, come sit down and relax. I know Vidya and I know where he is. I will tell you."

He took Ambika into his office closed the door. He told her Vidya's mother's illness, recovery, going home and sudden death. Upon hearing of Vidya's mom death Ambika broke down sobbing. Dr. Narayan consoled her. She thanked Dr. Narayan for all he had done for Vidya's mom.

"Now please Doctor Saab, I have to go see him please give me the address."

#

The sun was setting when she reached Vidya's village and followed the directions to his grandmother's house. The house was eerily quiet with a single lamp in the verandah. She went to the door and said "Vidya! Are you in there? It is Ambika."

She heard shuffling steps as the door opened by a woman in her eighties. "Ambika, please come in Vidya talked about you a lot."

"Is Vidya in or has he gone out? I am very sorry to hear about his mom's death. You must be his grandmother."

"Come in sit down. Consider this you home until Vidya returns."

She led Ambika into her home and showed her a room. "This is Vidya's room. Make this yours until he returns."

"Please tell me when he is returning and where he is. I will get in my car and bring him here."

"Beti, it is not that easy. His mom's death changed him. He was at a loss and did not know how to survive without her. He told me how he lost you; about all that happened; how he was falsely accused of stealing the money."

"Grandma! Can I call you grandma?"

"Yes, my beti, I like that."

"I have proof that Vidya is innocent. I have a written and signed confession from the guy who took the money. I came here to take Vidya back and clear his name."

"I admire your perseverance in getting and confirming what we in the family knew to be true. But first let me finish what I was telling you. Vidya packed some of his clothes, his mom's and your photo a small amount of cash and the cricket ball that never leaves his side. He left to face a tiger and slay the demon, in his own words. It made no sense."

The words struck a blow to Ambika's plans of getting together with Vidya. *Why is Vidya talking about tigers and demons? Has the stress destroyed his mind and made him raving mad? Is there any logical reason for a sane person to go looking for a tiger? And what about slaying a demon?* She took a few deep breaths to compose herself.

"Grandma I left my parents after my dad's treachery. I am not going back home, ever. The only person I love is gone. I have nowhere to go. Would you mind if I stayed with you until Vidya returned? I promise I won't be a burden on you. I can pay you rent. I will cook, clean and take care of you."

"Beti, I am old but am capable of taking care of myself and you, my grandson's future wife. Please stay here. Do not insult your new grandma by offering her money. Hold on to your money it will come in handy someday."

Both women held each other crying and laughing at the new relationship and the events that brought them to this union.

CHAPTER 23

Cave Dwelling

After bathing, yoga and breakfast of a banana and a glass of warm goat milk, Vidya retraced his steps to the cave and reached his destination, having walked that part of the forest with Kalu the day before. Two large boulders leaning against each other, obscured the 6x4 foot tall cave entrance. The interior of the cave had a strong animal smell. He tossed the ever-present cricket ball from one hand to the other and entered the cave, stood still to adjust his eyes. As he traversed deeper into the cave, the walls and ceiling closed in leaving a small opening through which he would have to crawl on his belly to move further. Since it was pitch dark in the deeper part Vidya decided to return the next day with a light.

He came with a candle and matches and crawled through the narrow opening. The size of the passage gradually narrowed as he progressed. He was worried he might get stuck. *Few more feet forward if it narrowed further, I would retreat and give up on cave dwelling.* He noticed the rock he was crawling on was no longer dry. Another few feet and he felt water trickling from the ceiling. Crawling further he entered another chamber with sounds of a water flowing. He stood up, stretched his cramped body and lit the candle. This chamber was larger than the one in front and a smoky smell replaced the animal's. He saw dry food, a makeshift bed, blackened wood and ashes where a fire was lit. Further down a stream of water flowing along the rocks, disappeared into the ground below.

Interesting! What does this mean? That night while trying to sleep he realized the significance of the findings in that cave.

#

Next morning Vidya went to see Narula. "I know what you did in the cave. I saw where you hid from the tiger, your source of water and the food you kept there."

Narula's pale face became paler and his eyes darted around looking if anyone was within earshot. "How do you know?"

"I went into the cave and discovered the myth you created. Why?"

"Vidya forgive me and do not expose me. I came here after I fought with my wife and children. Wandering around the forest, I found the cave, entered it and fell asleep. I heard a growl and woke up to see the tiger entering the cave, scrambled back and crawled through the tunnel to escape the tiger. I was lucky that despite it's trying, I got to the other side. I stayed there in the dark scared, until the tiger left. Hours later I crawled out. A villager saw the tiger and me leaving the cave and spread the news. Villagers regard me as a holy man and provide me with food and clothing, in return I bless them."

"You are not a holy man, and you are deceiving the poor people into giving you their paltry rations. Leave this village and promise me never to play this trick on these people or any others."

"Where would I go?"

"Go back to your family, enjoy your kids and grandkids. Be true to yourself and the others." Vidya, surprising himself of being assertive. *Has entering the tiger cave changed me already? I must continue my mission of facing the tiger and it will have a more profound effect, counteracting the black cat induced misfortunes.*

#

The next few weeks he spent exploring the jungle, its paths and landmarks from morning till dusk on all days except on Saturdays. That day he waited for Prakash Khan and helping Kalu and his mom in their daily chores. He and Prakash lunched together, in the restaurant, always the same rice and dal, sometimes supplemented with a piece of raw onion or homemade pickle the owner's wife made. Once Prakash left, Vidya walked, exploring the forest. He saw deer, antelope, monkeys and an occasional snake. He never came across a tiger or its kill and worried he will never come across one. The closest to danger he encountered was, a feral sow with half a dozen piglets heading to the watering hole. Seeing him, the sow grunted, stepped in front of its litter and lowered its head with its six-inch tusks pointing at him. Vidya stopped in his tracks and backed out, ready to climb a tree. The feral pig grunted a few times, never charged, and led its brood to the water.

Vidya found peace in the stark beauty of the forest, the struggle of the living to find food and water; the hunt of the predators; the cycle of life and death; the ferocity of mothers to protect their offspring; and the sounds and silence of the forest. He realized this eco system, was like a breathing, living and evolving gigantic organism governed by natural forces and the beings it harbors.

CHAPTER 24

Encounter

Kalu perched on a tall tree, about twenty feet off the ground kept his vigil for the tiger most days. Somedays he saw the wandering Vidya, but never called out to him. Kalu did not know Rudra with the broken tip of the spear lodged deep in its paw that and festered left it limping. Unable to use that foot for running or grabbing, it waited for the prey come close and jumped with the power of its hind legs to attack. This hunting method was not as successful as charging at full speed.

One day Kalu saw Rudra hiding in the grass, waiting for an unsuspecting prey to come by. Rudra was camouflaged, its golden yellow coat merging with the dry grass and the black stripes merging into the shadows cast by the westerly sun. The tiger yawned exposing his glistening sharp teeth sending a shiver through Kalu. *I better keep quiet. Last time it noticed me, it attacked. I will stay silent as a rock.* Rudra's head swiveled and its ears perked up. *Its sensitive ears probably recognized the sounds some animal was making..* Kalu looked around but failed to see or hear anything. A few minutes later he spotted movement, in the direction the tiger's ears turned. *Thanks to God, it is not looking in my direction.* Kalu saw a person, waving his hands up and down. *Who is that? What is he doing, walking toward the tiger?* Kalu watched with fascination the developing tableau until he recognized it was Vidya and the strange arm movements were to throw and catch an object; one to the other and back again, almost hypnotic in its rhythm. Kalu did not know what to do. Shouting to alert Vidya may turn the tiger's attention towards him, but if he didn't, Vidya would walk into the beast. In the end, Kalu did nothing. *Vidya came into the forest with the express intent of facing a tiger. He is not my responsibility.*

#

Vidya returning to the village took the shortcut by the lake. He was throwing and catching the cricket ball, in his hands. He was oblivious of his surroundings, despite the repeated warnings of many villagers for vigilance in the forest. This was his last week in the forest. *Like everything I attempt this will end in failure.* The ball he threw up hit a branch, did not come down on his outstretched hand and fell to the ground. As he bent to pick it up, in the evening light saw a vague movement in the grass about two hundred feet away. *Is that Rudra?* The eerie silence of the always noisy forest spooked him. He felt a primal fear. The hairs on his arms were erect. *Why am I afraid? To survive, I must leave this place.* He picked the cricket ball and was ready to retreat.

Rudra catapulted out of the grass with a mighty roar and ran towards him. He realized how foolish it was of him to come to the jungle to face a tiger. The beast was enormous, much larger and ferocious than he imagined. Time seemed to slow down as he saw his life flash before his eyes, and thoughts of Ambika, his only love floated in. He tried to bring her face into focus in the last few seconds left of his life.

Rudra stormed about halfway to Vidya, stood its ground and snarled, teeth bared.

Vidya froze in midstride. *Should I run in the opposite direction from the tiger? No, the old man said tigers attack from the back, I should not show him my back, he will pounce and make a meal of me.* Vidya stood his ground, facing the tiger.

Rudra moved cautiously toward Vidya, the muscles rippling under its orange skin and the golden eyes holding Vidya's. Survival instincts clicked in; Vidya's heart rate increased and muscles tensed as he watched the tiger creep closer.

#

Kalu moved from his perch facing the lake to a higher branch, which offered him a better view of the unfolding tragedy. He saw the tiger and Vidya facing each other. Run Vidya, run, he said silently, unable to help, engulfed in indecision and trepidation.

#

Vidya noticed the tiger's limp when it stopped is left forepaw was off the ground. Vidya's senses heightened, and time seemed to crawl at an infinitely slow pace. He saw no large tree he could try to scramble up, looked around for something to fend off the beast. *I am holding it in my right hand, the cricket ball. If I can hit the wickets 45 yards away, I can hit the tiger about 30 away.* Vidya's right arm extended back holding the cricket ball, as the left leg extended forward, and his body swiveled sideways, and the left arm extended forward in a classic throwing stance.

A primal scream erupted from, that reverberated through the jungle, as Vidya swung and threw the cricket ball aimed right between the eyes of the tiger, with all his might.

The fast ball was no match for the keen vision and reflexes of the animal. Rudra took a swipe at it with its left forepaw. The hard cricket ball hit and impaled on the injured and fully extended claw, and sending shocking pain through the paw, foot and shoulder all the way to the tiger's neck. Rudra roared, jumped and disappeared into the forest, with the ball stuck on his claw.

"It got my cricket ball," shouted Vidya and rushed into the forest following Rudra and entered deep into its domain, the forest which it rules.

#

Kalu who saw the encounter sprang into action, scrambled down the tree and ran towards the village screaming, "Tiger, tiger, Vidya went after it. He is in the forest. Everybody come, we must rescue him, before it kills him."

About a dozen men armed with wooden staves, axes and

whatever weapon they could get hold of, with two drummers to frighten the tiger away, followed Kalu into the forest.

#

Rudra limped into the forest and settled down in a bush and licked its wounded paw, grabbed the cricket ball with his mouth and pulled it off. The ball came off with embedded the claw, sending another wave of pain through its leg. Pus, blood, and the broken tip of spear poured out. and the pain lessened. Rudra moved into a thick bush, lay down, licked the oozing pus off his paw and closed its eyes.

Vidya tracked the tiger's path following the drops of blood deep into the forest, saw his cricket ball lying next to a thick bush and cautiously picked it up. In the failing light he did not see the tiger a few feet away. As he pulled his back heard a hissing sound and the tiger's front leg shot out and raked Vidya's forearm. Without a thought, Vidya bolted and retreated as fast as he could clutching the cricket ball, his forearm bleeding from three long deep gashes. He ran into the rescue party making loud noises to scare the beast aways.

CHAPTER 25

Fame

"Look his arm is bleeding. The tiger must have attacked him. He somehow fought it off. A young man fighting a tiger and winning; he must be brave and blessed," said one man, prostrating himself in front of Vidya, as others followed suit.

"What are you all doing? Get up. Let us go back to the village, it will be dark soon," said Vidya

A few men hoisted him on their shoulders shouting "Jai Ho! Jai Vidya Jai Ho!" The head of the village panchayat was waiting, invited Vidya to spend the night at his residence, one of the nicer homes in the village.

Vidya, still speechless at all the admiration, accepted the invitation. *Tomorrow is Prakash's day of visit, I will leave with him to the town and back to my village, leaving all this momentary fame behind and find Ambika.*

At the village leader's home Vidya washed his wounds, bathed, and cleaned the cricket ball. Looking at the embedded claw, he marveled at its beauty, almost jade like in its appearance, curved like the beak of a hawk, about four inches long and massive, attesting the ferocity and raw power of the tiger.

The elderly medicine man, who was summoned, was waiting for Vidya. He came in using a long walking stick, hunched over moving with a shuffling gait, carrying a cloth bag containing his medicines hanging over his right shoulder. He walked over to Vidya and touched his feet. Vidya jumped backwards. "Please don't do that. You are old enough to be my grandfather, it is I who must touch your feet."

"It is not age that determines a person's stature, it is his actions and deeds. I have heard of what you did today and that deserves recognition and respect. I brought a poultice made of medicinal herbs, honey and turmeric." The medicine man applied the poultice to Vidya's wounds, covered them with a banana leaf and tied it down with a cloth. "Keep it dry for the next five days, remove the leaf and wash the wounds with warm water. Use the poultice, to dress your wounds. Change dressings every five days, three more times. By then the wounds will heal. Mind you there will be scars will stay with you till your last breath. When you have self-doubt or face unsurmountable obstacles look at those scars to remind you of your bravery, strength and blessings."

#

Next day, the village gathered for puja at the temple to celebrate Vidya's encounter. The mela with music by the village drummers, a solitary sarod player; male and female vocalists; folk dancing by everyone; a young man performing tricks and magic to entertain the small children; a snake charmer with his cobra and a man with his pet monkey that stole trinkets and food from the unsuspecting kept everyone attentive. An outdoor kitchen was set up where men cooked rice, dal, a variety of vegetables and kheer for dessert. As the celebrations proceeded, the head of the village pulled Vidya to a side. He pointed a young woman singing folk songs and said, "How do you like that girl? She is my daughter and if you are interested, I will arrange your marriage and you can live in this village with your new wife."

"I am sorry. I committed to marrying another woman. You have a very beautiful daughter and will have no difficulty in finding a suitable match for her."

The music and singing stopped as a bunch of motorcyclists rode into the village led by Prakash Khan, saving Vidya from having any more marriage proposals.

"There he is," screamed Prakash Khan, pointing at Vidya. The bikers and their pillion riders jumped off their bikes, rushed towards Vidya, holding cameras and microphones surrounded Vidya. The cameras clicked and microphones were shoved towards his face. The questions poured out.

The questions kept coming, the cameras clicking and the lights flashing. Vidya raised his hands and said, "I came here to face a tiger, the tiger took something of mine. I went after it and got it back."

A middle-aged well-dressed man stepped forward form the trove of people asking questions and said, "My name is Laxman, I am a reporter for the All India Radio in Nagpur. I would like to interview you for tomorrow's national news. Do you accept?"

"Only if you get rid of all the others except Prakash Khan."

"Ok, this is what I will do, you go with Prakash Khan, I will catch up with you in town and record our interview. What is your name?"

Vidya decided not to give out his name and said "Tiger Wallah."

#

The mela continued for another hour, ending with lunch. Vidya and Prakash Khan rode the motorcycle on the first leg of his return journey.

"You can expect a big welcome party in town. The word of your heroics spread through the town like a swarm of locusts. A large gathering is expected outskirts of town. Once we get there you are on your own. Come back to my place tonight to sleep and next morning, I will put you on the Ravi Bus."

Two miles from the town, on a stage was a white clothed man belonging to the ruling party, making speeches to a large crowd for their votes. The crowd roared not because of his words; the man who went after a tiger bare handed and came back to talk about it, appeared on the stage.

The politician placed a garland around Vidya's neck. A priest came up on the stage and recited a few Hindu prayers lit camphor on a brass plate, waved it clockwise in front of Vidya's face and put a red holy sindoor mark on his forehead. The crowd sounded their approval. The politician handed the mike to Vidya.

"I am a man of few words. I will not take much of your time. Thank you all for this great welcome. This is overwhelming, and I do not deserve such accolades. Yesterday I was a lost soul wandering the depths of the neighboring forest, today by some strange quirk of fate here I am. I came to these parts to face a tiger. When the tiger charged me, I was paralyzed with fear for a moment. But some inner voice told me not to run, face it with what is in your hands a cricket ball. When the tiger retreated into the bushes, with the cricket ball, I went after the tiger, and got the ball back. It raked my arm and in return I got its claw." Vidya held the cricket ball high above his head.

The grounds reverberated with the sound of the crowd chanting, "Tiger Wallah Zindabad! TIGER WALLAH ZINDABAD!"

When the crowds quieted down Vidya Continued "Friends! The only advice I can give you is, when you get an opportunity, most times it will last only a few moments, here this instant gone the next, so do not waste that moment, grab it and make it your own. Do not waste time, act. Now it is time for me to go, for I have a long week ahead, traveling back to my village and then one more mission to find someone much more precious I lost."

Vidya tried to leave, the crowd surged forward and surrounded him some wanting to touch their hands to the sindoor on his forehead, others to touch him or his feet and some who wanted to see the tiger claw embedded in the cricket ball. After about an hour in the crowd, Vidya extricated himself and went to Prakash Khan's house.

CHAPTER 26

Home Bound

Ambika made a routine for herself, at grandma's home. She woke up early and went for a four-mile run; bathed and fixed breakfast for grandma and went to teach young kids, in a small school she and another college graduate started. Both women took turns and held classes in a house owned by a rich farmer who let them use a verandah. Granny had lunch ready by noon. They conversed about Vidya, the agony of not knowing his whereabouts and wellbeing. They were terrified he may not return.

At her last visit, Hari Ji said, "Vidya was in a small village, next to a tiger preserve and was wandering alone in the forest from daybreak to sunset looking for the tiger." *I will get more information today.* Ambika cycled to Hari Ji's.

"Hari Ji any more news of Vidya?"

"None, Ambika. I expect Ravi will call with an update. I will send word to you. Do not worry. Vidya is a very resourceful and intelligent."

"Thank you, Hari Ji, I don't know what granny and I would do without your support."

"I talked with your granny some time ago at the temple. Her desire is to get you both married upon vidya's return. I will have your wedding at my place here with…"

"Daddy did you see this in the paper today?" Rani interrupted, handing him the two-day old newspaper.

Hari picked up the paper and read for a minute and said, "Oh my! This is not Vidya, is it?"

Ambika felt faint, expecting a tragic news. Hari was frowning and looking at the paper.

"Hari Ji, what is it? Please tell me." Ambika had tears in her eyes and panicky.

"Here, look for yourself." Hari passed the newspaper into her trembling hands.

Ambika looked at the paper with trepidation saw a grainy picture of a man with long unkempt hair and face obscured by a shaggy beard and mustache. She tried to read the small type through her watery eyes. The words were swimming and she could not focus enough to comprehend the text, except the word 'Tiger Wallah' in bold print. Ambika took a deep breath, wiped her eyes and read the story and realized that it could very well be about Vidya. *But who is this unkempt fellow in the picture? Is this Vidya? If he is, why is he calling himself Tiger Wallah? Is he thinking of joining a circus?*

Rani peered over her shoulder said, "Yuk, this guy is not him. Vidya is clean shaven and always dressed in nice clothes. This is some bum."

Hari Ji chimed in. "This could be Vidya. If a guy is chasing after tigers for two months in jungles, that is how I expect him to look. What do you think, Ambika?"

"I for a moment thought he could be Vidya, but looking at the eyes in this picture, so intense and strong unlike Vidya's soft look. Hari Ji, can I take and show this it to granny see what she says?"

"Yes, let me know what you decide. I think it is time for the sounds of shehnai."

Back at home in the fading light granny looked at the picture for a few seconds and pronounced, "This is Vidya. My prayers are answered."

"But look those eyes are not Vidya's."

"Beti, you didn't know him as a child. When his dad was alive, that is the look he had. With his dad's passing, something changed inside Vidya. Now I see my grandson as I knew him as a child. My Vidya has woken up, and I am so glad. It is time to get ready to welcome him home. Let us clean up this place and cook some of his favorite things. I will talk to Pandit Ji, to find an auspicious day for your marriage."

Seeing grandma flitting about the house cleaning, arranging and humming to herself, Ambika thought she is so energetic like she was twenty years younger. She joined in the hectic activity, her heart filled with joy, expecting the return of now famous Vidya, her Tiger Wallah.

#

While the women were cleaning their home, getting ready, Vidya arrived in Bombay. Just like previously, there was a crowd to mob him at the bus station, only ten times larger. There were photographers, movie cameras, a band playing popular music, singers, dancers, khadi clad politicians and celebrities from Bollywood. A shower of flowers and petals welcomed Vidya, and garlands were draped across his neck. Vidya stepped on to the large stage and addressed the crowd. He delivered the same message he delivered a few days ago. The politicians begged him to join their party and run for office and when he declined, to campaign in support of their party.

"I have no interest in your politics."

"You are so famous now, please capitalize on it, run for the Parliament, you can be a minister may be even the Prime Minister. We need you to lead our party to victory in the next elections."

"Sorry, I have another mission to fulfill."

"What can be more important than being a minister?"

"It is very personal, and no business of any of you."

#

Vidya went to Ravi's home. He and his host sat down and talked about his experiences. Ravi examined the cricket ball with the embedded tiger claw "If it was not for this, I would not have believed anything you said. How did you survive and obtained this?"

"I am as surprised as you are, came close to death and saw my life ending. I threw that ball, with my mind blank except for the open mouth of the tiger and its sharp glistening teeth. It slapped at the ball like it was chasing away a flea."

"Well, it got you a lot of recognition and fame. What are your plans now?"

"First is to find Ambika. We both were discussing marriage when my life fell apart. It is my desire to make sure she is well and happy. Second, I will visit the town where I was accused of stealing money, confront my accusers and the police inspector who arrested me without proof."

"Then what?"

"While roaming the forest, I realized it's a great natural resource, with its animals, trees and birds, a microcosm of the world and its struggles. I will be a champion of the forests and all its living creatures, especially tigers."

"You are not expecting to make a living out of that, are you?"

"No, I will start a school in my village to educate the children and any willing adults. That will be enough for me and my granny."

"What about marriage, wife and children? Will you be able to sustain them?"

"It all depends, if Ambika is married, then I will stay single. If she is single and willing, we will get married."

"What is this Tiger Wallah name?"

"I wanted my identity to stay private, when asked my name I just blurted out what came to my mind. By the time I reach my village, people will forget Tiger Wallah, and I will just be Vidya," not realizing the name Tiger Wallah will stick to him like a barnacle on a ship.

#

Vidya on his way to grandma's, stopped in the town from which he was expelled by Srinivas and the corrupt police. At the bus stop there was a frenzied crowd chanting "Jai Ho! Tiger Wallah!" No one in the crowd recognized him as the teller at a local bank. The parade of politicians was by now a familiar occurrence for Vidya, as were the speeches and music. During his address to the crowd, Vidya noticed the familiar corpulent

133

figure of the mustachioed inspector Cholu Das in the crowd.

As he ended his speech Vidya said, "Inspector Cholu Das come on the stage."

What a great day, this famous Tiger Wallah, not only knows my name but has invited me to the stage. This is the opportunity I am waiting for seeking my next promotion. The inspector was ecstatic.

"Do you recognize me, inspector?"

"Yes sir, the whole town recognizes you, most of this nation does. You are famous, and I am honored that you know my name and have invited me on to the podium." Cholu Das folded his hands in supplication.

"You are not thinking of arresting me, are you?"

"Honorable sir, you must be joking. Why would I want to arrest you? I am your humble servant."

"Look at me, you may recognize me."

The crowd was silent, staring at the drama on the stage, not knowing where this was headed.

Cholu Das looked at Vidya's face intently, and his face went pale as recognition dawned on him.

"You ... you," he stammered. "You came back."

"I challenge you to arrest me inspector. Are you ready to arrest me, Cholu Das?"

"You lay a hand on Tiger Wallah, if he doesn't, we will break them. We will break your legs too inspector." The crowd roared, knowing the corrupt inspector's history.

A trembling Cholu Das fell at Vidya's feet, pleading for safety.

Vidya turned off the microphone and asked the inspector to rise, "If you reveal my name to anyone, I will come back with my tiger in tow and let him loose on you. Promise me that you will never say my real name to anyone."

"Never sir, never. My lips are sealed. Anything else you wish me to do?"

"Yes, one week from today I want you to come to my village and bring the thousand rupees you received from Srinivas. On second thought, bring me an additional thousand for all the trouble you caused me. I want a written statement from you about your and Srinivas' role in that affair. Remember never a word about my real name."

Vidya turned on the microphone and addressed the crowd, "Let the inspector pass unharmed. If any of you were victims of this man, let me know and I will make sure he makes amends. Do not harm him, he learnt his lesson."

Cholu Das left to the jeers and hisses from the crowd, glad he escaped without bodily harm. After the crowds departed, Vidya went to Anand's house to meet Amma. She looked at him, not recognizing him with long hair and beard covering his face.

"It is Vidya, Amma, Anand's friend."

"Oh Vidya, I did not recognize you. You have changed so much. What brings you here? Are the police still after you?"

"I came to see you, being in town. The police will not bother me anymore. How are you doing? How is Anand? He doesn't write or call." Vidya was relieved, Amma did not hear of the Tiger Wallah episode.

"I am well, just older. I am very sorry to hear about Padma. She had a rough life, poor lady. I think of her often and pray for her soul. Anand rarely writes or calls. I wonder about that girl Zahina, such a nice and pretty girl. I hope he is at least in contact with her."

"He better be. If he causes that girl any grief, he will answer to me."

"Did Ambika ever find you? I got the letter you wrote to me and went looking for her. She fought with her parents and left town, looking for you. I don't know where she is."

Vidya's hope of getting together with Ambika was dashed. He stayed for dinner, took leave of Amma, promising to return soon and return the money. He caught the late-night bus to his village. *It will be an early morning surprise for granny.*

CHAPTER 27

Reunion

Ambika was on her early morning run, which cleared her mind of the previous day's thoughts.

Dawn was breaking when Vidya alighted from the Ravi bus at his village. Vidya slung his bag of clothes, a few possessions and the cricket ball. He walked towards his grandmother's home. He was halfway through when he saw a person running towards him, too far away to even make out if it was a man or a woman. A minute later he recognized the runner was a woman. *Never seen a woman running in this village; how things change in a few weeks.* A minute later his pulse quickened as did his pace. *Can it be? Am I hallucinating? Is it Ambika?* He ran towards her waving his hands. He saw her stop for a moment with her cupped hands shielding her face from the rising sun.

A big smile broke on her face, and she screamed, "Vidya. Oh my god! It is you. Welcome back." Ambika ran into his arms; he wondered how she got there. They hugged and held on to each other. Vidya stared into her eyes; beyond words or thoughts of journeys completed, each in search of their true destiny, together at last, never to separate again. They held hands and walked towards granny's home, the early sun rays warming their backs, the path taken, taking them to the happiness they deserved.

Three days later they were married in a simple ceremony at Hari Ji's house with shehnais blaring and grandmother beaming.

#

One week after the wedding Cholu Das arrived, with the two thousand rupees. He bowed to Vidya and gave him the money in an envelope which Vidya handed over to granny for safe keeping.

"Aren't you going to count, if it is all there?"

"Inspector I know you are a scared man, not the fearless crime fighter you portray to be. You will not cheat because you know what will happen if you do. If ever I hear you or your police demand money and victimize the innocent, you will answer to Tiger Wallah."

"Yes, Vidya Ji, I renounced my old ways and will practice my profession with honor and dignity."

"Did you bring me the document I asked you?"

"Yes, Vidya Ji, here it is." Cholu Das handing over a typed signed document in an envelope, "Vidya Ji, I have a ..."

"I know what you want. You want me to keep this document a secret. I will, but if you revert to your dishonest ways, I will make this public and make it my mission to send you to prison."

"I swear on the soul of my dead mother, I will never go back to the old ways."

"Remember I will be watching, one slip and you will end up where you have sent many innocent people."

#

"Ambika, I am going to Amma and return the thousand rupees. Then I will fulfill my promise to my mom."

"What promise Vidya? I did not know you made a promise to your mom."

"I promised her to repay the person she believed was instrumental in my release that day."

"Who did your mom think was instrumental in that?"

"Your dad, Sri. Srinivas."

"Do you want me to go with you? I have a few choice words to say to him."

"No, I will do this alone, and make him pay for his nefarious deeds."

"Do you want to take the car?"

"No, I will go by Ravi bus, this time as a paying passenger."

Vidya met with Anand's mom and returned the thousand rupees she gave for his release. She gave him a solitary diamond pendant on a gold necklace for Ambika as a wedding gift.

"You both got married without notice, I am sorry I missed your wedding."

"Is Anand married or Amma? I haven't heard from him or Zahina after he left for USA."

"No, he is not married and doesn't want to get married. I heard that Zahina is married and is living with her husband in this town. I haven't seen or heard from her."

#

At Sri. Srinivas's residence, the gate keeper stopped him. "Master is busy. No visitors today."

"He will see me," Vidya showed him the cricket ball with the embedded tiger's claw. The gate keeper folded his hands and opened the gate.

Vidya walked into the mansion and straight into the Srinivas' study. Srinivas was reading and did not notice him. Vidya slammed the cricket ball on the desk in front of the man. Srinivas looked up startled. "Who are you? Can't you see I am busy?" Srinivas's eyes turned to the ball on the table, saw the tiger claw and, as recognition dawned on it, stood up. "Welcome to my home, Tiger Wallah. What can this humble man do for you? Please take a seat."

"I am not here to sit, like the last time when you tried to destroy me."

"How could that be? This is the first time I am meeting the famous Tiger Wallah."

"Because the last time you met me, I was just a teller in your bank."

Srinivas looked up into Vidya's face and his demeanor changed.

"You, you are the Tiger Wallah? Where is my daughter? What have you done with her?"

"Your daughter renounced you. She is now my wife, happy and safe."

"How dare you come here, with an arrest warrant pending and Inspector Das ready to arrest you?"

"Go ahead call the inspector and have me arrested."

"Do not for a moment think I won't, just because you married my daughter. I will have you rot in jail and bring my daughter home."

"Go ahead. Your threats will not scare Tiger Wallah."

Srinivas picked up the phone, dialed the inspector's number, "I have the guy you promised to arrest if he ever came back, in my office. Come now, arrest him and throw him in jail."

Srinivas listened to the inspector's response, and the blood drained from his face, and he seemed to shrink in his chair. When he looked up the arrogance in his face was replaced with fear, brow wet with droplets of sweat. "What do you want from me?" Srinivas' voice was shaky.

"I want to look at the last annual statement of your bank."

"Why do you want that?"

"Because you must pay for your misdeeds, and I intend to cause you as much misery as you have caused your daughter and my family."

"If you think I will empty the bank for you, you are mistaken. I am not scared by your empty threats."

"When Tiger Wallah makes a threat, it's not an empty one." Vidya pulled out two documents from his pocket and threw them on the table. "These are certified copies of two originals I have in my possession. Read them and decide how empty my threat is."

Srinivas picked up the documents with shaky hands and read them. "Publicizing these will destroy my business and standing in the society. I will pay you ten thousand rupees for the originals and all copies."

"There is no amount of money that will get you the originals. I will decide how much it will cost you to keep this private."

"How do I know that you won't release them once I pay you?"

"You will not know, but I know, because when I make a promise, I will honor it."

"Tell me how much it will cost me?"

"I need to look into your books to decide what would be the right amount."

Reluctantly, Srinivas pulled out a fat folder and passed it to Vidya., "Can I get you something to drink or eat, while you are studying the ledger."

"No."

Vidya spent about 30 minutes studying the ledger, closed it and looked at the banker sitting in front of him. Vidya looked at Srinivas who averted his gaze at the intensity of the look.

"You will give half of your wealth to Ambika, for her to use as she pleases. Donate a quarter of your wealth to build a school in my village, under my supervision. I will grant you one visit with my wife. If you convince her, she may rekindle your relationship, otherwise, you and your wife will not contact me or my wife ever again."

"You are asking for three quarters of my wealth, with nothing substantial in return. That is not fair."

"You are in no position to decide what is fair, after what you have done to Ambika and me. You destroyed my livelihood, threatened my freedom and took a thousand rupees from my destitute mom. Time for discussion is over. I will be back in two days with my wife. Have all the paperwork and money ready by then. If you meet all my demands, I will leave my wife here for an hour, for you to make amends." Vidya picked up his cricket ball and walked out.

That evening Vidya told Ambika about his trip, his interaction with her dad and the financial restitution..

"What do we need all that money for? We are happy with

140

what we have."

"Ambi, you belong to a rich family. I wanted you to have a nest egg as an insurance. You can leave your share in a bank and not touch it until a need arises."

"What are you going to do with the share you asked for?"

"I have a plan and a vision. I will use that money to build a proper school in our village. Your friend and we both will run the school not only for our village but also from the neighboring villages. Ravi Ji agreed to bus the children for free."

"I am so proud of you, Vidya. What are you going to call the school?"

"I am thinking of 'Padma Niketan' after my mom, if that's ok with you."

"Great idea Vidya' reminds me of Tagore's Shanti Niketan."

CHAPTER 28

Present – Captive Anand

Amma learned of the roadside explosive that disabled the jeep and injured Anand on his drive to their village. Let me find out which hospital he is in, and his condition, before I go to him. By the next day, she knew this situation was more serious than a simple roadside accident. A rebel group kidnapped Anand. She heard of kidnapping and extortion by this group. She was pondering her options. If the kidnappers demanded a ransom, she would pay to get Anand released. Being a woman of action never letting events around dictate her, Amma decided to act than react, contacted her village elders and asked what influence they can exert on the rebels. Amma telephoned Durga to inform and seek her opinion.

"Amma contact Vidya who lives in a village close by and seek his help. I heard he is a respected person in those areas and has many followers. He is Anand's friend and will help."

#

Amma met Vidya next morning in his village. She found a remarkable change in Vidya, the meek young man with slumped shoulders and a defeatist look was now a handsome well-built man with broad shoulders, with long hair and well-trimmed beard covering most of his features. The most remarkable was the change in his eyes, bold and piercing look that continued to assess the environment and the people around him. Vidya introduced Ambika, their seven-year-old daughter Uma, and Amrit his nephew, a fair skinned boy of five with shy looks.

"I came to ask for your help, Vidya."

"Amma, you do not have to ask. Tell me what to do and I will do it."

"It is about Anand." Amma saw see the sudden change in Vidya, his brow knotted, and a fierce look appeared in his eyes. A moment later Vidya's looks returned to normal. *What was that about?* "Naxalites kidnapped Anand, please get him released."

"I will do anything you asked, though my heart and mind tells me I should leave Anand to his fate."

"You and Anand were best friends. Your words surprise me."

"I loved him like a brother and would have given my life for him. He broke that bond."

"Vidya you are way out of bounds, it is my son you are talking about."

"Amma, forgive me, I apologize, meant no disrespect. Anand has done something egregious and broke our friendship."

"Tell me what he did and what you will do to get my son released. What can I do to repay you?"

"Let me bring Anand home first. What Anand did, let him tell you. His actions, destroyed a person, I admire and respect."

"I am staying in my village to until this is over. Please keep me posted."

Two days later after meeting with the rebel leader Vidya went to Amma's village to update her on the status of Anand.

"Amma, I met the Naxalite leader Murali. Anand was still unconscious when I left this morning. The doctor who accompanied me, did not find any broken bones or internal injuries. Anand needs to be conscious and recover his strength before he can be moved, He is being taken care of in a primitive setting. The doctor is very competent. I have no doubts Anand will recover and we can get him out. I am negotiating with Murali for Anand's release. I will let you know once I know their demands."

#

Voices of a man and a woman talking, was the harbinger of regaining consciousness, though I couldn't understand their conversation. The words I heard were 'Anand' and 'recovering'.

I mumbled "Let me sleep."

"It is time to wake up Dr. Anand!" uttered a man's loud voice, forcing me to open my eyes.

As I focused my eyes, on the blurry shape in the room, I realized that his was face covered, only eyes visible. He was tall and well built, and I looked around to see who the woman he was talking to was and saw no one.

"Who are you? Where is she? Where am I?"

"People call me Tiger Wallah. I do not know who you meant by 'she'. I am alone and you are deep in the forest in a rebel camp."

"I heard a woman's voice. I know the voice. I know her. Where is Zahina?"

His eyes turned feral. "There is no woman in this room. You suffered a nasty head injury and are hallucinating Dr. Anand."

"How do you know my name?" I was angry and frustrated.

"You had a passport on you with your name and profession."

"Am I your prisoner? When are you releasing me?"

"You are not my prisoner. The rebels. Captured you I do not know if or when they will release you?"

"If you do not release me, I will cause a great deal of trouble for you and the rebels. I give you a fair warning."

"Dr. Anand, you don't understand the precarious situation you are in. There is nobody here to help you except me and I am trying to get you released. *Behave!*" Tiger Wallah's anger was reflected in his voice and his eyes.

I felt a terrible headache and I closed my eyes. Through my half-closed eyes I saw him take something out of a bag on his shoulder and toss it from one hand to the other repeatedly. *A grenade?* I fully closed my eyes and heard him walk out of the room, close the door and secure it with a chain. Weariness and anxiety gave way to deep sleep.

On waking up, I noticed that my head was bandaged, all the blood and grime on my body cleaned and I was wearing clean clothes. An hour later Tiger Wallah arrived to check on my welfare.

"How many days have passed since my capture?"

"This is day four, you were unconscious most of the time, just mumbling and saying words nobody could understand."

"Why am I kept in a locked hut? When can I go home?"

"Dr. Anand negotiations for your release are ongoing. You are in no shape to travel even if the rebels release you. The forest is a dangerous place, and to keep you from wandering away, you were locked up. If my plans succeed you may be on your way in a day or two." Tiger Wallah walked out.

#

In a minute the door opened and a boy about five peeped in. His eyes were large and inquisitive, dark curly hair and a shy smile on his face. I beckoned him to come in, surprised to see a child in this encampment. He walked in hesitantly, eyes focused on mine. He looked at my bandaged head. "Does it hurt? I once fell and hit my head on a rock. It hurt a lot. I cried."

"I am sorry to hear that. What is your name?"

"I am Amrit."

"What a nice name. Do you live in this forest?"

Amrit laughed, "You are funny. Why would I live in the forest? I live in the village with my uncle and aunt."

"Come and sit next to me." I was starving for friendly human contact.

"Can I touch your bandage?"

"You may, be gentle, if you press on it, it will hurt."

His gentle touch and cool hands soothed my anxiety. I took his hands in mine and looked at him, his steady eyes holding mine, innocent and somehow reassuring to my troubled soul. I felt an unexpected connection with Amrit in the rebel camp.

"Please tell me a story?"

I thought for a moment and told him the story of Gunners and the victory over Prabhus. He listened aptly.

145

"Will you teach me to play cricket? I play soccer with my friends and scored two goals. I want to play cricket."

"Let me get better and I will"

"Promise?"

Before I could answer, a woman's voice summoned, and Amrit left.

A few hours later, Amrit came back and sat next to me on the bed. His hands touched my face and forehead. Amrit, nectar of the gods, gives immortality and revives the dying to full health. The company of this child magically influenced me, an elixir to curb my despair of being imprisoned and controlled. One soothing ray of hope in an otherwise dreary captivity; somebody to talk to even it was a child; free of adult presumptions about captives and controllers.

"You don't have fever anymore."

"No, I am feeling better, no fever."

"My ammi told me when you have fever you are fighting bad things. When the fever goes away it means you have won."

"Where do you go to school, Amrit?"

"We have a school in our village. Lots of kids come from all the villages to our school. They come on a bus. It is free."

"What do they teach you in your class?"

"I am in first grade. I am learning English ABC. I can read Telugu and Hindi. My teacher says I am excellent with numbers. I know multiplications one to five."

"You are a very intelligent kid, Amrit, I am proud of you."

"My uncle says I should go to America, where I can learn a lot."

"Yes, when you grow up, come to America, I will show you around."

"Do you live in America?"

"Yes."

"Do you have a car?"

"Yes."

"Did you go on a rocket?"

"No, that is for Astronauts."

146

"I don't know what that means."

"These people sit in a rocket and go way high up."

"How high, do they go to the stars?"

"No, the rockets don not fly that high."

"Please tell me another story."

I held Amrit close and told him the story of a cow, a calf and a tiger, my grandfather told me, when I was his age.

"So, the tiger let the cow go in the end? It must be a nice tiger."

"It is not a true story. The moral of the story is, if you give your word, make a promise, you must fulfill it, even if it threatens your life."

"Do you do that always?"

"No, I am not such a strong person or good person. I never fulfilled many of my promises."

"Don't feel sad, maybe one day you will," consoled the child in his innocence and wisdom.

The next few days Amrit came many times to my hut and I told him stories from Ramayana, Mahabharata and of Birbal.

"You tell good stories. I like you." Amrit gave me a hug.

What is my attachment with this kid? Will I break this, once I am well? His presence in this dangerous place was like a beacon on a dark stormy night, soothing my fears, and giving me hope and optimism I will eventually be set free.

Being true to my nature, I never asked Amrit about his parents or his uncle and aunt or their names. *My philosophy in life is less people I know better it is.*

CHAPTER 29

Life in Rebel Camp

It's the tenth day of captivity the last six conscious. My faculties have returned. Seeing my face in a mirror saw the professional way my scalp wound was sutured. How did they take such good care of my injuries in the middle of the forest? What resources do they have? Who sutured my wound? Was there a lady with her face covered? Was it a hallucination, or did I hear Zahina's voice as I was coming out of unconsciousness? It must be my imagination running wild —Zahina the woman I abandoned a decade ago would be in the same rebel camp, at the same time, caring for me.

I was planning an escape, when the door opened and I hoped it was Amrit, but to my disappointment it was the Tiger Wallah. "The rebel leader and I have agreed on a deal for your release. It is a little complicated. Have you recovered well enough to understand, Dr. Anand?"

"Yes, I am ready to get out of here? How much money are the kidnappers demanding? What is your share of the loot?" I was frustrated.

His eyes flashed, I averted my eyes at their intensity. "Do not insult the people holding you and I, who negotiated your freedom. If I leave now, you will be a captive the rest of your life, however short it may be."

"I am sorry. This captivity has upset me. I will listen to what you have to say with an open mind."

"First, and most importantly is for you to adapt a child here and take him to America and bring him up as your own."

"What child? What would I do with a child? I work sixty hours a week and I don't have time for a child. I am single, who will care for this child when I am at work?"

"The child is Amrit. You both have already met. The rest is for you to resolve."

"Amrit! He is a happy child, why would I take him from his aunt and uncle. He may not want to go with me."

"During difficult times we are compelled to do what is unpleasant. The child is in danger, and his safety is of paramount importance to his family. He needs to be unreachable to the person threatening his wellbeing. If you love him and take care of him, he will get used to you. You must promise to love him as your own and not go back on your word."

"I will let you know by tomorrow. What else do you want?"

"Your mom has already agreed to those. They are not your concern."

"Where is my mom? What have you done to her? Why is she involved in this at all? How is she?'"

"Your mom is well, eager to see you. She asked me to negotiate your freedom. Your mom is a remarkable woman. She may tell you all she has done for your release. Let me remind you, if you do not agree to take Amrit with you then the whole deal is off."

"What about Amrit's parents? Don't they have a say in all this?"

"Amrit does not have a dad and his mother is lost. His uncle and aunt have bought him up since he was an infant. I will be back tomorrow same time. Be ready with your decision, and make the right one for everybody's sake," said Tiger Wallah and raised his hand in goodbye.

As he raised his hand the loose sleeve slipped down revealing three long scars on his forearm. *Did a tiger cause those scars, that gave this fellow the name?*

#

Once he and Murali agreed on terms for release of Anand,

Vidya went to Amma's village and told her Murali's demands.

Amma listened and said, "You want Anand to adopt and take Amrit to America; I stop selling timber in my forest lands so you can relocate tigers. Is Amrit Zahina's son? Where is she? Why is her son for adoption?"

"Amrit is my sister's son. This is not the time to discuss Zahina, Amma. When this is all settled, and we send Anand off to USA, I will answer those questions. I want you to persuade Anand to take Amrit with him. I request you not to talk or discuss Zahina with Anand. It is not good for him to find out about Zahina. Once he recovers, he should find out on his own.

"Remember Amma, there is more to this story and this group of rebels. Ravi is a college educated fellow who took upon himself to fight against the economic injustices facing the poor. He is their champion and not a violent man in the true sense. Of all his demands, the one I cannot figure out how to accomplish is for his people to be self-sufficient and join the society as mainstream citizens. I am at my wit's end with this demand."

"What exactly does he mean by mainstream? These are people who shunned the rules and lived as rebels in the forest. They should renounce their way of life and move back to their villages. I do not see how it is anybody's problem, but theirs."

"If they move back to their villages, they and their children will starve, they have no means of survival."

"I sympathize with their plight but cannot see what you or I can do about it."

"Amma, we are in a conundrum, with Anand's release hanging in limbo. I will be back tomorrow and maybe you can figure out a solution."

"Vidya, I don't understand. You are you championing the kidnappers and wild tigers, while my son is languishing in the forest?"

"Amma the forests are disappearing in our country, and it is essential we protect them. I have envisioned tigers roaming freely in this forest and discussed with forest rangers and conservationists. They agreed to move Rudra, and a tigress to your forest, once timber harvesting stops. The forest will still belong to you and your children, except it will be Rudra's home.

"Amma I am forever indebted to you for all you did for my mom and me. Nothing I do will erase that debt. I am using all my resources and influence to free Anand. Believe in me and be patient."

"What guarantee would I have that they will release Anand?"

"I give you my word Amma, I always keep my promises."

#

Amma wasted no time to express her thoughts the moment Vidya arrived the following day. "Vidya I could not sleep last night thinking of my son, my family and the ancestral property in our family for ten generations. It will be Durga's and Anand's, after my demise. I am eighty years old and do not have energy to continue managing it. Anand and Durga have shown no interest in the lands. These lands will have no caretaker after I am gone. I have a solution for satisfying Murali's demands. Of my three hundred acres of land, I will set up two hundred as a co-op, my five current workers and Murali's people will be members of the co-op. You and Murali manage the business aspects, 15% of the produce will be mine to support me. After my demise, the co-op gets 100%. The co-op will also farm the other 100 acres with 50% of profit to my children and their heirs. If the co-op fails all lands return to me or my heirs.

Vidya was speechless for a moment. "Amma, I have no words to express your generosity and an enormous sacrifice. Are you sure this is what you want to do? It is such a monumental decision. You may regret it later."

"Vidya, I have thought this through. I never second guess my decisions and there will be no regrets. But I too have a demand. This whole action is subject to one clause. The deal is off if my one demand is not met."

"What is it Amma? If it is in my power and capability, I

promise to fulfill it."

"It is a simple demand Vidya. It is my belief that education is the pathway out of poverty. I demand that all my workers send their children to school. The sane applies to co-op members. I want their children to get an education and move on to better lives; have opportunities to fulfill their dreams. Anyone wanting to be a member of the co-op, must send all their children to school until they are seventeen."

With tears flowing from his eyes Vidya folded his hand in namaste. "Your wisdom and sacrifice are beyond words Amma. This co-op should bear your name."

"No Vidya, it will not bear my name. Just call it Amma's Co-Op. Now get me an attorney to write up the deed."

"No need for any paperwork now, first let me bring Anand home. Amma please do not bring my role or Zahina with Anand, it is essential that he does not know, for Zahina's safety."

CHAPTER 30

Freedom

I decided after soul searching that night, to take Amrit America with me if the rebels release me. I was not sure how it would work, with visas and the paperwork involved in bringing an adopted child home. I had no other choice, accept and go free or decline and stay captive. How did Tiger Wallah involve mom? Is he for real? Or is he a charlatan using a few well-placed scars on his forearm for personal gains? I bet he is in cahoots with the kidnappers!

I told Tiger Wallah "I will adopt and take Amrit."

"Glad to hear, I wasn't sure if you would and make another blundering mistake?"

"What you mean by that?"

"Amrit told me about the promises you did not keep. Anand, I expect you to keep this one. If not you will have to deal with me."

Until that moment he had been addressing me as Dr. Anand. *Why this sudden change? Why does that sound familiar, a voice from the past.* Once again my mind was out of control. I felt a headache coming on and asked Tiger Wallah to give me an hour to rest. He left and I lay down and closed my eyes. A few minutes later the door opened and Amrit walked in with a glass of water and two pills.

"Amrit stay with me."

"Yes, I will stay. Are you feeling better?"

"Not yet. The medicine will take time to work. Thank you for bringing them?"

"Uncle asked me to give them to you."

I never paid much attention to the word 'uncle' since it was commonly used to address elder men in India. Amrit stayed with me, and I told him a funny story of Birbal, a minister in Akbar's court.

After the story Amrit laughed and said, "Did the horse really grab the minister's white beard in his teeth and yank it?"

"That's what happens when you starve an animal. It mistook the beard for hay."

Amrit left because Tiger Wallah came in to resume our conversation.

"Tomorrow you and I will leave to do the paperwork for Amrit's adoption. Afterwards I will drop you at your village. Amrit will join you in a day or two. Once I drop Amrit I will be out of your life. You are responsible for all travel arrangements to America. Is that okay with you?"

"Yes, I agree. Why do you cover your face, what are you hiding? Did the tiger disfigure your face?" I was fed up with his overconfident attitude.

"I only show my face to people I trust. You do not belong to that category."

"What do you know about me? Why are you so narrow-minded judging people, mere acquaintances, you hardly know?"

His blazing eyes turned on to mine, he opened his mouth to say something, turned around said, "Be ready in the morning."

#

Tiger Wallah arrived. "I will leave on my motor bike and will meet you in town. You travel with Murali, the rebel leader. You have to walk to the road where he will be waiting."

"Why do I have to travel with a kidnapper? Why are you ordering me around?" living in America, I was spoiled, with nobody to tell me what to do or how.

"If you open your eyes to see and listen to what is around you, you may learn something, DOCTOR Anand." The words sent a chill through me, having heard the same words from

Zahina more than a decade ago.

Too many coincidences to ignore. I wanted to get in a verbal duel with the Tiger Wallah but caution and my habit of avoiding confrontations won over me and I nodded my acquiescence. The journey started with Murali, in the driver's seat and I in the passengers'. Ten minute later, we passed Tiger Wallah on the way, with a woman sitting on the pillion and a scarf wrapped around her face. I stared at her as we passed them and for a moment our eyes locked and the same feeling I had the last few days gripped my mind. In a flash they were out of view.

"He doesn't have a high opinion of you, Dr. Anand," said Murali

"I do not care what he thinks."

"He sought and won your release. You should be thankful."

"I should thank you too, for blowing up my jeep, injuring and kidnapping me."

Murali sighed and kept quiet. We drove for another hour. We stopped on the way to stretch our legs, got out and walked in the forest breathing fresh air.

"You are a doctor, committed to taking care of the sick and injured, aren't you?" Murali looked at me.

"Yes, though I do not directly take care of patients, I am committed to their wellbeing."

"Then you understand, taking care of people, is noble don't you?"

"Yes."

"Tell me Dr. Anand, how is that different from taking care of the poor and the neglected? You see me as someone who injured and captured you, but I see myself as a champion of the poor and the exploited; fighting the wrongs imposed on these people; fights for their freedom from economic shackles and unjust laws. Do you see the poverty around you? Do you hear the despair in their voices? The blast that injured you was directed at someone else. You were in the wrong place at the wrong time, and I am sorry for what happened to you."

I had no answer for him. Why is everybody reminding me I am out of touch with my surroundings? Is that so obvious? Murali who I met a scant hour ago had figured out my greatest shortcoming.

"Dr. Anand, I did not mean to offend you or rebuke you. We all see the world through colored glasses of our own making. I was no different ten years ago." Murali told his story while we walked.

"If you are a wanted man, why are you going into town? Aren't you afraid of being captured?"

"We are traveling in the Tiger Wallah's vehicle, no one in the town dare stop it. I am safe as long as I am in this vehicle."

"Is the Tiger Wallah, real? I think he is hiding behind a mask."

"He is as real as it gets. There was a time a few years ago the whole state and this nation was in awe of him. He has followers everywhere, who believe there is nothing he cannot do."

"He must be extremely rich, capitalizing on his fame."

"On the contrary, he lives a simple life with his wife daughter and grandmother in a small house with his grandmother. He runs a free school for the children and works as an accountant for one of the rich folks in the neighboring village. He is a great soul, with an iron will, always helping the needy."

I had nothing to say. *I am a very poor judge of character.* We got back in the car and drove.

#

We waited on the outskirts of the town until Tiger Wallah arrived. I was eager to meet the lady on the pillion and to my disappointment, he arrived alone, his face covered by a bandana. We proceeded to the Tahsildar's office to complete the paperwork for adoption of Amrit, and all the other deals worked out between Murali, Tiger Wallah and my mom. The last two were completed with no delay. We ran into trouble with the adoption with clerk refusing to proceed with adoption of the boy in the absence of parents or legal guardian.

"Sir this is highly irregular, no documents of any kind and you want this gentleman with an American passport, to adopt an Indian child. You must produce valid documents."

"Is the Tahsildar in the office, I want to talk to him." Tiger Wallah insisted.

The clerk sighed, got up from his desk and asked the Tiger Wallah to accompany him. Through the open door I saw a middle-aged man sitting behind an office table. He and Tiger Wallah engaged in conversation. A few minutes later Tiger Wallah, pulled an object form the bag hanging around his shoulder and thrust it in front of the Tahsildar's face. *Is he threatening the government official? What is wrong with this guy? He will get all of us arrested and thrown in jail.* The Tahsildar get up from his chair, bowed his head and beckoned the clerk, who rushed in. Both the clerk and Tiger Wallah came back out. Another ten minutes later the stamped and officially signed documents by the Tahsildar were in my hands and I walked out a free man with a newly adopted son.

#

We drove back to the place where the Tiger Wallah parked his motorbike. Murali bid farewell and left in the. I rode with Tiger Wallah. We neared my village. He stopped by the road that goes into the village.

"Dr. Anand, this is far as I go. Can you walk the last mile to your home?"

"Yes, I want to ask you one question? Will you give me a truthful answer?"

"Depends on what you ask, if it is something I can answer without breaking confidences of people, I will."

"Do we know each other?"

The serious look in his face softened for a moment and he said, "Please go. Your mom is waiting anxiously."

"Thank you for protecting me and getting my freedom back."

"Don't thank me. Thank your mom." His eyes flashed, and

he was gone.

I watched him as he sped away on the motor bike and when he disappeared, I turned and walked towards the village and my ancestral home. When I reached my destination, I found the place I haven't visited in many years was still standing but worn and weathered showing the neglect of the rightful heirs too far away and the matriarch caretaker too old. *Houses are like people, they thrive when there are living souls within, and wither away when neglected.*

Mom was sitting on the porch, on an old reclining chair belonging to my paternal grandfather. She got up and hugged me, with tears in her eyes.

"I should have never asked you to tackle the village problems; called you from America to get in this mess, injury and captivity. I am sorry."

"Don't blame yourself, Amma, what happened was by chance. I was in that place at the wrong time. This experience had opened my eyes to many things."

"How is your wound? They said you were unconscious for days. Are you ok?"

"The wound is healing well, somebody in the camp had medical skills, did a professional job and took good care of me. I am back to normal."

"You lost a lot of weight."

"The first few days I ate nothing being unconscious. Later they shared their meager rations."

"Did they treat you right those rebels?"

"They are very poor and are fighting for their existence and their rights; are no different from people here in this village, or the city or America, just the same."

"Glad to have you back. Your old room is ready for you. Go wash up and let us eat."

#

That evening after dinner I discussed my plans for taking Amrit with me and all the paperwork, and bureaucracy involved. Amma wanted to come with me to look after the child. I declined. "I must do this on my own. You are welcome after I settle with Amrit and stay with us for as long as you wish."

"Do you want to talk to Durga?"

"She won't talk to me Amma, my doing, not her fault," I said and remembered the slides I was reviewing when Durga's call came. I must call Sun, as soon as possible and find out about Diana.

"Where is the nearest phone? I have to call America."

"There is one in the village post office. It is closed now. Opens in the morning at eight. You can make your call in the morning," said Amma.

#

I went to the post office and booked my call. After pleasantries, Sun assured me that all is well with his wife Diana; the positive node was removed; no other tumors found on CT and PET scans; oncologist decided to watch and wait, than subject her to therapy which she may or may not require.

"When are you returning?" asked Sun.

"A few more weeks I must get visa for my son."

"You have a son in three weeks, that is fast work. Who is the lucky lady?"

"It is a long story. I adopted him, there is no woman."

"Bringing up a child as a working single parent will not be easy. Better find yourself a wife."

"I have a plan, to make it work. I will need help, may be from you both until I get all this sorted out."

"You don't even have ask Anand. We will for as long as it is necessary?"

"Thanks, and goodbye. I will let you know when I will arrive, once the travel arrangements are complete."

#

Amrit was with Amma when I returned, brought in by his uncle and aunt with all his belongings that fitted into a small worn suitcase. I took him to my room and asked Amma to have another cot put in so Amrit could sleep with me.

"I would have loved to meet his aunt and uncle. You should have asked them to wait."

"They were getting late for school and could not wait."

"Maybe I should visit them before I leave with Amrit."

"That is not a good idea, the child was reluctant to leave them. You must spend time with him and get him used to you."

"Okay. I will take Amrit to the town with and get a cricket set to play with."

Amrit and I went to a sports store, and I bought him a junior cricket set. The next few days we spent most of the time together playing cricket and getting to know each other.

CHAPTER 31

USA

Two weeks later, having completed all the formalities for a US visa we boarded a flight to America. The business class seats were comfortable, and Amrit was fascinated by all the buttons on the seats, his first plane ride. I ordered a vegetarian Indian meal for him, and the regular menu for myself. When the food arrived, he looked at my plate and wanted to try every dish on mine.

"Your food is better than my food. Can I get what you have for my next meal?"

"Yes, Amrit whatever you want. Would you like to exchange your plate with mine?"

"Really, will you give me yours?"

"Yes, anything for you."

"I like you a lot, you are nice. I like living with you."

"I will take care of you. You are my son."

#

We arrived in USA eight weeks after I left. When I look at him, I feel a connection I cannot fathom. Something about his looks and eyes make my paternal instincts rise. Amrit fills a void that existed in my life, since I came to this country a decade ago. My job is no longer important. Within a week, I moved to a part-time position, giving up the chairmanship of the department. *The need to focus on this child, for he is lonely like me, is of paramount importance. I will devote my time and energies for his care and wellbeing and not let go of this child as I have done with my other acquaintances and friends. Life is more than success at work or wealth.*

I enrolled Amrit in a private school. I drop him off at school, go to work, and by early afternoon I sign off from work and be waiting for Amrit at his school. We eat ice cream together, roam the parks, and do Yoga together in the evening.

"I learnt Yoga from my uncle, and I will teach you."

He has not called me dad yet; I am optimistic that someday he will.

Will this one act, exonerate me of my past misdeeds and absolute self-centeredness? I do not know the answer, nor do I know what the future holds. Content with my life, thoughts of Zahina flood my brain, having felt her presence during captivity. The regret of abandoning Zahina, my only love, consumes me.

#

Lying in bed, trying to be at peace, I struggle to fall asleep. A decade of pain, anxiety and immense upheavals my actions and inactions have caused haunt me. *Have I learnt a lesson? I hope so. My thoughts always turn to Zahina when I cannot sleep. Where is she? Does she ever think of me? Does she hate me? Or has she driven me completely out of her thoughts? Do I still love her? In the deep recesses of my heart, I do. Will I ever get to see her again? Can I even muster the courage to look her in the eye and ask for forgiveness?* The pursuit of my ambitions gave me professional satisfaction and a prosperous life, at the expense of love and happiness These thoughts float through my mind, most nights as I drift off to sleep.

Two knocks and the door opened. I saw the face of Zahina in the dim light of the night lamp.

"It is time we finish what we started a decade ago, Anand," said Zahina slipping into my bed. As I felt her warmth next to me, I turned towards her when....

Knock! Knock! The sound woke me up, realizing that Zahina was just a dream and the Amrit, my adopted son was crying and knocking on my door. I opened the door and grabbed him in my arms and hugged him.

Amrit said, "I can't sleep. Saw ammi in my dream. I want my

ammi. I miss her."

"Your Uncle told me your mommy was lost. We don't know where she is."

"No, I did not lose my ammi. She told me she was going back to the hospital where she works." Amrit's tears flowing down his face.

"Amrit, where is your mom?"

"My mom works as a doctor in a big city. I love her. I want her to be with me. Please go get my mom."

"When did you see her last?"

"The day we left my village, to come to yours. I should not have left my ammi."

Amrit looked into my eyes beating his tiny fists on my chest. I looked into his eyes full of sadness and anger. It was a bombshell exploding - my connection and affection for this child. That look sent me back into the past, the same eyes, the same look that scorched my heart a long time ago.

Oh Lord, what twist of fate has brought this child to my care.

I hugged Amrit, my precious Amrit, tightly to my chest and whispered in his ear, "Is your ammi's name Zahina, Amrit?"

"Yes. My ammi's name is Zahina."

Is this my path to redemption?

Unlikely, but hoping is not a sin.

PART THREE -
I ZAHINA

CHAPTER 32

Past – Early Years

"Zahi wake up! Zahi! ZAHI!"

"Abbu, please let me sleep a little longer," I was in deep sleep, and was in no mood to get up. I rolled over, clutching my pillow.

"You will be late for school. Get up honey, Shabnam is up and ready."

Hearing the name of my sister, I sat up and said in an accusatory tone, "Abbu, you are always favoring her, you don't love me as much as you love her."

"You both are like my two eyes. How can I favor one over the other? I am proud of your sister, and you are the joy of my life. Now be a good girl and get ready for school. What would you like for an after school treat today?"

"Abbu, I want a red rose."

"A red rose, is what a husband would give you."

"I don't want a husband, just a red rose."

"All right, a red rose it will be. Now get up and get ready," Abbu said, giving a playful smack on my behind.

I loved those morning rituals with my Abbu; stayed in bed even wide awake, until he came in and he promised me a treat.

"I will be a doctor when I grow up, Abbu, and I will buy you a car and get rid of your bicycle," I promised.

"Inshallah!".

My dad's a devout Muslim and did his daily prayers and went to the mosque every Friday. We lived in a small house in a section of the town where most Muslims lived, near the

166

mosque, from the towers of which the muezzin's melodious voice called for daily payers. Abbu believed as a Muslim, you follow the edicts of Islam; follow your beliefs and be true to them; Hindus, Christians, Buddhists and every other religion conforms to the broad strokes of societal rules which we color with our values and practices; and every one of them is a brother or a sister. We are Indians first. Before Muslims invaded India, we were all either Hindus or Buddhists.

Shabnam, five years older, was overprotective of me. She and Abbu treated me like a princess at home, letting me get away with mischief and trouble making, to the great consternation of Ammi.

"You both are spoiling her, catering to her whims and demands. What will happen to her when she grows up, gets married and goes to live with her in laws? Which one of you will be there to help her?" Ammi fumed.

"My Zahina is a princess she will marry a prince and be happy ever after."

"I don't know what all this fuss is about. I am never getting married," I tried to put their disagreements to rest.

#

As I remember the past, my childhood was wonderful, loved by all. People used to tell me how beautiful I was and in return I gave them my squinty look and a lopsided grin. At school, I got in trouble, teasing girls and boys alike, never taking no for an answer. During those years, I discovered the pleasures of reading, got immersed in short stories and fiction by American, British authors. 'The Citadel' by A. J. Cronin had a profound impact on me, planting the idea in my mind to become a doctor and serve the poor. I did relatively well in school, in the top ten, but never the first. I had no interest in music or handicrafts; played soccer for my high school girls' team. Content with my books, I made no friends or developed binding relationships. Shabnam was my only confidant, and I shared my deepest thoughts, aspirations and worries with her. Shabnam's friend Durga would visit, and I would sneak in and spend time in their company. Sometimes they talked about boys, as they laughed and giggled, 'not for your ears,' Shabnam used to say as she hustled me out of the room.

#

I finished high school and was ready for college. I chose premed courses in pursuit of becoming a doctor to be the first one in the family and in the entire neighborhood. I joined the local college and Shabnam was away at the Andhra University to pursuing masters. During a visit home she said, "Do you remember Durga, my friend?"

"Yes, what about her?"

"Her younger brother Anand is in your class."

"Why are you telling me this?"

"Just so you would know. Maybe you can be friends with him, I hear he is very talented with a one-track mind."

"So?"

"Nothing, since you don't have any friends, it would be good for you to know someone. College life can be lonely."

"I have my books. I don't need any friends, especially a boy."

"Hey, I am just saying. Not trying to fix you with him or something. I had friends who were boys in college. You get a different perspective of life from boys."

"Shabnam! You are boring me with this conversation. Change the topic else or leave me alone."

"As you wish." Shabnam walked away.

#

To spot Durga's brother, I started scrutinizing the boys as they came in. Suddenly I became the center of attraction for the boys once they noticed me watching them. Most of them came in strutting to catch my attention. One day I noticed one guy trying to sneak in behind others. He was tall, well dressed and had long curly hair. *This may be Anand, unimpressive.* I did not have confirmation until after one of the tests, the instructor was handing out our test results.

"In this test only one student got a perfect score. Will that person stand up, please?"

Everybody turned their attention away from the instructor toward the back of the class to find the guy I picked out standing up with obvious discomfort, his eyed downcast and shoulders slumped.

"Please tell the class your name?"

"Anand sir." He was barely audible.

"Congratulations Anand, keep up the excellent work."

Anand nodded his head and slid back into his seat.

What is with this guy? If it was me, I would jump up and down, college or not; he looks like a naïve nerd, ideal for my teasing. Throughout the year I watched him, as he kept a low profile, shy and unassuming, always getting top grades and was the darling of most of the teachers. He seemed a loner, never mingling with the other students and never heard him talk loudly. The word spread around that he was bookworm spending most of his time in the libraries around town. Though I was always looking at him when he entered the classroom, I never seen him raise his eyes to mine. Different but not interesting, I decided to get his goat someday.

#

All that changed during the second year when Anand was challenged to participate in the Quiz Bowl and agreed.

The next evening Shabnam called and asked me to join Anand's team since he was in a pickle and needed a girl to join his team.

"Shabnam, let me think about it. I cannot promise you I will. Let me see how it goes tomorrow."

"Ok whatever you can do. He is a good kid and is eager to get the team together. Please say yes, please Zahina."

"I will let you know tomorrow."

"Sometimes you can be so difficult."

"Easy for you to say. You are not in my shoes."

"Have it your way. Bye," said my sister, miffed.

#

To join? Or not? I was undecided. Recently I started a book

by Leon Uris and did not want to put it aside for ten days. But the more I thought this seemed like a perfect opportunity to get to know Anand. I wanted to see how he can win the event. *Can this down to earth boy really be that confidant of his prowess to guarantee winning? What makes him tick?* I never thought about any boy or a girl as much as I did of him that night. I spent the night tossing and turning through restless bouts of sleep.

#

After class I planned to corner Anand and decide if I should join his team. After the last class I waited outside for Anand. From where I was, I could see him deeply immersed in his thoughts, sitting in the middle row. *Has he gone to sleep or is he waiting for somebody like a girlfriend?* That thought irritated me. Anand suddenly looked around like he just woke up, gathered his books and came out. I slid behind a pillar, ready to ambush. His relaxed stride suddenly tensed as his eyes found me, and his looks turned to the floor. *Why am I attracted to this bookworm?* I expected him to stop since he knew I was there, probably waiting for him, but he continued to walk looking at the floor.

"My dad says I should pursue my dreams with confidence. I want to join your team for the quiz bowl if your team is not full," I said.

His face went pale, and he looked flustered, turned towards me still looking at the floor and stammered 'yes and no' a few times and finally uttered, "No, my team is not full. Yes, please be on my team."

What is with this guy, and why is he stammering? Why doesn't he look up and look at me? I said, "I am just asking to be on your team not to marry me. You can look up, there is nothing interesting on the floor."

I gave him my squinty face and lopsided grin as he looked up. His jaw dropped at my looks. I laughed and regained my normal look.

I asked him, "Do you like what you see?"

170

As I looked into his large soft brown eyes and knew that he was a gentle soul. For a moment, I regretted the prank I played on him. As he continued looking into my eyes, I felt a little weak in the knees and broke the contact with his eyes and mumbled something about meeting for practice tomorrow and quickly departed. *What is wrong with me, I who took no prisoners when teasing others for a thrill, was going gaga over this fellow?* During the walk home, I could not get the soft brown eyes; the curly hair outlining the handsome face; the innocence of his gaze; his flustered appearance during our meeting and the gentle way he spoke, out of my mind. *The next one week will be interesting, after that quiz bowl, win or lose I will not see him again. How wrong I was.*

#

The following evening after the classes the team of four boys and I, met to discuss our strategy. Anand looked more composed than the previous day and announced the first order of business was to elect a team leader and proposed me as his choice.

"Why?" I promptly questioned him.

"Because you insinuated yourself into the team, that shows your assertiveness and composure,"

"I only came in and asked because you were getting ready to ask me and I just helped you."

"How do you know?"

"A girl has to keep her secrets. You should be the leader because you were stupid enough to fall in the trap Mahajan laid for you," I immediately regretted my choice of words seeing his crestfallen looks.

Rest of the team members immediately sided with me saying that Anand should be the team leader. Having settled the matter of leader, our next aim was to strategize how we would train for the quiz bowl, with only one week left we did not have the luxury of time on our side.

Anand assigned each of us a subject but did not say what his was.

Evasive and doesn't disclose his thoughts; looks laid back and indecisive most of the time, but when he decides on a course, I see his focus; he is more interesting than what I gave him credit for.

CHAPTER 33

Slippery Slope

Anand, the very name gives me goose bumps and makes my heart throb, even after all these years. Anand and I met in college, became fast friends that progressed to love and commitment. The rose he gave me, that day in the park, when he came running, is still in my possession, carefully dried and wrapped in cellophane.

I was heartbroken when Anand left for America to fulfill his lifelong dream. I vividly remember the day I invited him to come to my room in the nurses' quarters, how one thing led to another, I kissed him on the lips, first for me and Anand, we desperately clung to each other, passion exploding like the floods of Godavari River, struggling to get out of our clothes; the kiss neither of us was willing to end, slowly moving towards my bed, when the loud incessant knocking on the door put an abrupt end to our passion.

Once Anand left, I fell into a bottomless pit void of light and levity. I lost my passion for reading, my jest for life left me and my future seemed bleak and purposeless. The nights were sleepless, and the days were dark, filled with loneliness, despair and longing. I stopped interacting with colleagues, and the upbeat approach with patients I cared for disappeared. I was like a robot doing my duties as a nurse going through the motions of work unable to get out of depression.

As Christmas approached, I missed the last few Christmas Eve celebrations Anand and I spent at Thomas', Anand's friend. The simple joy of spending the day with Anand; chatting with Thomas and listening to the stories of their cricket team Gunners; the talents that earned him the name 'fox on the field'; his leadership skills in encouraging his players to their height of abilities and beyond for the victory over Prabhus; winning the district tournament championship. When I think of those times my depression releases me for a moment but returns soon after with a renewed vengeance drawing me into its deep dark embrace. The last few days, I have been thinking on a way to end this pain and suffering, I did not know how, except for the most drastic of all actions, forbidden by Islam and every other religion.

The opportunity came on Christmas Eve. My heart was heavy with longing and despair. That morning I woke up with a terrible anxiety and deeply depressed. I bathed and went to the work, spent the entire day tending to patients working like a zombie. Before the day ended, I went to dispense medications to patients. Just before leaving at 8PM, I went back to the medicine cabinet, emptied the bottle of sleeping pills into my purse. That night I did the unthinkable, without heed for my family or my friends, swallowed all the pills on an empty stomach, put a 'do not disturb' sign on the table next to my bed and lay down hoping that this would put an end to all my suffering. Little did I know that I embarked on a journey that would take me through physical and mental anguish that befell many unfortunate women in my country.

#

The first signs of consciousness were the sounds I was hearing, the earliest sense to recover; vague sounds sometimes soothing sometimes disturbing, limbs moving on their own volition; a distant brightness coming closer and closer as I squeeze my eyelids shut forcefully, to stop the assault; cool soft hands on my cheek cupping my face a voice whispering, "Please wake up. Zahina open your eyes."

I know this voice; this touch; I fought through the fog, opening my eyes. An out of focus face appeared in front of my eyes and as I tried to focus, the features slowly became apparent.

"Shabnam, I am sorry," I wanted to say but could only make a squawk.

"Praise to Allah! She opened her eyes and is making sounds," Shabnam's voice. I tried to reach and touch her, but my limbs would not respond. Wearily I closed my eyes and was asleep again.

#

Two days later, having recovered most of my senses if not complete control of my limbs and muscles, I was thoroughly ashamed of my botched attempt at suicide. However, the despair and depression persisted as before. To add fuel to the fire, the looks of my family and friends that came to visit, did nothing to raise my spirits. *The one person who can get me out of this quagmire was thousands of miles away, unaware of my plight.*

Durga, Anand's sister came to see me one day, and promised, "I will beat Anand to a pulp, for all the problems he caused."

I did not understand her fury or her blaming Anand for my doings. I was in no mood to talk to anybody and kept my silence. Shabnam as usual was there for me to lean on, despite my silence, seemed to know what I needed, whether it be a trip to the bathroom or a glass of water. The most difficult person to face was Abbu who appeared to have aged ten years in those few days, his usual upbeat and smiling face, which until now was also my trait, was replaced by a mask of pain and sorrow. Ammi's stoic face of a Muslim woman showed no emotion, except a little more shine in her eyes with suppressed tears.

I looked at their faces and get more depressed. If there was anything, I can do to make them feel better I would, but my mental state did not allow me to comfort others with my heart in darkness and agony. Friends would come singly or in groups and talk to me while I sat or lay there with no expression on my face and no happy thoughts in my mind. Hearing them tell me how lucky they discovered me before it was too late and how miraculously I recovered. All because a nurse had to leave on family emergency and the supervisor tried to summon me.

#

Once I was released, my family took me home. Weeks passed with no improvements in my mental status. One day Abbu announced that he has a marriage proposal for me. I did not look at him nor did I acknowledge his words, I just sat there looking at the floor drowned in my sorrow, and no will to respond. I should have told him "Abbu please do not go ahead with this, you always said, 'Follow your heart' and my heart is not in it'. The words never came out of my lips, frozen in despair, depression and inaction.

I never asked him who the man was or what his occupation was. It was Shabnam who raised these questions later when she found out about the marriage. Abbu and Shabnam talked in my presence, ignoring me, because by then the happy, smiling upbeat Zahina has disappeared and I was a shell devoid of emotion, who rarely uttered a word and never smiled; I became a nonentity.

"I am worried about her, if the word gets out, I can never find a suitor for her. This young man is 24 years old and runs his family meat shop."

"Abbu, you will not get my sister married to a butcher," said, outraged Shabnam, "Is he educated at least?"

"Yes, he went to high school with your sister but dropped out two years later to learn his family business."

"A high school dropout to marry my sister, no way," Shabnam was adamant.

"He says he was in love with your sister from the day he saw her, in school."

"He was in love with a thirteen-year-old girl then and now wants to marry her. Abbu, please think about it. Your precious daughter getting married to an uneducated meat vendor."

"Shabnam, this is a done deal. Their family is coming tomorrow to meet Zahina. I promised them a dowry of 50,000 rupees and some gold jewelry. I cannot back out now. I am getting old and have health problems. This is the best I can do. Look at your sister, who will take care of her when I am gone. What will happen if the word gets out that she tried to kill herself, no self-respecting Muslim will accept her? This boy comes from a good Muslim family and Zahina will have a safe place to live."

A wedding date was set, and invitations were mailed to family and friends. I picked up one and wrote a message to my love, signed it with a Z and mailed it to Anand, worsening my depression.

CHAPTER 34

Marriage Made in Hell

Six weeks later I was married in a simple Muslim ceremony. The only thing I remember is Abbu giving the dowry and jewelry carefully wrapped in a yellow silk cloth tied with a red ribbon, to my future mother-in-law. Later, I learnt that she put my dowry in a wooden box in her bedroom with all her other cash and jewelry. The night of consummation of marriage, Sayeed my lawful husband who reeked of perfume bought me a present wrapped in a brown paper. I took it and placed it on the small table in the room.

"Open it!" commanded Sayeed.

I, tore open, the package and my heart skipped a few beats when I noticed it was a burkha.

"You will wear it like a good Muslim, whenever you go out, or when any male person enters this house."

He came around near me, sniffed my hair and advised "You should use a stronger perfume."

He pushed me on the bed, lifted my sari, and plunged himself into me. A minute later he groaned, rolled off and went to sleep. There was no tenderness, words of love or light touches. Slowly I rolled out of bed to wash and when I came back, he was awake and ready.

"No need to wash. I want you pregnant soon."

"I was hurting, I had to go wash."

"If Allah wanted you to have pleasure, he would have made you a man. A woman is just for the pleasure of man and to bear children."

Thus started our first night as husband and wife, and it got progressively worse. He would come to bed reeking of offal, unwashed and the rough coupling would happen three to four times a night.

I was still depressed, but somehow, I weathered these encounters, paying no attention to the acts in the bed, my mind separated from my body, a distant observer, seeing my body being ravished.

#

The morning after the first night, I was sore. Sayeed's mother who ran the family with an iron fist told me, "From tomorrow you will get up early, not like today, before sunrise and make tea for the entire family and breakfast. You eat after we are done. Once Sayeed leaves for his shop, gather all the dirty clothes and wash and hang them in the backyard. After your bath, prepare lunch and serve when Sayeed comes home at noon; clean all dishes after you eat. Simi leaves after lunch to meet her friends. Afternoon you may rest or read the Holy Book. Prepare tea and a snack for me and my daughter by the time she returns. We eat dinner at seven in the evening, get the food ready. Clean up after dinner and go to Sayeed's room."

Her expectations flabbergasted me. Will I have any time left for me to read books I brought with me? What about my nursing career? What about time to go visit Abbu and Ammi? What is Simi's share of the workload? Simi spent all the time preening herself and demanding me to serve her whims.

She had her own room and would call 'Zahina, make me tea' or bring me water, or get me a snack. I cooked and cleaned and washed clothes, pans and dishes like a slave, never receiving a kind word from any of them. The family constantly harassed and cursed me for not cooking to their liking.

One day I was looking for my books, I brought with me and asked Simi if she has seen them. "Sayeed took them one day and burned them in the backyard soon after you came. I was cleaning your room and showed them to him," she answered.

"Why?" I said knowing she lied about cleaning my room,

179

because she did no cleaning, most likely spying on me. I was glad that some of my personal stuff was in a locked trunk in my bedroom I shared with Sayeed.

"Ask him yourself."

When Sayeed came home from the butcher shop, I asked him "Why did you burn my books? Those were the very best of the literature and fiction."

"Those books are not literature, those are about fornicating women enjoying it; they have pictures on their covers of scantily clad women, corrupting immature minds; they are blasphemy. If I see any more of those books not only, will I burn those, but I will beat you on the street for all the neighborhood to see what a sinner you are. The only book you should read is the Holy Koran, Allah's word to the faithful."

#

One day deciding there was nothing to lose I asked Sayeed "I am a trained nurse. I would like to find a job. When you go to work, I can go to work too."

"Honorable Muslim women don't work outside the home. They do not mingle with strange men. Your place is inside the house taking care of the family. I don't know what your father and mother taught you."

"Don't you blame my parents, they are much better than your family, and they are also better Muslims," my temper flared.

I did not see the fist that flew to my face, as Sayeed punched, knocking me to the floor, surprised and hurt at the violence directed at me, his wife.

Simi who just walked into the room encouraged her brother, "Kick her, kick her. How dare she raise her voice against you? Sayeed, you are too gentle with her, knock her teeth out!"

I stayed on the floor expecting more punches or kicks coming my way. Fortunately, none came. One side of my face was swollen, and I tasted blood from a cut lip. I was relieved he broke no bones or teeth. As I lay there on the floor too stunned even to cry, curled up in a fetal position, my mind switched into survival mode. I thought of the poem Invictus by Henley, 'Under the bludgeonings of chance - My head is bloody but unbowed'. I knew then what he meant by 'I am the master of my fate - I am the captain of my soul'. Through the veil of depression that hung on my life, I could see what my goals were. *I must survive and escape this hell.* My thoughts turned to Anand and a calmness descended on me. I didn't care if these thoughts of Anand were a betrayal of marriage vows, because in my mind, my marriage was void the moment Sayeed hit me. I hated them all and decided to go back to my Abbu and ask for his forgiveness and have the marriage annulled. It has been six months since I have seen Abbu, I decided to see him at the first opportunity.

#

A week later planning my visit, I quickly finished my chores and after lunch, when Simi stepped out and my mother-in-law went to her room for a nap, I donned my burkha, stepped out for the first time after marriage, hired a rickshaw and headed home. I went in, found my father laying on the bed, his eyes sunken, his hair disheveled and bones visible through his emaciated body.

He slowly turned his head towards me and said, "Who is it?"

For a moment, it stunned me he could not recognize me until I realized that I was in burkha and removed it.

"Zahina my child, why are you wearing a burkha?"

"I am trying to be a good Muslim, Abbu. What is wrong with you? Are you sick?" I asked, laying a hand on his forehead.

"Zahina come sit by my side. Your mom went to the drugstore to pick up my medicine. Tell me all about your happy married life. Are they treating you like the princess you are?"

Looking at him so sick, trying to change the focus of my questions, I realized that I could not do what I came for, to get my marriage annulled and to escape the hell I am in. This would surely kill him if he knew of my misery and inhumane treatment by my husband and in laws. I smiled and lied, "Abbu everything is great. No worries there."

The concern he had on his face when he saw me in burkha disappeared and a faint smile appeared on his face. I heard Ammi walk in, stood up and embraced her. She looked thin, having lost weight and worries and concern replacing her normally stoic facade.

"Let your father rest. We will go in the other room and have some tea," she said ushering me out, hugged me tight and started crying.

"Ammi what is wrong? Talk to me, please. Stop crying. Is it Abbu?"

Between heavy sobs she said, "He is dying, your Abbu has blood cancer, and they say he has a few months left at the most."

My legs turned to jelly, and I collapsed on the floor at her feet, tears flowing. Ammi sat next to me and pulled my head into her lap and ran her fingers through my hair trying to sooth me, like Anand did to console me a few days before he left.

"Zahina, I beg you do not tell him about your problems. When Allah beckons him I want him to go without worries. Hearing about your problems will disturb him. Let him live in peace, the few days he has on this earth. Please, my baby, promise me."

She saw the still healing bruise I received a week ago and figured out my life at Sayeed's.

"Ammi, I never will say anything to him. I promise."

Two weeks later I got word that Abbu was no more and has passed away in his sleep. *My Abbu is no more - the one who loved and cared for me more than anyone; taught and made me what I am; to be fearless and pursue my dreams; the one I was hoping would secure my freedom from this loveless marriage.* With him went my plan, to get my marriage annulled--without a male guardian the mullahs would never grant my wish. I was stuck in this hell for a long time, maybe forever, in a marriage I never wanted, a husband who never loved and in laws who only wanted a slave. My hope of survival depended on one person, Anand, who I believed will come one day and take me away. This thought strengthened my resolve to survive and to endure the privations doled out by the in-laws.

I asked Sayeed permission to visit my Abbu's funeral.

"Go ask my mother."

I asked my mother-in-law she refused and said, "The day you got married you belonged to this house and this family. No need to go to the funeral of the person who gave you away."

CHAPTER 35

Life of an Abused Wife

I planned my future without them, get free and pursue my dream of becoming a doctor. I remember my promise to Abbu about the car I would buy for him on becoming a doctor. With him gone, my resolve now was to become a doctor and serve the poor. This provided me with a goal and a positive outlook. The false hope that someday I would reunite with Anand, helped me survive those awful years.

Days turned to months and then years, Anand never came to rescue me, Sayeed never treated me like a human being, the in laws never relented their psychological assault on my senses. The only relief I got was the decrease in frequency of the rough sex, to once every night. By this time my body was used to this assault, with neither pain or pleasure or pregnancy. The two women used this to berate me on my failure to produce an offspring. Calling me names and labeled me a cursed soul, who defied Allah's wish that women should bear children. During this time, I lost my Ammi, for she did not have the will to live after my Abbu's death. Shabnam and her husband moved to middle east, where they were teaching in a university. I was as lonely as any human being could be, like a sailor lost at sea. Years rolled by and the opportunity to escape never materialized; my resolve to be free never weakened. I bided my time waiting, for a chance to break the clutches of Sayeed and his family.

#

In the fourth year of my marriage, I missed my period. I

was ecstatic with the possibility of new life budding within my womb and worried about the family I am bringing this child into. I decided to wait another month or two to confirm my pregnancy, before telling Sayeed. he next month also I did not have my period and decided that if I miss it the third month, I will announce my pregnancy. *May be that will grant me some reprieve.*

Two days later Simi announced during dinner one day, "Zahina has missed two periods. I have been watching her, she is hiding the pregnancy from all of us."

What was to be a cheerful announcement, set the family against me, angry and confrontational instead of congratulatory. I escaped their wrath, withdrawing into my own world, not even letting their words reach my brain, in fact I shut them out. When things quieted down after a few hours I asked that I like to go see a doctor to monitor my pregnancy.

My mother-in-law immediately nixed the idea, "There is no need for a doctor, having a baby is natural. I had two healthy babies, with no problems. When the time is right, I will call the local midwife to take care of the delivery."

Being a nurse working in a busy hospital I saw many cases of women with no regular care during pregnancy, presenting with severe complications, resulting sometimes, in the death of the baby or the mother or both. *I must keep myself healthy with the knowledge I have, not only for my sake but also the new life growing inside me.* For the first time in many years my hope rekindled, filling my heart with a joy that I cannot put into words.

When the bouts of morning sickness started, I did not get any help from the two women. They expected me to do my chores so they can relax and enjoy the fruits of my labor. Nothing has changed in the bed either, Sayeed was inattentive to my physical needs of pregnancy. The frequency of couplings that had decreased over the years, renewed with vigor, my pregnancy probably bolstering his sense of manhood.

I asked Sayeed many a time to let me get proper prenatal

care during the pregnancy which he declined and said, "My mother says women need no doctor's care."

#

Pregnancy brought me the happiness that I am bringing a child to give me the companionship that I craved. There were many nights I stayed awake thinking of these matters and eventually decided that once the child was born and I regained my strength, to escape with my baby. Find refuge, hide, get legal divorce, leave the town and fulfil my promise to Abbu attend a medical school and become a doctor!

#

I calculated from my last period, the delivery day. This was one secret I did not divulge to anyone. As months passed, I got over my morning sickness and I showed. I could now feel the baby kicking inside me, reminding me he or she is there, and to be careful. As I grew larger, it was difficult for me to perform my chores and to keep the two women happy. A constant stream of complaints and curses rained on me those days. The only time I was free was in the afternoon when Simi went out and the old one took a nap.

I decided to get checked up at the neighborhood municipal clinic one day and ventured out when Sayeed and Simi went out after lunch. I hired a rickshaw to the nearby maternity and child welfare center for a checkup.

The nurse examined me and said, "Today is your lucky day, the doctor is in, she comes here every Tuesday. If you can wait a little longer, I can get her to examine you."

"Yes, I will wait."

A few minutes later the lady doctor walked in, I remembered her from the quiz bowl.. She asked me to undress so she could do a pelvic exam and check on the position of the baby in my womb.

As I was undressing, she looked at the chart the nurse had prepared and suddenly said looking at me "Zahina. Weren't you with Anand that quiz day?"

"Yes doctor"

She examined me, took some measurements and proclaimed that, "You and your baby are healthy and progressing as expected. You are due in eight weeks, I advise you to limit your physical activity, especially bending and lifting. I recommend you do leg ups to strengthen your abdominal muscles. Come and see me every week until you deliver."

I was elated the baby is doing well. *Hearing Anand's name was a good omen.*

#

My labor pains started a few days before the expected date. In the beginning, it felt like abdominal cramps, but soon the pains became severe, came like clockwork every half hour slowly increasing in severity and duration. This lasted throughout the night and next morning, the duration between contractions lessened to ten minutes, I was gasping and moaning, but no human hand touched mine to comfort me. My water broke that afternoon and the contractions increased. Finally, the old woman sent for the midwife who arrived promptly and assured that everything was under control. She lifted my sari, looked under and announced, 'not yet'.

The contractions were coming in waves now and I moaned and groaned, while Simi stood at the foot of the bed with a smirk on her face. I prayed to Allah to get her out of there. My prayers were answered; the midwife asked Simi for a bucket of hot water and a cup of tea for herself. Simi grumbled and went out.

After a bout of particularly strong contractions, I felt a flood of warm liquid gushing out, wetting the bed. I screamed at the midwife to look. Something was not right. She peeked under my sari again and went pale.

"You are bleeding profusely. There is nothing I can do. You must go to a hospital immediately or you may lose your baby and maybe your life."

"Please go to the City Clinic two streets down and ask the doctor to come immediately. Tell her it is Zahina. She knows me, she is at the clinic today, Tuesday."

#

The doctor came and examined me and said, "You have placenta previa, meaning the afterbirth structure is over the opening of the birth canal preventing the passage of the baby. We must do a cesarean section immediately, to save you and the baby."

She summoned a taxi, and they picked me up in my bloody sari, frightened for my unborn child, thinking, if I lose my baby there is nothing more to live for.

"Allah if you take my unborn, please take me too," I prayed.

I asked Simi and if she would be kind enough to bring me fresh clothes and gave her the key to my trunk.

#

Simi hated her sister-in-law from the day their entire family went to meet her. She was jealous of Zahina's good looks, education and poise. She envied Zahina being a nurse, independent and successful. She attributed Zahina's mild manners as weakness of spirit and her outgoing nature unbecoming of a pious Muslim woman. Simi decided that she and her mother, would make Zahina's life miserable.

The moment Simi got the keys, she knew what she would do — break Zahina's privacy and search for her secrets. No sooner the taxi departed Simi rushed to her brother's room. Her hands were shaking with excitement, and she struggled to insert the key to unlock Zahina's trunk and secrets. In a frenzy, as soon as the lid was up Simi's hands dove in, she scattered clothes around on the floor, going through each one shaking and dumping. Simi reached the bottom of the trunk and was disappointed not finding any juicy tit bits of Zahina's past. The last of the clothes were out and Simi noticed a flat piece of cardboard lying on the bottom of the trunk. Simi pulled the cardboard off and saw a dried rose in a sleeve. She moved the rose aside and pulled another sleeve of documents, a stack of diplomas and certificates. She pushed them back in the sleeve and while placing it back in the trunk noticed an envelope under the certificates. She opened the envelope to find a stack of photographs. Looking at each she realized they were all her family pictures showing Zahina with her parents and sister. She threw them back into the trunk in disgust and noticed one with some writing on it; she picked it up and with great difficulty read the writing-

Remember Our Good Times,

Anand

Simi turned the photo over to see Zahina standing shoulder to shoulder with a handsome young man. She concluded that the guy in the picture was her lover. She had the evidence of Zahina's misdeeds. *If I can get my brother to get rid of this unfaithful wife, I will have done this family a favor.* She quickly threw, the rest of the stuff back in the trunk, picked some cotton clothes along with the dried rose and the photo walked out of the room. She ran into Sayeed, who just returned from work.

"What were you doing in my room? Did I not tell you not to go in there?" Sayeed said, his voice rising with anger.

"Look at these Sayeed, look at your wife cavorting with her lover. You must divorce her. She has brought shame to our family."

"What are you talking about? Where is Zahina?" said Sayeed, ignoring what Simi was showing him.

"She is in the hospital. Doctor said there was some problem with the delivery. They took her in a taxi. She was bleeding."

"If anything happens to my child, I will not forgive her."

"You will not forgive her if you look at this picture."

Sayeed looked at the picture, shouted obscenities and turned towards Simi, raised his hand and said, "Where did you get this? Who gave it to you?"

"Your wife was hiding these in her trunk all these years, the unfaithful woman. Don't raise your hand against me. I gave you information to act on."

"I will slit her throat, that infidel and unfaithful woman. She has betrayed Allah being unfaithful. I am in the right to spill her blood."

"Don't be a fool and attack her in the hospital. They will arrest you and hang you for that. Just grab her child and divorce her and you will get rid of her from your life. She will suffer enough by losing her child and end in hell for defying Allah's wishes."

"Simi, sometimes your dumb brain comes up with brilliant ideas. Come with me, let us go to the hospital. We will bring the baby home, away from the clutches of this faithless woman."

CHAPTER 36

Talaaq

"**Z**ahina wake up! Zahina!! ZAHINA!"

"Abbu (dad) please let me sleep a little longer," I was in a deep drug induced sleep, dreaming of my Abbu waking me. Not wanting to get up I tried to turn around to hug the pillow at my side. A sharp pain in my lower abdomen woke me up, groggy from the medication, a hand on my shoulder shaking forcefully and a woman's loud voice, "ZAHINA! WAKEUP!".

I looked around with a drugged mind, still too foggy to realize I was in a hospital. I looked frantically around to locate my newborn son.

"Where is my son? I don't see him in his crib. Why is the crib empty? What happened to my son?" I was frantic, the anxiety bringing my senses to sharp focus.

As I looked at the concern on nurse's face, I became more frantic and tried to get out of bed only to find that I was restrained and an IV was dripping into my vein. When the fog cleared, I sensed what I thought was a bad dream, in fact was my husband Sayeed, walking into the hospital room with my newborn son on my bosom, proclaiming 'Talaaq' three times, wrenching him from my hands, and walking out of the room, with his smirking sister in tow.

As she walked out my sister-in-law said, "You have no place in our home, you have betrayed your marriage vows, brought disgrace to our family and to Islam. Live on the streets where you belong," and she threw what she was carrying at the foot of the hospital bed.

Seeing my son snatched from my arms and taken away, I started screaming and tried to get out of the hospital bed. The nurse who just walked into the room to see me struggling to get out of bed, quickly pushed a strong sedative into the running IV, to calm me down lest I rip my sutures.

I looked at the nurse and pleaded, "Please let me go. I must get my baby. Help me, nurse, help me. I am a trained nurse and I can take care of myself. Please let me get my baby back."

"If I let you go, your sutures will pop. What will happen to your baby if you injure yourself or worse, die? I cannot let you go for another 48 hours; I will ask the doctor to sedate you and keep you in restraints until then. Sorry, nurse or not, you are not going anywhere."

"Are you not a mother? Don't you have any compassion? I am ready to die to save my baby. Please plea..." I pleaded as the nurse pushed another dose of sedative.

Finally, after 48 hours, the doctor proclaimed that the wound is healing well. I knew exactly what I must do to recover my son and break out of the clutches of Sayeed and his family.

#

I was discharged upon my request. The nurse brought my clothes and a dried rose and a picture of me and Anand, Simi threw on the floor. I bathed, dressed and left the hospital carrying my meager belongings in a small paper bag. Until I saw the rose and the picture, I did not know where I would go. *I must stay out of sight of Sayeed, recover my son and leave the town immediately, destination unknown.* I hired a rickshaw and headed to Anand's house.

#

On the way to Amma's, I noticed two burkha clad women sweeping the streets. Seeing them gave me an idea and I asked the rickshaw wallah to go to the market before heading to my destination. I entered a clothing store, bought a large burkha and two yards of soft white cotton fabric, headed to Amma's. I knocked on the door wishing Anand opens the door.

Amma was surprised to see me after so many years.

"Zahina come in. You are beautiful as ever. I hoped you and Anand would get married. I knew what was going on between you both, sneaking on to the terrace, thinking I wouldn't notice."

I blushed and said, "We were so young then, full of optimism. Sadly, time has a way of delivering its own reality."

"Are you unwell? You look tired and worn out. Is there something wrong? What can I do?"

Vidya told me many a time about the generosity of Amma. Her genuine concern struck me, the pent-up emotions boiled over, breaking down my poise, and I clutched her crying and hung on to her tiny frame. She gently led me to a sofa, sat with me until I regained composure, brought two glasses of cold orange juice. Pluto came wagging his tail. *The old dog still remembers me.*

Looking at the bag I brought with me, she said, "I see you came prepared to give me company for a few days. Where would you like to stay? You know both Anand's and Durga's rooms. Stay in either. Go relax for a little while I attend to some of my chores, we will have an early dinner and you can tell me what brings you here. Stay here as long as you want."

"I would like to stay in Anand's room, have so many fond memories of that room. I will stay here only for two or three days and then move on. If you don't mind, please look at my incision. It is throbbing. I did not bring much with me, can I borrow a sari from you?"

"You can borrow whatever you want. I still have many of Durga's clothes here. Take whatever you want with you. What do you mean by incision, did you have surgery?"

"I had a C-section three days ago, my husband divorced me immediately after my son was born, literally snatched my baby out of my hands and left me. I plan to recover my son and disappear, Amma. Can I call you Amma?" my tears were flowing again, and I saw tears swelling in her eyes.

"Come with me, my child" said Amma, taking me to her bedroom, "Lie down. Let me look," loosening my sari and with a gentle touch removed the bandages, "I will be back with some warm water and some sterile supplies."

Few minutes later she gently washed the wound with warm water, let it dry and applied an antibiotic cream and bandage.

"There was a little reddening around one suture, I cleaned it off and applied antibiotic cream. It should be ok by tomorrow. If not, I will remove the suture. Go, change and rest. I will call you when dinner is ready".

#

After dinner, I explained my plan to Amma, "I must leave town immediately after I get my son. I will go to Vidya. He promised Anand, to take care of me, if ever the need arose. The only problem is that I do not know where he is."

"I know where Vidya is. Vidya is living with his wife and his grandmother in a village. My driver will take you there. Do you realize that if you fail, and get caught, I may not be able to help?"

"Yes, I understand. I will succeed. It is about time my luck changed. I need a broom. May I take one of yours. I don't think it is coming back."

"Do you need any money?"

"No, if everything goes as planned, I should have more than enough to tide me over."

#

I slept in Anand's room. His cricket trophies were displayed on the wall shelves; his books arranged in neat rows; a picture of me from college days under the glass on his table; his clothes in the closet and his cricket bat in one corner. I changed and lay down on the bed trying to sleep, exhausted; missing my son; my breasts ached for his lips to suckle nourishment from them.

Next morning, I bathed and Amma change my bandages. With her help I fashioned a sling around my upper body to hold my baby securely. I picked up a large broom like the street sweepers were using. Eleven o'clock I headed to my destination, in Amma's car with her driver. A few streets before my destination, I got out.

"Park under this tree and be ready to leave at a moment's notice," I said to the driver. Donning the oversized burkha, I walked towards Sayeed's house carrying the broom. Started to sweep the street, as I watched the front door. I planned surveillance for two days, and on the third, to execute my plan. I watched Sayeed going in at about twelve and leaving about 1:30. Simi, all dressed up, left thirty minutes later and the old lady peeped out and went back in. I kept watch until Simi returned home two hours later and went inside. The next day the family followed the same routine,

On the third day, I bid my farewell "Amma, words cannot express my gratitude and thanks. If all goes well, you will not see me again because I will be hiding, if not you will hear about in the town gossip or the news. I will send word through Vidya if I succeed. I hope my coming here does not put you in Sayeed's crosshairs. Please pray for the wellbeing of my son."

"My prayers will always be with you, Zahina. If you ever need help, please get in touch. I will be here until I die. Don't worry that your ex-husband bothering me. I am old and physically weak, but tough. If he ever comes here, he will be in for a surprise, I know how to handle bullies."

I got out two streets away from Sayeed's, "I will come back between 2:45 - 3 PM. You should be ready to take me to Vidya's village. If I am not back by four o'clock, go home and tell Amma that I never came out."

"Yes, Mem Saab, I will be here and ready. Our destination is a long drive, will get you there safely and comfortably. Madam, packed supplies for the baby and you in a basket."

You are two steps ahead of me Amma, I never thought of baby supplies. How can I ever repay you? I walked with my broom towards the house, that I served like a slave for four years, to take what is mine, embark on a journey fraught with danger and an unpredictable future.

I waited, sweeping the street until Simi left and let another twenty minutes pass for the old one to be asleep. Nobody paid any attention to the burkha clad woman sweeping the streets. I dropped the broom and walked into the house, straight into the spare bedroom next to the old lady's, found my son sleeping soundly on a cot. I took my burkha off, picked him and placed him securely in the sling. He opened his eyes and stared into mine for a moment, sending a shiver of joy throughout my body. He was snug against my chest with his head nestling between my breasts. I paused for a moment, enjoying the sensation of his tiny body against mine. This is not the time to waste, I reminded myself, donning the burkha. I had one more thing to retrieve, my dowry and jewelry given at my wedding. I walked into the old woman's room. She was snoring with her mouth half open. I opened the wooden box holding my dowry. It made a creaking noise; the woman stopped snoring.

"Is that you Simi," she said with her eyes closed.

"Uh.... uh" I replied, my heart thumping.

"You are early," her eyes were still closed.

"Yaa. Yaa," I whispered grabbing the dowry bundle still wrapped in a yellow silk cloth and tied with the red ribbon, hid it under my burkha and walked out with my son, and my Abbu's hard-earned money. My dowry given for my welfare became mine, on the day of divorce. I walked to the waiting car, got in, wiggled out of my burkha and gazed at my son, peacefully sleeping against my chest. Happiness and content filled my being, wiping away years of pain and abuse. I gently ran my fingers through his hair and face, waking him. He looked at me with large eyes and my heart melted as he held my gaze. At that moment, I felt us bonding together. A few moments later his face showed distress and he cried. My poor baby is hungry, I realized and pulled my up top and let him suckle on my breast. He immediately latched on, and I felt the real joy of motherhood. I will never let you go back to that hellish place, I promised him. I name you 'Amrit' nectar of the gods.

I looked out of the back window and saw three motor bikes following us. I worried Sayeed or his buddies following me to end my brief freedom. Every few minutes I looked back to see the same motor bikes behind me. Even when we left town, they were still behind, sending waves of fear.

"I see three motor bikes following us," I told the driver.

"They are here to make sure we have a safe journey to our destination, Madam arranged these Vidya Ji's friends for your safety. They were watching over you, the last three days when you thought you were all by yourself sweeping the roads," said the driver.

Thanks again, Amma, for your concern.

I sat back and relaxed enjoying the sensations of the suckling and dozed off.

CHAPTER 37

Reminiscing

The misfortunes of the last five years of isolation and abuse are behind me now. I will restart my life, pursue my ambition of becoming a doctor and reestablish my connections with the only people left, after the demise of my Abbu and Ammi, with whom I shared the best years of my life. I wasn't sure if I will ever reach Anand, my only love, not knowing where he is and what he is doing. Does he even think of me ever, or has he forgotten me, got married and leading a carefree life with his family? Once I settle, I will get his whereabouts from Amma and contact Anand. Immediately I saw the flaw in my optimistic thoughts about meeting and rekindling our relationship, and put such thoughts to rest, buried them deep, never to surface.

#

About six months into our relationship, Anand's laidback style frustrated and angered me. In the beginning, his lack of presence amused me, but later it bothered me. He doesn't notice me like he used to or focus into my eyes, giving me goosebumps. Has he lost interest in me? Is he looking for or found another girl? However, much I control my negative thoughts, they would not leave me. I started having sleepless nights.

Abbu noticed my irritability, "What is bothering you, Zahi?"

"Nothing Abbu, I am just fine."

My growing discontent with our relationship reached its peak one evening, I was telling him about when I was five and

Shabnam ten. I was teasing her with one of my dolls. Shabnam grabbed the doll and hurled it into our backyard where the doll lodged high in a tree. To retrieve it, I quickly scrambled up the tree and plucked the doll from its precarious position and did not know how to get down. I jumped from about ten feet above the ground and twisted my ankle and was in a cast for a month. I looked at Anand, expecting some sympathy for my injury. Anand was lost in his thoughts, looking through me.

"Anand, so what do you think of that?" I was loud.

Startled he regained focus, and looked at me and said, "That is good, very good."

I gave him a piece of my mind, grabbed my bag and walked out. Shabnam called that evening and I told her what happened and said, "I am tired of his lack of attention and lack of initiative. I will not see him or meet him anymore."

"What if Durga and I, both sisters coming to rescue the love stricken?"

"I hate you, Shabnam," I hung up.

#

When he thought or knew he was right, Anand never backed out of defending or confronting the opponent, whoever it may be. This was very clear when he was a new intern, in the hospital where I worked as a nurse.

One early morning as I was ready to go to my ward for the day shift, a nurse who was working the day before said, "You don't know what your boyfriend said to his professor, on his second day of internship. During the morning rounds with his professor, the one with the bad temper, your friend disagreed with the professor's diagnosis, causing an explosive situation in the ward, with the professor storming out mumbling to himself."

Oh Anand! What have you done? "What happened next?"

"Well, Dr. Anand's diagnosis was confirmed, he took the patient to surgery for evacuation of a blood clot on the brain. The doctor and the patient are in the post-op ward, where they have been all night long."

I exchanged my duty with the nurse in the post-op ward, went to check on the patient and the doctor. I found Anand on a chair by the bedside sleeping and the patient stirring in the bed. I checked on the patient first and took a penlight and shone it on to one of the patient's pupils. I lifted the other eyelid and repeated the same to find both pupils reacting well to light.

I exclaimed, "His pupils are reacting to light!"

Anand woke up with a jerk, promptly pushed me aside and examined the patient and proclaimed, "He is on the way to recovery. Nurse keep me apprised of his condition every six hours, I will get a cup of coffee, a shower and nap for an hour before getting back to my duties," not recognizing me in the heat of the moment.

I gave him my squinty look and said, "Whatever you say, master."

He glanced at me, laughed and said, "Zahina, what are you doing here? How did you get here?"

"A girl has to keep her secrets, doesn't she?"

#

I have seen firsthand during those tumultuous years with highs of our love for each other, to lows of despair I felt the day I saw his face beaming for his success in ECFMG exam.

I knew then, that when he leaves me and goes to America in pursuit of his dreams, I will slip out of his thoughts and his memories of our time together will fade, because in a way he is like a child whose attention is on what is up front. That day I left his presence with a heavy heart, my life and destiny changed forever. If there is one thing I want to do before I die, I must see Anand and apologize for my doings.

I must and will break out of this rut, for my son, so I can make sure he grows up in a healthy home. Inshah Allah.

CHAPTER 38

Sayeed's Frenzy

Sayeed's mom woke up from nap, saw her cash box open and discovered Zahina's dowry missing. She ran out, her grandson forgotten and headed to Sayeed's meat shop. Sayeed hearing the missing dowry flew into a rage and cursed his mom for being careless with the dowry.

Simi returned from her visits with friends, noticing the absence of her mom she stepped into the spare room to check on the baby, found the crib empty. Simi looked all over the house with no success, decided to let Sayeed know before she got blamed for the missing baby.

She entered the store, noticed Sayeed literally foaming at his mouth and loudly screaming at mom.

Noticing Simi Sayeed "Why are you here? Did you lose something?"

"Yes, your son is missing."

Sayeed figured it must be his treacherous ex-wife who somehow got into his home and took his son and the dowry given to him for marrying that no good woman, "I will kill that pig, that scheming woman I divorced," he grabbed a butcher's knife and stormed out.

The two women looked at each other, locked up the shop and headed home. They prayed to Allah the Merciful to bring Sayeed and his son safely home and punish the evil woman.

#

Sayeed asked neighbors if they knew or saw anything. A teen aged boy said, "I saw a burkha clad woman who was sweeping the floors enter the house. I thought she went inside to probably to clean the house to earn extra money. But she came out hurriedly, after about five minutes, and walked away. I don't know where she went."

The last time I saw her she was in the hospital; must go there and inquire if anybody knows where she went. Sayeed went back to his home tore the wedding picture of him with his bride and, shoved the half with Zahina in his pocket and went to the hospital. He showed the photo around to the nurses and doctors demanding Zahina's whereabouts. When they finally told Sayeed to leave or they will call the police, he moved to the hospital entrance, where jatkas and rickshaws were standing. He continued with his inquiry until one rickshaw driver told him he saw the lady in question get in Abdul's rickshaw 2-3 days ago.

"Who is Abdul? Where can I find him?"

"Probably getting drunk, in the slums over there at six every evening."

In the liquor shop, he found a single patron sitting on the floor and drinking country liquor.

"Are you Abdul?"

"Yes. What do you want?"

"Tellme where you took my wife? The one I divorced."

"I know nothing about your wife, I just pull rickshaw to make a living."

Sayeed pulled out the butcher knife from under his shirt, and shouted, "Tell me now or I will cut you."

"I don't know your wife, that is the truth, Allah is my witness. Don't hurt me."

Sayeed thrusted the picture of Zahina in his face, "This one, three days ago."

"Oh, that one. She got in my rickshaw and asked me to take her to the officer's colony; on the way she changed her mind and asked me to take her to the used clothing store."

"What happened next?"

Abdul told to which house he took her and Sayeed went

there. *I am an honorable Muslim and will not tolerate any affront to my manhood.*

#

When the bell rang, Amma pruning the flowering plants in her front yard, wiped her brow, slowly stood and hobbled up to the gate. Before she opened the gate, she gave three hoots on her silent dog whistle, commanding the dog to stay put wherever he was.

"How can I help you?" she said to the tall heavy built man, who appeared very agitated.

"I am looking or my wife. I need to talk to you."

"Why don't you come in and have a seat. Let me wash my hands. I will be back in a moment.

Amma returned to find the man was sitting stiffly in the chair, "Tell me how I can help you find your wife?"

"I was told my wife came here?"

"Lots of people come here, I am not sure if she is one of them. What is your wife's name?"

"She is not my wife anymore. I divorced her three days ago." Amma realized that this was Zahina's ex-husband.

"I am not sure how I can help, have you gone to the police, if she is missing, your ex-wife?"

"She stole my baby and my dowry and disappeared."

"There is no one here with your baby or your dowry."

"I know she is here, you are lying," Sayeed said raising his voice, "I want to search your house."

"Listen, whoever you are. I am telling you nobody is here with a baby and stolen dowry and never was. You are not searching my home. I suggest you leave."

"What? You old woman, you think you can stop me? I will do what I please. You are lucky I am not planning on causing you any physical harm."

"I am serious when I ask you to leave. You will not search my home or stay here any longer."

"I will decide what I do, you are in no position to stop me," said Sayeed angrily getting up from the chair, as Amma

203

brought the dog whistle to her lips and gave a single long silent whistle.

Sayeed took one step forward towards her when he saw a black streak and heard a low growl as the huge German Shepherd charged into the room and stopped between the man and his master with its teeth bared and hackles raised.

"Hold, watch" Anand's mom instructed her dog and turned towards Sayeed and said, "I suggest you sit down slowly. Make no sudden moves. I will be back in a few minutes."

She stepped into the next room and called her neighbor, the inspector of police who is a good friend and explained the standoff with Zahina's ex-husband.

"I will be right there and take care of him, just got back from the police station and still in my uniform," said the inspector.

#

I will slowly move my hand and grab the knife under my shirt and cut the dog's throat in one sweep, before it can react. He moved his hand slowly towards the knife, grabbed the handle and pulled it out in one sweep. With no sound and in a flash the dog's jaws clamped on his forearm in a vice like grip. Pluto looked at Sayeed as if to say what other stupid tricks do you have. Anand's mom returned and saw a terrified Sayeed with the dog with its jaws clamped on Sayeed's forearm.

"If I say the word, the dog will bite through your bones. I asked you not to make any sudden moves and you ignored me. You will now stay until the police inspector arrives to take you into custody. I have work to do so I will leave you in the company of my dog. Have a good day and never come back."

The inspector arrived a few minutes later and asked for Sayeed's full name and address, "I can have you arrested and thrown in jail for threatening this lady with a knife. I warn you if I see you here again, I will arrest and prosecute you. If any harm comes to this lady ever, I will come looking for you."

The inspector escorted Sayeed out and let him go, warning again about returning to this location ever again.

CHAPTER 39

Light at the End of Tunnel

Amrit was nestled against my bosom sleeping peacefully as we traveled in Amma's car. It was midnight by the time we reached the outskirts of Vidya's village. I asked the driver to stop and let me out and give me the directions to Vidya's home. I wanted to walk the rest of the way. No point in leaving a trail in this village, arriving by car at midnight. I got out with Amrit safely tucked in the sling and my meager belongings in a bag and started walking toward the village. Within a few minutes I saw a man walking toward me, in the moonlit night.

As he got closer, a loud voice, "Is that you, Zahina? Amma called me and said to expect you tonight. I couldn't wait any longer had to come to take you home."

Approaching closer he flicked a flashlight first at my face and then on to his own. I saw a bearded man with long flowing hair and a broad smile on his face. *Is this Vidya? What a change?* The meek young man I knew has changed into a handsome man with a confident stride. The soft, hesitant eyes were now intense and piercing.

"Yes Vidya, I am so glad to be here."

"Zahina, welcome to my humble home. We were waiting for you since Amma's message. How are you? Where is the little one? Come on, let us go home." *The man of few words has changed indeed.*

"Vidya it is very generous of you to take me in. I hope I am not inconveniencing you. Is it ok with your family?"

"I promised Anand that I would be there for you if you needed it. I am honored that you thought of me. Let's go and meet my family."

We reached a small brick house. Vidya introduced his family who were waiting on the porch, "This my grandma who owns this house, my wife Ambika and my daughter Uma."

I nodded my head at all of them and said, "Namaste."

"Beti, you look tired, please sit down. Have you eaten? We have some food for you, sorry we ate," said granny hugging Zahina. "Wash up, eat and go to bed. It is late, you must rest, and we can talk tomorrow. Sleep as late as you want. These three will leave by seven in the morning for school."

I haven't felt so at home since I left my parent's home, at Anand's and now Vidya's. Old friends from the past showering me with hospitality and safety, welcoming me to their homes as one of the family. A small ray of hope that the worst is behind me and that this will blossom into a rosy dawn, and a new beginning.

#

By the time I got up bathed my baby and got ready, Vidya, Ambika and Uma had left for school. I stayed with granny and helped her with her chores and told her the story of my marriage, the mistreatment, getting pregnant, divorced the day I delivered and the desperate action to kidnap my son.

"Beti, you have suffered a lot. You are free now and we will do our best to help you. You knew Vidya from before, but he has changed a lot in the last four years. When he sets his mind, nothing will stop him. He is determined to care for you. Think about what you want to do with the rest of your life. You are still young, marriage is something you should consider, despite your experiences."

"Thank you, grandma, for listening and for your advice. Marriage is not my priority. I wanted to become a doctor when I started college. After talking to Vidya and Ambika I will decide, how to go about it. I would like to leave my dowry money with you for safekeeping."

"I wouldn't mind holding the money for you, but I

206

recommend that you open an account and deposit it in a bank. It is not only safer but easily accessible wherever you are. Let Vidya advise you."

#

After dinner, I sat down with Vidya, while Ambika looked after Amrit. Vidya listened to my story for the last five years, his brow knitting and his face turning red with anger. I was astonished to see his eyes burn with fury.

"Do you want me to put the fear of god in that man, Sayeed?" Vidya said.

"No Vidya, I don't want him to find out anything about us. I want to disappear from his life and thought. Knowing him, he would search forever, just to take my son away and kill me for what I have done. I see him as the laughingstock of his neighbors, friends and relatives, for letting his wife get the best of him. I know he is planning his revenge as we speak. My worry is that he would somehow find that I went to see Anand's mom and I am concerned for her."

"I am going to Hari Ji's this evening, and I will call Amma and ask her to be on guard. If she wants, I can ask a few of my followers to keep watch."

"What followers Vidya? What are these people following you for?"

"When we have time, we can talk about that. It is not important. First you tell me your plans for the future and how I can help you."

"I need to regain my old self and take care of my baby. Please let me stay here during that period. For Amrit's and my safety, I will move far away, out of Sayeed's reach. My heart's desire is to use my dowry money to go to medical college and become a doctor. Someday I want to meet Anand and apologize for abandoning him."

"Zahina, I do not approve of you ever meeting Anand. He abandoned you and was responsible for your misfortunes. Forget him, he does not deserve your apologies or affection. He doesn't know what commitment is."

#

It was close to midnight by the time Vidya came back from his other job; I was waiting for him, unable to sleep. Amrit finally fell asleep in Ambika's bed, enjoying the attention of his aunt and cousin.

"Why are you still up, rest," said Vidya.

"I am too keyed up. I cannot believe I escaped the clutches of Sayeed. Until I got pregnant, I thought I would die in that house. When I realized I was pregnant, I decided to escape for the sake of my child."

"Amma said that Sayeed was there a few hours ago demanding your and the baby's whereabouts. When he got nowhere, became aggressive and threatened her. Amma let her big dog loose on him. "

"For a petite old lady, Amma is a force you don't want to mess with," said Zahina. "I wish I had some of her mental strength."

"You do, Zahina, you do. You survived hell, you suffered through the last five years and broke free, a testament to your strength and grit. Never underestimate it. Hari Ji, is anxious to meet you soon."

#

"Vidya told of your desire to be a doctor and be faraway. I admire your determination and vision, but it is difficult for a woman to be alone, especially a single mother. It would be best if there is a helping hand nearby; With that in mind, I took the liberty and called my good friend Ravi in Bombay. He is willing to help you," said Hari.

"Thank you, Hari Ji, it is very gracious of you to help me. Please convey my thanks to Ravi Ji for his generosity."

"The reason I wanted to meet with you today, is to arrange for a telephone conversation with Ravi. He is expecting us to call him today. You can thank him personally."

Once the pleasantries were over Zahina said, "Thank you Ravi Ji for your offer to help. My name is Zahina I am a registered nurse. I haven't worked for the last five years because of family issues."

"Oh my! You have such credentials. I know a few people here in the medical field. I will talk to them and get information on how to go about getting an admission in a medical college. In the interim, please send me copies of your diplomas and certificates. It is likely to take some time to work through this."

"Thank you, Ravi Ji for all your help," said Zahina with trepidation; all her all her degrees and diplomas were still in Sayeed's house.

#

"Vidya, all my important papers are in Sayeed's house. Without those I don't see how I can go forward with my plans," Zahina said on their way back home.

"Tell me where all your papers are in that house."

I told him where they were when I left that house.

"I have a plan to retrieve those, if they are still there."

A week later Vidya brought me all my certificates and papers.

"I even have the trunk, minus the clothes. Your sister-in-law is prancing all over town in your clothes. She had no use for these papers, they were in the unlocked trunk in the room you said it would be. The man I sent told the old lady in the house that he buys old trunks and she sold it to him for 10 rupees. He picked up the trunk with the papers."

"Thank you, Vidya. I will keep the trunk it will come in handy when I move."

Two weeks later a message came from Hari Ji asking me to come for a telephone conversation with Ravi Ji.

"Do you know about Lokamanya Tilak Municipal Medical College and Municipal Hospital?" asked Ravi.

"No Ravi Ji I have never heard the name before."

"It is one of the premier medical colleges in the state. I know Dr. Khan, chief surgeon and associate dean. He said that they are starting a new program next year. This program is for their hospital nurses who want to be doctors. Instead of the usual five years, this course would be three and a half to four years

209

to get the MBBS degree. He said he could offer you a nurse's job as soon as you are ready. Once on staff, you will be eligible for applying."

"Ravi Ji, I do not need a few days, I am ready. How do I apply for the nursing job?"

"I will arrange a telephone interview with Dr. Khan. You both can discuss the details."

"Yes, Ravi Ji, that would be perfect? How do I repay you for help?"

"When you become a full-fledged doctor, give some of your time and service to the poor."

"Yes, Ravi Ji and thank you again."

CHAPTER 40

Steep Climb

"Vidya, Dr. Khan offered me staff nurse job, and six months later I will be eligible to apply for medical school. I will have a private room in the nursing quarters and a monthly salary of Rs.250. I cannot accept this because the nurses quarters are for adult women only, I cannot take Amrit with me."

Vidya stayed silent for a moment and said, "Zahina don't make a hasty decision. This is the opportunity you waited all your life for, a guaranteed job and then admission to medical college. Time will pass by so fast you won't even know it. Ambi and I will look after Amrit like our own. Uma will be his sister. We will love and take care of Amrit."

"How can I leave my only baby and live that far away? He will grow up not knowing his ammi."

"Whenever you get a few days off, come and visit. We will make sure he will not forget you. If you cannot come I or Ambi will bring him to you. In a city like Bombay, where you have no family and friends, how are you going to take care of an infant?"

"What about Sayeed? If he finds out my son is with you, he will come here and will take Amrit away."

"I am not afraid of Sayeed. I have a vast following in the neighboring communities, villages and towns. Nobody can force me, not anymore. Those days are long gone."

#

Three weeks later I arrived in Bombay, Ravi Ji received and

took me to his home where I met with his wife, two lovely children and his dad.

"Please stay here for a few days to get your bearings. We will be available for you if the need arises. Consider this as your second home," said Ravi, a multimillionaire who lived in a simple, nondescript four-bedroom house, thoroughly impressing me with his simplicity and down to earth manner.

"What are your plans, I know that you are a trained nurse and aspiring to be a doctor. How would you like to help people who cannot afford it? Zahina are you willing to provide basic healthcare for the poor in your spare time?"

"Thank you for your offer of extending your family home and welcoming me. Once I settle down in the new job, I will do whatever I can to help the poor, but you realize that I am only a nurse, not a doctor. What I can do is very limited."

"The people I have in mind, have no medical services or healthcare available to them. They let illnesses fester and seek care when they are beyond help. Any care they get is a step in the right direction. Let us talk about it in a few months."

#

I moved into the nurses, quarters in the hospital, a third-floor room with a view of the neighboring hospital buildings, a single bed, a table and a chair. There were communal bathrooms and a mess hall on the ground floor. I was in orientation for a week where experienced staff nurses showed how things worked in their hospital, location of various departments etc.

I met with Dr. Khan a tall, distinguished looking older man with a mop of silver hair and a perpetual smile on his face.

"Welcome Zahina, Ravi talked a lot about you, and I am glad you have accepted my offer. I will help you as much as possible in the pursuit of your dream to be a doctor. One thing I want from you and all those who work for me in this hospital is dedication to the work and care of the patients. I always treat my employees fairly and expect the same of others. If you experience mistreatment or see it happening to others, let me know."

"Dr. Khan, thank you for giving me this opportunity, you do not understand what this means to me. I have been away for a little over five years from nursing and it will take me some time to freshen up my skills. I will not disappoint you."

"Ravi also said that you plan to serve the poor whenever you have time, and I applaud your decision. I am planning on setting up a small clinic in Dharavi it will be a free clinic to provide the most basic of services to the poor. Any way we will talk about this in a few weeks. First, get used to this facility and its staff. Okay Zahina?"

"Yes, sir, I would like that. In a month or two I should be ready to assist you, with that project."

"May Allah bless you my child, I pray for your success."

CHAPTER 41

The Mother of All Slums

I entered Dharavi two months after starting my nurse's job. The clinic was a rusty tin shack with a worn tin roof. It had two rooms, one for patient examination and the other for minor surgical procedures.

Dharavi was inhabited by a million people and occupied about one square mile of precious real estate in the heart of Bombay. It was like an overgrown mythical beast belching fire and smoke and emitting noxious fumes and fetid odors from its potters' kilns and open sewers. It was a Mecca for recycling most of the refuse generated by the city; by hand; by innovation and by the necessity to earn a meager living. The residents represented a microcosm of the diversity of India, by ethnicity, religion, and talents. In this slum, children went to school dressed in clean clothes, came home, and played in the streets, or worked recycling trash. There were churches, temples, and mosques to fulfill the spiritual needs. This was the situation in the world's second largest slum when I went to Dharavi to deliver basic healthcare.

#

My brow was sweaty in the sweltering heat even after sundown, as I examined the six-month-old infant. He was very thin, with sunken eyes, a protuberant belly, and sparse reddish-brown hair. *Looks like kwashiorkor.* The mother looked equally malnourished.

"My husband died when this child, my first one, was born. One day after work he complained of body aches. Next morning, he woke up with fever and headache. By evening he was lethargic, went to sleep and never woke up. He was unconscious for two days and passed away. He is the sole breadwinner for my family, I have been living on scraps and my milk has dried, so there is no milk for the baby," she said.

I gave her a two-pound bag of milk powder, courtesy of UNICEF, told her how to mix it with water for feeding the baby. Unfortunately, I had nothing to give her for nourishment, so I gave her two rupees. She was reluctant to take the money, but I insisted she takes it to buy some rice and lentils. I asked her to come back when she has used up all the powdered milk. She thanked me profusely and wanted to touch my feet as a sign of respect, which I refused.

Wherever I look there is poverty, malnutrition, disease, and despair. It was gut-wrenching to see it every day, and the only reason I stayed there, was the realization that if I did not, there was no one else to help them. It was two weeks since I started coming to this shack bearing the sign 'Municipal Health Clinic'. I work here from 6PM to 9PM, after working a full shift from seven in the morning to 3:30 PM in the hospital. I get to my hostel room around 10PM, a quick supper of the hospital food, left for late comers. I get up around 5:00AM do some stretch exercises, shower, grab a quick bite and head to my work. By the end of two weeks, my presence as a nurse spread throughout Dharavi and people came in to see me, pay their respects and bless me. When the illnesses were beyond my ability to diagnose or treat, I directed them to the hospital. Dr. Khan encouraged me and gave pointers on the cases I sent, and I found his knowledge and insights very educational. Dr. Khan asked me to join him in the surgery suite one afternoon, where he was repairing a deep laceration on a patient's leg. He taught me how to debride and suture wounds.

"I usually teach this to my interns. This skill may come useful in Dharavi," he said.

I spent the next few weeks with him in the surgery suite, learning to suture wounds and set broken bones. He was a very patient teacher, never getting angry when I made a mistake, always encouraging and explaining how to avoid mistakes. This training was immensely helpful.

The clinic had a treatment room in the back, which was in disuse since the doctor who worked there retired. Locals refurbished it under the guidance of Dr. Khan. The hospital supplied basic sterile supplies and instruments to provide first aid along with a stock of medicines. The slum dwellers named me 'Kudi Doctor' and were happy for the medical help I provided. Ten to thirty patients waited for me each evening. I set up a system by which I would see the severely ill first.

One evening a man bleeding heavily from his upper arm and in great distress was carried in by four men. I quickly got him into my treatment room. He was in his forties with a sweaty face a weak pulse. and was going into shock. I saw the deep cut of the brachial artery in his upper arm close to the armpit *I must stop the bleeding to save his life. It was too high up in the axilla to place a tourniquet and stop the bleeding.*

I shouted at one of the fellows, "Go get a car or a taxi, to take him to the hospital."

I held a sterile pad on his bleeding artery with pressure, with my other I grasped a hemostat from the tray of sterile instruments. In seconds the pad was soaked in blood. I quickly got the hemostat open and in position, removed the pad, thrust the hemostat over the pulsating artery and clamped it down. The bleeding immediately stopped. I knew I was taking a chance, that he may lose his arm, but at least he had a chance at life. I started a fast iv saline drip checked the hemostat, placed large sterile pads over the wound and secured it with tape.

The car arrived I got the injured into the car and told his friends, "He lost a lot of blood. Ask for Dr. Khan. He does not leave until 9 or 10 at night."

Next morning, I was doing rounds in the pediatric ward when Dr. Khan walked in.

"Good morning, Dr. Khan," I said, turning toward him.

"Good morning, Zahina, can I talk to you for a moment privately?"

Mortified that I messed up yesterday, trying to save the patient and scared he would fire me, walked with him to an office. I looked apprehensively at Dr. Khan ready to take whatever he unleashed.

"Congratulations, Zahina, your quick thinking and prompt action saved not only the fellow's life, but I could also restore circulation to the arm. He has an excellent chance of full recovery. Most of my interns would have panicked and made a mess of it. Using a hemostat was brilliant, it prevented the artery from retracting into the axilla; would have made my job that much more difficult. I admire your cool and collected handling of this patient without panic."

"I did not have any time for panic Dr. Khan, I just acted on instinct."

"I came here to tell you also, my office will accept applications for the medical college from tomorrow, I want to see yours in my office and you can designate me as a reference."

"Yes Dr. Khan, Thank you. I will get mine in."

#

I arrived at my clinic, to find crowds waiting that evening. *What catastrophe has brought this many people to the clinic?* As I walked closer the four men from yesterday cleared a path for me through the throng. At the entrance to the clinic was a well groomed middle-aged man.

"My name is Dada Tommy. I keep the peace in this place and drive away the scum. These four are my men who patrol the slum and keep order. The one you saved yesterday is one of them. Thank you for saving his life," he said.

"I was just doing my job. I do not deserve any special thanks. That he survived is all I need."

"You are very humble, but you saved the life of another human being and that is admirable. Step forward and meet the man's wife and his three children, see how grateful they are. Without your help, the woman would be a widow and the children fatherless," said Dada pointing to a woman holding a garland and two girls and a boy looking at me with smiles on their faces.

The woman stepped forward and placed the garland around my neck and the children bowed their heads bent down and touched my feet, embarrassing me, as the crowd clapped and whistled.

"You have my word I will do my best to help you in serving the people of Dharavi and you are welcome to my home anytime. Now tell me what is that I can do for you now to show my gratitude," said Dada.

"If you really want to help, I need a person in the clinic to assist me and keep track of the patients. I like a few volunteers to clean this place, a few chairs and tables. Fix the leaking roof. And if you want to do more make an extension to this building with five or six beds to admit the sick."

Dada Tommy stared at me as I was listing my demands was quiet for a few moments burst out laughing, "You drive a tough bargain Kudi Doctor, if you allow me to address you so. By the time you come in tomorrow I promise I will get the roof fixed and you will have chairs and at least one table. If I cannot find an assistant, I will send my wife Punam, she is the educated one in our family, having completed high school and can read and write English. The extension building will take some time so be patient."

"Thank you, and I apologize if I was too greedy."

"You only asked for items to better this center, and not a thing for yourself. That in my world, attests for your selfless commitment to these people. You will be under my personal protection, I will have one of my men escort you every night to your hostel," said Dada Tommy.

Of all the help Dada Tommy provided, Punam, sent to assist me, was a godsend; a person to trust and lean on, during the turbulences yet to come. The next day when I came to the center, the clinic had a new roof; and the interior was clean. A few months later Dada had the extension to the clinic built, while I went to visit my son.

CHAPTER 42

Dream Come True

The day I got admitted to medical college was both a very joyous, attaining the first step in my lifelong goal to become a doctor and a day of sorrow, thinking of my Abbu and Ammi who were not with me to celebrate. I thought of the past five years that sapped the life out of me. I missed my son.

The January session I got admitted was limited to 45 students, fifteen women and thirty men. Only a few were nurses. Most were younger than me by almost a decade, coming straight out of college. I continued my nursing job on weekends, did not give up on Dharavi.

The mornings started in anatomy dissection hall. We worked in pairs dissecting a body part. My partner was Sharma. In the beginning, he would read from Cunningham's manual, and I would do the dissection. I realized if this continued, he would not pass tests. I pushed him to assist me in the dissection and after a month of struggle he started dissecting.

Little did I know that this soft spoken, mild mannerism was a disguise to his true nature and cause me immense trouble.

#

Two weeks into medical college, Dr. Khan suggested that I quit the nursing job.

"This is my livelihood, and I cannot give it up. This job provides me with shelter, food and a paycheck. Please, Dr. Khan, let me continue," I begged.

"I am concerned about your wellbeing, Zahina, You, are working seven days a week, for over fourteen hours a day. No one can go on like this for four years and expect to get through medical school successfully, consider what I am telling you; for the work you do in Dharavi I will pay you the same per hour that you make in nursing."

"Sir, I work as a volunteer, and I cannot accept remuneration for that."

"Look at this way, by living in Dharavi, you will be there for the people most of the day, except the hours you are in classes. The room in the clinic is free. So, use the salary for your food and necessities."

This is how Dharavi became my home for the next five years and I became a savior of the ill in that slum. There were days I would think of my son Amrit and become morose and quiet. Punam was the person I leaned on those days to regain my focus. Slowly I opened up to her telling my story, my lost love, my torturous marriage, the uncaring in-laws and now my far away son.

"Zahina in all this adversity you stood strong and made a life for yourself, I am amazed at your strength, tenacity and resolve."

"I have this dreaded feeling that my ex-husband Sayeed will find me and come here to seek revenge and steal my Amrit."

"The people of Dharavi have a great respect and admiration for you. Nobody will harm befall you, and nobody will ever reveal your whereabouts. I promise, Tomar will spread the word that there may be a person searching for you and to be on the lookout and misdirect him."

I felt reassured and relieved by those words. My work continued and the people of Dharavi brought me whatever they made, the shoemakers shoes, the weavers clothing, the woodworkers, a cot, and a cabinet. Some took turns cleaning up my surroundings and the center. Many would invite me to their homes on Sundays for lunch or dinner. I tried to refuse, but most insisted until I relented. I made many friends visiting them. It surprised me that living in that polluted slum, their homes, whether a shack or a more robust building, were clean, organized with small touches that made it pleasant. I felt that I found my life's calling in this slum, that has become my home and I was content. However, a new situation arose at the medical college, that I was not sure how to handle.

#

During anatomy dissections we crowded around the cadaver a pair on each limb and one on the head and neck, ten people, trying to cut and pull and dissect. We were constantly bumping into each other. I was the only female in that group and most respected my personal space. My partner, Sharma however, would keep contact with my body until I moved away. I noticed that when I was dissecting, he would lean close to me, his body pressing against mine and occasionally as he was pointing at the dissection his arm would brush across my breasts. When it happened, the first few times, I did not think much of it. As weeks passed these unwanted contacts became more frequent. One day I was dissecting the foot and tracing the branches of the sural nerve, his hand extended to point at one of its branches, his forearm pressed against both my breasts with increasing pressure, and he would not break contact. I leaned back and fell off my stool. The other students came to pull me up. I noticed a leering smile on Sharma's face. I felt revolted and violated. *Next time it happens, I might wield the dissecting scalpel on him* but put that thought out of my mind.

At the end of the classes, I went to Sharma and said, "I want to talk to you in private."

His eyes lit up and said, "Any time Zahina, I like that."

We walked up to a quiet corner, and I waited until all the students left and said, "I want this touching and pressing to stop."

He moved closer to me and said, "Don't be a prude, Zahina. These things happen when we work in close quarters."

"You are doing it intentionally. I want you to stop that."

"I am telling these are accidental and they are likely to

happen. What are you going to do about it?"

"I am warning you, keep your hands to yourself," I said with rising fury.

"You look so beautiful when you are angry, I feel like kissing you," he said leaning towards me.

I moved back until the wall stopped my retreat, and Sharma crowded, pushed me against the wall with his hands on my shoulders and his face was leaning towards mine. I dropped my handbag, clenched my fist and landed a punch on his face, mustering all my strength. Pain shot up through my hand and shoulder and he reeled back, holding a hand to his face. I slipped past and walked away and heard him say, "There is nothing you can do to me Zahina, I come from a powerful family. You may escape today, soon you will be mine to do as I please."

#

I came back to my room in the center, shook up and distraught. Punam immediately recognized my turmoil and asked me, "What happened Zahina? Why are you upset?"

"Nothing to worry about, just a bad day at the college. I will be fine in the morning," I replied, thinking there is no need to drag Punam into this.

That day I just had a few patients, and I went to bed early, determined to bring it to the attention of anatomy department chairman and put an end to this. Next morning instead of going to dissection hall I went to Dr. Mohan, the chairman. I waited about thirty minutes before he would see me. I finally got in, he was in a chair behind a desk stacked with books and papers and a skeleton hanging from a hook behind him. Dr. Mohan was about five foot three, overweight with a balding head and teeth stained by chewing paan.

"What do you want to see me about a young lady? I am very busy. It better be important."

"Sir, I have a problem...," I started.

"I only deal with problems of the academic nature, if it is a personal problem you have come to the wrong person," Dr.

Mohan interrupted.

"A student is harassing me," I blurted out.

"You all are adults, not high school kids. Take care of it yourself."

"This guy is touching me inappropriately and said he would have his way with me."

"You are a beautiful woman, that is his hormones talking. Don't worry."

"He is making unwanted advances and tried to kiss me."

"You are a much older woman than the kids here, married and divorced, take that as a compliment and make the best of it, than complain and make trouble. These things happen, adapt than fight, if you want to progress. I am busy. Please go back to your station and take care of it yourself."

My temper was flaring, and I wanted to give this slime ball a piece of my mind, but reluctantly backed out. I went back to Dharavi, skipping my classes for the day. I was clueless how to stop Sharma and not ruin my lifelong ambition of becoming a doctor. I thought of talking to Dr. Khan, but decided against it, since Sharma is from an influential family, and it might get Dr. Khan in trouble. I heard a knock on my door and Punam walked in.

"How come you are so early today?" I asked Punam.

"Word reached me that Kudi Doctor is in the clinic with a frown on her face and in deep thought. As your didi, I came in, talk to you and see if I can help. You were distraught yesterday and same today. Please talk to me, Zahina. I cannot see you this way," said Punam with tears in her eyes.

I hugged her and cried. She dried my tears and held me as I told her all about Sharma and his behavior towards me. She listened to me and said, "Don't worry about this anymore, Tomar will take care of this once for all."

"This guy comes from a wealthy and influential family. I do not want Dada to get in trouble."

"Not to worry, Tomar knows how to handle this kind of kutta. Wait and rest, let me talk to him. Tomar thinks of you as a god given gift to this community and will take care of this today."

Punam came back an hour later and said, "Tomar wants you to go with him today to your college after classes and point out this guy."

"I do not want this guy maimed or killed, he is, as my professor put it, a young man with hormones."

"He is worse than a pig. Tomar will put the fear of God in him. They will not kill or maim him, maybe slap him a few times. He will deliver street justice - *when you threaten one of ours, you are dealt with!*"

I went to the college with Dada Tommy that afternoon, on his motorbike, and pointed Sharma as he was walking towards his Vespa scooter. Dada looked back and pointed at the guy again, nodded his head, started his motor bike and returned me to the clinic.

#

I did not find Punam at the clinic, which was unusual, but this was an unusual day. I got busy with seeing the patients and when I was about to close the clinic, Punam rushed in with food. She insisted I eat while she waited and updated me about operation Sharma.

"They took care of him. He will never bother you again."

"Is he dead or beaten badly?" I was afraid to hear the answer.

"Tomar was furious and was ready to beat the guy to a pulp. I told him you did not want hurt. Tomar pointed him to his four guys waiting outside the college. While Tomar was bringing you back, the four guys got hold of Sharma put him in an autorickshaw and took him to the outskirts of the town, gave him a couple slaps. Sharma started crying and offered them money, his scooter or anything they wanted. They asked him to drop his pants and told him they would it cut it off, if he ever misbehaved with any woman. He peed in his pants and cried like a baby. They left him there crying."

I never saw Sharma him again. A few weeks later, the episode of what happened to Sharma surfaced on the rumor mill. Dr. Mohan called me to his office and said he was sorry for how he behaved that day I complained.

"I was having an awful day and did not realize how offensive I was. I meant no harm. I apologize if I offended you."

I stared into his eyes, my eyes conveying my fury and disgust, until he broke eye contact. I walked out without accepting his apology. Word got out that I had connections and not to be messed with, and that was fine with me.

CHAPTER 43

The Singing Sikh

I fell into a routine, up by 5AM, get ready and out of my room to check on the admitted patients and provide them medications for the day. I would be in the medical college by eight until the classes were over and back to my patients. Once a week a doctor came to oversee my care and spent their time teaching me the subtle diagnostic pointers and were helpful in increasing my knowledge and confidence. As months progressed, I became more confident and comfortable in handling patients.

One day a burkha clad woman came to my center with a high fever. She was blind in one eye and severely disfigured face. I gave her pills to reduce her fever. She told her story - after one serious argument her husband threw acid on her.

In this great land, the plight of women takes many paths, spans across all socio-economic classes, religious boundaries, and education levels. Some women are abused while others attain pinnacles of success and acceptance. My experience and this woman's were a sample of abuses ranging from neglect, psychological and physical abuse, unrestrained violence, disfigurement and in extreme cases loss of limb or life.

I reserved Friday evenings for going to the Jama Masjid. For that trip I always wore my burkha not for camouflage, worried of Sayeed. Saturday, I spent at somebody's home for lunch.

Returning from the mosque I usually stopped at a dhaba, ran by a Sikh man, to pick up hot naan and spicy chicken curry.

One Sunday, I walked over and see if the dhaba was

227

open and was pleasantly surprised that he was singing one of my favorite songs from my college days, 'Mera jutaa hai Japani…' (my shoes are from Japan … but my soul is Indian), his back towards me and chopping vegetables. I stood there listening and thinking of happy days. He turned around and saw me and stopped.

"Please don't stop, it is one of my favorite songs."

"I was not expecting anybody on Sunday this early. I was just getting ready to make mirch masala to go with the roti."

"I am sorry, I will come back later," I said.

"Don't go, please sit here, I will make you a cup of tea."

"Only if you continue to sing, I am Zahina."

"What a beautiful name, I only knew you as Kudi Doctor. I am Charan Singh, the sole owner of this grand establishment in this perfect setting." He laughed.

I sat while he sang and made me tea, a pleasant experience the likes of which I haven't experienced in a long time. I stayed there for two hours listening to his songs and inhaling the aroma of his cooking. He packed two roti with the mirch masala and refused payment.

"You give so much to this community, and I will be honored if you accept this little token of appreciation."

"Thank you very much, but only once, I do not believe in being a freeloader. Next time you must accept my payment."

"Yes, Kudi Doctor Ji."

From that day I visited his dhaba every Sunday, sat and enjoyed the tea and his singing, troubles fogotten, transported to a carefree world, a true heaven in contrast to the world I was in. In between songs he told me about his place of birth Jullundur, about his parents and his elder brother. I told a little about myself omitting the last five years except to say that it was a marriage gone bad. It was a unique friendship that developed between us. Two lonely souls enjoying each other's company for a few hours every Sunday. Sometimes I worried if I was getting deeply rooted in this community when I did not know what the future holds.

One day Charan said, "I notice a sorrow in you Zahina and I am very troubled by it. Talk to me and let me help you."

I told him everything holding nothing back, Charan came around and hugged me. "Zahina, consider me your big brother. I will be here for you whenever you need me."

"Charan bhai, you know all about me. Tell me how a Sikh from Jullundur ended up in Dharavi running a dhaba."

"I was sixteen and went to play hockey with my older brother Devinder and his friends. On the way home, we stopped to get cool lassi and were caught up in a fight between people protesting for Punjab statehood and the police. A tear gas shell landed in our midst. Devinder picked it up and threw it away. It unfortunately landed amongst police. who charged us. Our group scattered the police caught and started to beat me. Seeing my plight Devinder jumped in using his hockey stick to fight the police. I got free. My last look of Devinder was fighting the police with blood running down his face. Word came that the police put him in a truck and drove away. He was never found. My father searched for Devinder day and night. My mother, who taught me to sing, stopped singing and went into depression. My younger sister, unable to deal with this, emigrated to UK. When I heard that police were searching for me, I left my hometown and came here. Worked menial jobs for a couple of years and opened this dhaba."

I got up and hugged Charan. No words to console – there was enough sorrow around to drown us all.

CHAPTER 44

Blast from the Past

I graduated from medical school in three and half years and became a full fledged doctor. A happy day for attaining my childhood dream, convinced my Abbu and Ammi were beaming from heaven. My routine continued at Dharavi as a doctor. Dr. Khan recommended the years I spent with him and other doctors at the clinic and my experience in handling all kinds of cases count for the year of internship.

#

It was a glorious Sunday morning. My clinic opens at 11AM, and following my daily routine after bathing, I dressed in my favorite red churidar pajamas and a matching top, I went to Charan's dhaba. Charan handed me a red rose and a cup of masala chai and sang my favorite songs. I sat there sipping the hot spicy tea, enjoying his songs and missing Amrit. A sound of running feet behind me interrupted my daydreaming. I saw Punam running towards the dhaba.

She stopped near me, waited a few seconds to catch her breath and said, "Your sister just called for you. She said it is important and she would call back in half an hour and asked me to bring you to the phone."

Shabnam calling early in the morning, at 5AM from Iran, sent a chill through my body. *Why would she be calling so early if it was not a dire emergency?* My body would not respond to my desire to accompany Punam to her home, and I froze. Charan came around and placed a hand on my shoulder to reassure me. By now he has learnt to read my emotions. I leaned on

Punam for support, and we made our way to her place.

#

"Zahina, how are you doing? Is Punam with you by your side?" asked Shabnam.

"Why? What is the matter? Are you all ok?".

"We are all fine. Please sit-down Zahina, we need to talk. I have news of Anand and I wanted you to be sitting down, knowing how emotional you get with this topic."

Tears started streaming down my face as I imagined the worst, knowing this news would be devastating. I started praying silently, as my senses shut down, holding the phone to my ear and my breath.

"Anand was ambushed and kidnapped by a rebel group on his way to their farms and taken into the forest. He sustained a head injury in the process. Vidya is helping Amma to secure Anand's release."

Hearing the name of Vidya brought me back to reality and I knew what I must do to save Anand. I bade goodbye to Shabnam, interrupting her advice to be careful and not venture into the unknown.

I said to Punam, "Please take me to the train station. I must go to Vidya as soon as possible."

#

I rushed to see Dr. Khan to seek advice on how to deal with Anand's injury. He listened and said, "Dealing with a head injury, requires neurosurgical experience in most cases, and is difficult even in a hospital setting, but to deal with this in primitive conditions in the middle of a forest is almost impossible. But you have to play the cards dealt. If there is anyone, I trust with such a task, it is you, Zahina. My advice to you is to do nothing heroic, just stabilize your friend within the limits of the supplies you have. Once stabilized, move him to a better equipped facility and have the experts take care of him. If you can wait, I will have the operating room nurse pack sterile supplies and medicines you might need."

"I am eternally grateful to you for your support and

understanding. May Allah grant you a long and productive life," I humbly bowed my head.

#

Thirty-eight hours later, thirty on the train, two hours waiting and six on a bus I finally got to Vidya's place, unannounced.

"Anybody home?" I hollered.

Amrit came running, "Ammi! Ammi! I love you," and hugged me.

I picked him in my arms and saw how much he has grown since the last time. *I must find an apartment and take him back with me.*

"Uncle is not home, and Ambika Aunty is fixing lunch. Grandma is doing her puja," Amrit updated me on everybody's status.

I sat down on a cot, hugged and kissed Amrit and gave him his treat. He went running into the kitchen to announce my arrival. Grandma and Ambika came into greet me and Amrit sat in my lap, beaming. We were chatting when the sound of a motorbike announced Vidya's arrival.

#

"How and when did you get here?" asked Vidya.

"I just got here. Any news about Anand?"

"Why are you concerned about that scoundrel? Are you here because of him? You must be out of your mind to think I would let him near you again. He caused you enough pain," Vidya was furious.

"Shabnam told me of Anand's accident, kidnapping and head injury. I must see and take care of him whether you approve or not. I must apologize to Anand for abandoning him. This is my only chance to do that, I don't know if I will get another chance."

"You have a very twisted understanding of abandonment. I see it as exactly the opposite. He went to America, left you alone, never communicated and did whatever he wanted, and you say you abandoned him."

232

"Vidya, this is something between Anand and I, do not butt in. I am determined to do what I said, and no amount of your opposition will change that. Tell me, where is Anand?"

"He is injured and is a captive of the rebel group, Naxalites."

"How will we get him out and take care of him?"

"We, meaning you, will not do any such thing. I am going to the forest hideout of these folks to seek his release."

"What if he needs medical attention? I am a doctor in the largest slum in the country and have treated all kinds of injuries and illnesses. You need me to bring him back safe. It is decided we both are going."

"I am concerned about your safety. You should not have come here, without letting me make the arrangements, not just for your safety but of Amrit's."

"Why what is wrong? How is my safety and Amrit's affected?"

"Sayeed has been probing and searching for you all this time to get his son back and is getting closer. He was here in this village a fortnight ago, asking the villagers if they have seen you or a boy who would be five now. He implied he knows somebody here is hiding them and he is planning on coming back with his buddies."

I felt faint and my heartbeat at a furious pace and I said, "I will die before I let anybody touch Amrit. Do something, Vidya. You cannot let Amrit end up in that family. Please protect my son from that illiterate boor, who will bring him up to be a butcher."

I knelt and started praying "La illaha illa-Allah ..."

"I have a plan we will talk about it after we get Anand back. Like you said, Anand needs medical care and I promised Amma to bring him home safe," relented Vidya.

"What if Sayeed comes to snatch my son when we are not here?"

"The people in this village all know I want Amrit safe. They will be on the lookout for Sayeed and his gang and will hide Amrit in a safe place, if necessary. Sleep well tonight because we leave at four in the morning. You will be a pillion rider on my motorbike."

CHAPTER 45

Tending Anand

Vidya explained to me the rules of this meeting, "You will remain silent until I ask you to say something when we are with the kidnappers. We meet their party, a few miles from their camp. They will blindfold our eyes to protect their secret camp and take us in a circuitous route to disorient us. They don't know I know it's location. Do not appear anxious or afraid, just follow my lead."

"Don't worry about me I live in the slums of Bombay for the last five years and dealt my share of scary characters."

"Ok, let us go" said Vidya, bidding farewell to Ambika and the two kids.

About two miles from our destination, four rough looking men searched us for weapons, blindfolded, and led us through the forest on foot. After an hour's walk, they removed the blindfolds. We were in a clearing with about thirty thatched huts with mud walls, and a stream on one side of the clearing.

"The chief is waiting in that hut over there," said one, pointing to a larger hut.

We went in and found a tall, heavyset man dressed in a worn and patched military uniform, holding a gun and a sword in a scabbard on his left hip.

"My name is Murali, and I am the commander of this camp. Who are you and why did you want to see me?" he demanded in a deep voice.

"My name is Vidya, and this is my sister Zahina. We come to seek Anand's release."

"An odd pairing, a Hindu and a Muslim, how come you are brother and sister?"

"I am not here to discuss my family. I want Anand released."

"You mean the guy who fell out of a jeep? He is in no shape to be set free, never regained consciousness."

Noticing me take a sharp breath, Vidya placed his hand on my shoulder and said, "I heard of his injury. I came with my sister, a doctor. With your kind permission, may we would tend to his injuries?"

"A doctor? How fortunate! Since you are a doctor, you must have taken an oath to treat the sick and injured without considering their religion, skin color or beliefs. Will you extend this courtesy to the sick in my camp?" Murali asked me.

Vidya nodded and I responded "Commander Murali, would you like me to tend to your sick before or after I take care of Anand?"

Murali burst out laughing, "You are smart answering my question with a question. You may tend to your man first. He lost a lot of blood and is unconscious. Just because we don't agree with the current government doesn't mean we are terrorists and living in the jungle doesn't make us savages. After you finish with your man, I will have the sick come in for a checkup. Your fellow is in the third hut on the right. We'll talk later."

#

The sight of Anand unresponsive on a bamboo cot, his hair matted with clotted blood, clothes torn, pale with sunken eyes was shocking. *His outcome depends on my skills and care. No time to get emotional.* I checked Anand's pulse and blood pressure and was satisfied, that he is not in shock; checked his face and could detect no fractured bones or broken teeth; checked his abdomen and found it to be soft and pliant; no sign of internal injury; checked his limbs and chest and found no evidence of any fractures. *He is lucky to be alive with no fractures.*

I asked Vidya to fetch some hot water and snipped off Anand's matted hair to examine the six-inch ragged scalp laceration on the right side, deep, but not all the way to the bone. I gently ran hands all over his scalp and could not detect any abnormal depressions indicating fractures. *He either has a concussion or brain injury. If it is the latter, he needs immediate neurosurgical intervention.* I cleaned the wound with sterile saline and Anand moaned and moved his arms to stop me. I sighed in relief, realizing that he is responding to pain and can move his arms.

"Anand, can you hear me, it is Zahina, your friend, can you hear me my love?" My tears flowed again, when Anand's left eye slowly opened a little, the right eye still shut with clotted blood around it, and broken words "Za..Za..Za" escaped from his lips. The eye closed and he reverted from the semiconscious to an unconscious state.

Vidya arrived with hot water and watched as I carefully cleaned and derided the wound, sutured it, applied a sterile pad with antibiotic cream and finally a bandage. I cleansed all the blood and dirt from Anand's face. After finishing, I sobbed and hugged Vidya, unable to suppress the turmoil in my heart.

Vidya consoled and led me outside and after I recovered my composure, took me to the hut housing the temporary clinic. A dozen patients of all ages and both sexes were waiting for me. Vidya informed me he would stay with Anand and watch over him, assuring he would come and get me if there was any change in Anand's condition.

#

Murali invited us for the evening meal, "Today's menu is roasted yams and plantains, both abundant in the forest around the watering spots, we live off the land."

"Thank you for sharing this with us. We came unprepared to spend the night here," said Vidya.

"This guy must be something very special to bring a doctor like you to tend his wounds," said Murali.

"Yes, he is," I replied.

"No, he isn't," said Vidya and I gave him an angry look.

"Thank you, doctor, for taking care of my sick. I will send for the medicines you prescribed tomorrow. Is it possible for you to visit my camp to check on the sick periodically?"

"I do not live here, but visit Vidya regularly, and I can come and hold a clinic."

"Thank you for agreeing. Accept me as another brother."

"Yes. Tell me why you targeted Anand."

"Let me tell you my story before I answer your question. Like you both, I went to college and have a BA degree in economics and a second one in philosophy. I was happily working as a lecturer in a college, married to my sweetheart. One day I was riding my motorbike on the same road you came on, hit a big rut and crashed about five miles from here. The villagers rescued me, took me to their village and nursed me for two weeks until I recovered. Those two weeks they shared their meager rations with me, sometimes starving when there was not enough.

I saw their plight, working from daybreak to late evening in the fields and orchards of landowners, coming home with a rupee or less. Our society, I realized was structured to keep the poor and the rich segregated in their places and exploited the poor. I met with others who believed in me, and we created a political movement for the fair distribution of wealth. The government declared us a rebels hunted, jailed, tortured and killed us. We transformed slowly from the peaceful movement, to an armed one, to protect ourselves. That's how our movement ended up in the jungles. We fight for the poor and oppressed.

"Now your sweetheart, was in the wrong place at the wrong time. We were trying to ambush a police operation against our camp that night when your friend's jeep came in. My folks mistook it for a police jeep and triggered the explosive. I am sorry that we injured and captured the wrong person."

"Brother if so, are you willing to release Anand?" I asked.

"It is not that easy. I need to show my people what I got in return. We capture, and once ransom is paid, release. That is economics side of the equation, we use the funds to build our huts and improve our living conditions. I must show some tangible return to release Anand. I am sorry, but that is the reality of our existence."

Vidya turned and said, "Zahina, why don't you stay with Anand. I have a few things I need to discuss with commander Murali."

#

Vidya looked at Murali and said, "I have a plan and after I explain it to you let me know if it suits you."

Both men talked through the night agreeing on some points, disagreeing on others, sometimes calm and other times with voices rising. By midnight they agreed on some and disagreed on some and decided to continue next day.

#

"I am going to see Amma and inform her. I think you should come with me." said Vidya.

"Anand has not regained consciousness, I cannot leave him without medical supervision."

"Your safety is my responsibility, more than Anand's. I hate to leave you in this isolated place in the forest."

"I trust Murali, he is an honorable man. I am safe, do not worry about me. Please bring Amrit with you. I will spend time with him while you deal with Anand's release"

"I will send a few people to help you take care of Anand as soon as I get to the village. I will send Amrit with them. They will be here by late afternoon with food supplies for the camp. We shouldn't be dipping into their meager supplies. Remember if he regains consciousness, Anand should not see you or hear your voice."

"Send these two antibiotics for Anand'."

I checked on Anand after Vidya left. He was still comatose, not as deep as before; he was groaning, mumbling undecipherable words, and responding to painful stimuli. Following Vidya's advice, I wrapped a chunni around my face and head with only eyes showing.

#

Vidya returned a day later and met with Murali for a few hours. He outlined the deal agreed upon between the men and what my role would be "This deal will give everyone what they want. Amma wants her son back, Murali wants resources for his people, his people get something for capturing Anand, you want Amrit safe from Sayeed and Anand wants to go back to America, everybody should be happy."

"What about me, I can't let Anand go without apologizing to him and I cannot let go of Amrit never to see him again?"

"My chief concern is safety of Amrit. Sayeed has located Amrit to my village and is working on legal means to get custody of Amrit. I cannot fight the legal system. That is the reason for Anand to take him to USA. He will be forever free of Sayeed. Amrit will make him come looking for you. Zahina my dream and desire was to see you and Anand get together again. I do not know what made you both go different ways. You have showed your commitment to Anand and came for him. Similarly, Anand must prove his love towards you, come searching, face the hardships involved and then you both will have a union that will last. If you meet him now as you say to apologize to him, the relationship you seek will likely fail. I do not want Anand to break your heart again. I can never excuse or forgive him, whom I loved like a brother, for what he did to you. Believe me right now you are better off, Anand not seeing or knowing that you took of care of him."

"Alright, but I will not give up Amrit. Once I find a suitable job I will go to USA and get my son back and disappear again. Until then Anand can keep him safe from Sayeed's reach." I said with a heavy heart.

I returned to Dharavi with a heavy heart. Punam as usual consoled me. I told her all that happened and my sorrow of agreeing to Amrit's adoption. I also told her my ex is on my trail and likely to end up here to exact revenge. Punam said, "I will ask Dada to be extra vigilant on the lookout for persons searching for you Zahina. He will protect you."

PART FOUR - CONVERGENCE

CHAPTER 46

Redemption?

resent-USA

"Yes. My Ammi's name is Zahina."

Anand heard the words from Amrit, and it took him a few long moments to comprehend. His first thoughts were of disbelief. *How can it be? How can Zahina's son be an orphan and be living in a tiny village? Is this some trick Tiger Wallah is pulling? But for what means? If the child's words were true, where is Zahina? What happened to her husband? When and how did she become a doctor? Was she the one he saw on Tiger Wallah's motor bike?*

The answers can wait, first order of business was to get Amrit to sleep. Anand hugged him as they sat on the bed. Finally, Amrit stopped crying.

"Amrit I will find your mom and will bring her here. If she doesn't want to, I will take you to her, promise,"

"Will you break your promise?"

"Whatever happens I will not break this promise."

"Tell me a story before I sleep, the story of the cow, the calf and the tiger."

Anand repeated the story and halfway through, Amrit fell asleep. He did not stop but completed the story talking in a soft voice realizing he needed to reaffirm for himself the moral of the story, 'Truth shall set you free.' He carried the sleeping boy to his bedroom and tucked him in, returned to his own room and lay down. He wasn't sure what this meant, and how it would unfold. Highly strung, he tossed around in the bed for about thirty minutes, gave up on sleep and started on finding Zahina. It can't be too difficult, Durga, his sister can tell him in a minute where Zahina is, if she will relent and talk.

Anand made himself coffee, picked up the phone and called Durga. *It is about three in the afternoon in India. She should be home.* The phone rang for a while and got disconnected and realized that he does not have her office number. He called Amma.

"Amma, how are you?"

"Why are you calling in the middle of the night? Is everything ok?"

"Yes, Amma, we are fine. I couldn't sleep. Do you have Durga's office number?"

"Let me get it for you. Why do you need to talk to Durga?"

"To find out whereabouts of Zahina?"

"Why? Is Amrit asking for his mom?"

"You knew. Why keep it from me?"

"I did not know for sure, but suspected he is her son."

"Do you know where she is? Amma, please tell me."

"Sorry Anand, I don't know where she is. She came here seeking help about five years ago, trying to recover her newborn son from her ex-husband. She asked for transportation to Vidya's village. She stayed with me for a few nights and left to get her son back and disappeared. I don't know where she went from there."

"Why go to Vidya?"

"She told me that Vidya promised you he would take care of her if the need arose."

"How can I get in touch with Vidya, immediately?"

"Vidya is somewhere in the forests of Madhya Pradesh and is out of reach."

"I will find out from Durga."

When Durga picked up the phone Anand said, "Durga this is Anand."

"Why are you calling me?"

"Let bygones be Durga, I need help?"

"With what?"

"I am trying to locate Zahina."

"After a decade you have the nerve to call me about Zahina's whereabouts. What makes you think I know where she is? Even if I knew why would I tell you? You have caused her enough trouble to last a dozen lifetimes."

"If you don't know, maybe her sister can tell you."

"Shabnam is somewhere in the middle east with her family, teaching. I haven't talked to her lately."

"Please help me Durga, please," he begged.

"Can't and won't."

Having exhausted his only contacts in India, Anand was no closer to finding Zahina. He raked his brain for the next half hour until a thought came to his mind. If he can locate her parents, then they would tell where she is. He could not think of her father's name. He concluded that he never asked Zahina, his love, her father's name or where he worked. His lack of interest in the people around him, has finally caught up with him. Must find Zahina's address when they were in college. But where would he get their address? He never went to her home when in college. Never even had the interest to walk with her to see where she lived. He was getting angry at himself when suddenly a thought came to him. Those letters that Zahina wrote him when he first came to USA. Those unopened letters, he put them away somewhere had the answer to finding Zahina.

He went through boxes of papers accumulated over the last decade in vain, every scrap of paper he came across was in those boxes, but not the ones he was seeking. It was almost daybreak *I must get ready for work and take Amrit to school soon. I might as well try the last two boxes before I give up.* He opened one and finally came across the three unopened envelopes, two letters and one Zahina's wedding invitation. The first two letters had two had a return address for her room in the nursing quarters. The third had a 'Z' instead of the return address. He opened the first and read it over years after she sent it, in which Zahina apologized to him for crying on the last day he came to see her. I should have been as strong as you were, but I could not control my emotions. I am sorry for ruining our last day together, she wrote. The second was a rambling letter dated a week later in which she poured out her anguish at their separation. It was clear from that Zahina, very upset, was not coping with their separation.

He opened the wedding invitation last, read it without comprehending any of the words. He turned the card over and read the brief handwritten message and his world collapsed around him and he fell on the bed, realizing the enormity of his mistake, how for ten years he was living a life untouched by the calamity he forced on Zahina, whom he promised to love and go back for. I cannot live with this knowledge. I don't know how I can survive and what for.

"Dad why are you crying?" the voice of Amrit broke him out of the spell of despair. "Did you also have a scary dream?"

"Yes, my son, my precious Amrit, I am awake now" said Anand hugging his son and regaining his composure.

The card with the handwritten message lay on the floor,

Anand, please come and take me away.

Rescue me and save me from this marriage.

The word marriage smeared by Zahina's tears.

CHAPTER 47

Clueless

T he only living link to Zahina was Amrit, a five-year-old, who knows that his mom lives in a big city and is a doctor.

Anand talked to Amrit to get more information that will help his search. The conversation did not offer any clues. Amrit's description fit many cities in India. No idea where to start the search. That night over a simple dinner of pan-fried salmon and steamed vegetables, Anand resumed the conversation with Amrit.

"When your mom comes to visit you, did she bring you any gifts?"

"Yes, she brings me coloring books and story books."

"Anything else?"

"She brings me new clothes always and chocolates sometimes. I am only allowed to eat only one, after the evening meal. Chocolates are bad for my teeth, my Ammi told me."

"Does she bring any special food from there?"

"No, she doesn't bring any food, but she made this special food one day for all of us in uncle's house."

"What is it? Does it have a name?"

"I don't know the name. But it has lots of cooked vegetables put on a bun. It was very good. I liked it and ate two."

That answer was the first clue, Anand realized, though he could not put a name on it or associate it with a place. There was something in the back of his mind from a long time ago that he was trying to recollect. I know this dish; I have eaten it.

Where? Anand was racking his brain.

"We went to see the gate?"

"Uh! What?"

"The big gate, Mom took me there in the city."

Why did Zahina take him to see a gate? Is it at a fort or a palace? Maybe some remnant of a historic place. The word gate did not help.

"A man with a camera took our photo in front of the gate. Mom paid him money to give her two pictures. I have one."

"Where is it?"

"It is in my suitcase."

"Amrit, I emptied your suitcase when we came here. I did not find any photo in it."

"I hid it in a secret place in the suitcase and my ammi told me not to show it to anybody. She said it will get us in trouble."

"Will you show it to me Amrit?"

"Mom said not to show it to anybody. Promise there will be no trouble."

"Yes, I promise."

Anand brought the old worn suitcase down from the attic, glad that he did not throw it away. Amrit ran his hands along the edge of the cloth lining the interior, found a spot and pulled on the fabric and it peeled away revealing an envelope. He carefully pulled the envelope and gave it to Anand.

With trembling hands, he pulled the photo out of the envelope and looked at the photo of Zahina, for the first time in a decade, standing with her son in front of the monument "Gateway of India" in Bombay. The woman in the picture was skeletal thin. Gone was the carefree, smiling and exuberant Zahina. There was a forced smile on her face, but the usual sparkle in her eyes, no longer visible. There was an intensity in her look that was her trademark whenever her temper flared. She looked as if she was bearing the burdens of the entire nation. A weary Zahina stood there with her arms around Amrit, who was standing in front. She looked much older in that picture than what Anand expected her to be.

Anand knew where the search would begin and how he would find Zahina. *There will be no peace of mind or rest for me until I find Zahina.*

#

Anand did not know what to do with Amrit, before traveling to Bombay. The boy was just settling down and going to school. Who will care for him? The only people he could ask were Sun and his wife Diana. What does he tell Amrit, who just bonded and has called him, dad for the first time? He must check with Sun and Diana first. He picked up the phone and dialed. Diana answered.

"Hi! Diana, I am in a bind. I must return to India. I was wondering …."

"We would love to keep Amrit, my twins would love it and he will be happy and safe here."

"Don't you have to ask Sun?"

"I know he would love to have Amrit here."

"Any way, you be careful. We will take care of Amrit for you. I recommend that you get an attorney to write your last will and testament, naming Amrit as the sole kin, just in case. Please come back in one piece."

"Thank you for your concern. Please. take care of Amrit as your own, I will name you both as legal guardians in my will."

Having solved the problem of where to leave Amrit, next on the list was let the child know of his decision. That evening after dinner and reading him a book at bedtime Anand asked him, "Would you like to stay with your sisters for a few days while I look for your mom?"

"I like that, they play with me a lot, and give me new toys. Will you come back soon?"

"I don't know how long it will take to find your mom. As soon as I find her, I will bring her here."

"Will she come in the same plane we came in?"

"It may not be the same one, but it will be a big plane."

Anand tucked Amrit in, bade goodnight, went to his bedroom and lay down wondering what the future holds for him and Zahina. *Will she take her son and return to India, creating a void in his life that Amrit filled? If she stayed, will she stay in this house with him, or unforgiving, move out of here. What about her husband, will he be an obstacle in her plans, or will he accommodate her wishes?*

CHAPTER 48

Needle in a Haystack

A nand took an extended leave of absence from his job and got Amrit situated with Diana. He got multiple copies and enlargements made of the picture of Amrit and Zahina. A few days later he arrived in Bombay, got a room in the Taj Intercontinental and slept for six hours, and woke up middle of the night. He stepped onto the balcony and saw the lighted Gateway of India. He wondered if Zahina was somewhere close by. Where are you, Zahina? I am coming to find you, please be on the lookout for me. He pulled out the phone book and looked up the names of medical colleges. This is where I am likely to find whereabouts of Zahina, in the rosters of the medical colleges and her acquaintances. Should be able to accomplish this in a week.

#

Anand first visit was to a nearby medical college was a bust. He went to the office and asked a clerk about locating a medical student who probably attended their college. The clerk refused.

After back and forth for thirty minutes, the clerk looked at him suspiciously and asked, "Sir, is this person a man or a woman?"

"A woman. You help me I will give you five hundred rupees."

"Sir, why didn't you say it in the beginning? What is the lady's name?"

"Zahina."

"Sir, I have been here twenty years. I promise you I have

250

not heard the name. I have an excellent memory for names, especially unusual ones."

"Maybe she registered under her family name."

"What is her family name, sir?"

Anand suddenly realized that he had hit an unsurmountable obstacle. When they were together, he never asked Zahina what her family name was. He knew her as D. Zahina, did not know what the D stood for. "It is D."

"Dee, sir?"

"No, just a D."

"Sir you are making no sense again. You say Dee, Justad and Nodee. I don't think anybody will match those names."

"Listen, I will give you another two hundred rupees, please help. The first letter of the family name starts with the English letter D."

"Sir you have a very convoluted way of expressing yourself. Anyway, thank you for the additional two hundred. To be clear, you want me to find a lady student whose family name starts with D and an initial Z representing the first name."

"Yes, you got it right."

"Sir, do you know how many years I have to go back?"

"Ten to twelve years, would do just fine."

"I only have access for two years here. The rest are in storage only accessible by my supervisor's authorization. Talk to him about this. And please sir, say the important thing first, if you get my drift. He won't be satisfied with a mere seven hundred. If everything works well, I will have your answer in fifteen days. Go through the door on the left that is my supervisor's office."

The supervisor authorized the search of the records after receiving one thousand rupees. Anand's head reeled from this morning's interactions and shattered his optimism of locating Zahina. He had no energy left to tackle another medical college that day. He returned to the hotel, ate a quick lunch and crashed in his room.

#

When he woke up refreshed, it was dark and about 10 PM. He immediately placed a call to Diana to inquire about Amrit's wellbeing and update them on his progress so far. Diana cautioned Anand to watch his step and avoid trouble, in pursuit of an old love. Amrit wanted to know if Anand found his mom.

Anand took a shower after the call, ordered room service. It was midnight in Bombay, but because of the time difference it was daytime in his hometown. He was fully awake and rearing to go. He wasn't sure where to go, when he remembered Amrit telling him his mom worked with poor people. Maybe I should find a taxi and drive around the city to view poor areas, he thought as he dressed and went down to find a taxi. He got in one. Asked the driver in Hindi, to drive him around town and show him the poor areas and slums.

"Sir my name is Chakravarty. People call me Chak" said the driver.

"I am Anand."

The conversation started in Hindi, but soon changed to English when Chak stated to answer in English.

"Chak, your English is very good."

"Anand Ji, I have a master's in economics. The only job I could get is driving a taxi," replied Chak.

#

For a few hours they drove around the city with Chak pointing the various poor sections. There were no clinics in the areas they visited. *How do these people living here get healthcare?* The midnight travel provided no clues to locating Zahina.

"We just covered a small fraction of the city, Anand Ji. There are hundreds more of these poor areas in this city," said Chak quenching any hope Anand had about quick results to his search.

Next morning Anand rented a car after Chak agreed to drive him around. Chak dropped him off at a medical college and waited until Anand returned. They went around various slums asking about Zahina. This routine of going to medical colleges, parting with money to have them look for Zahina's admission records continued for the next few days. He did not know whether to search Ayurvedic and Homeopathic colleges also.

He spent about twenty thousand rupees bribing clerks and their supervisors in medical colleges. No one found any sign of Zahina ever being admitted to their college. Chak and Anand continued their surveys of poor areas and found no clinic or doctor's offices. They got out at these places and showed the photo of Zahina and Amrit around. Nobody recognized her. Every place they visited, they stuck posters with Zahina's photo and an announcement of reward for five thousand rupees for information of her location. By the end of the week Anand lost whatever little hope he had of this approach succeeding.

Chak suggested that the only large slum left to investigate was Dharavi about an hour and a half drive from their location. The next morning, they reached Dharavi. They parked the car, took a handful of posters and entered the slum.

"In the eighteenth century this was an island and later a fishing village. As pollution in the adjacent Mithi River destroyed the fishing sites, the fishermen and others moved away. This slum was built over many decades," said Chak.

"It smells awful, and the fumes are noxious," complained Anand.

"Anand Ji, you haven't entered the belly of the beast yet. This is nothing."

They showed the picture to anyone who would talk to them, explaining that she is a doctor, and they were trying to locate her. No one responded in the affirmative. They stuck posters on utility poles and bare walls, progressed deeper into the slum until they ran into a hefty, well-built person, better dressed than most in the slum. When he saw the picture, Anand noticed a momentary flash of recognition on the face of the man which quickly disappeared.

"You seem to recognize her," said Anand.

The man thought for a minute and said, "I saw her

somewhere a few months ago, I am not sure where?"

"Please, this is very important I have been searching for her a long time. Anything you remember, any little will be very helpful in my quest."

"I saw her at another slum, probably Baiganwadi."

"Chak, do you know this place? Have we already visited it?"

"We went there the first night. We never went again or talked to anybody."

"Let us go now. We have the best lead so far," said Anand, ecstatic that there was light at the end of the tunnel. Little did he know that if he had ventured another hundred feet into the slum, he would have come across the place Zahina worked, with the sign 'Municipal Health Clinic'.

Dada Tommy's man, assigned to watch over Zahina, suspecting that her husband had come searching for her, misguided them to another slum. The man went to his boss to report. Chak and Anand walked back to their car, moved away from Dharavi, home to Zahina for the last many years.

#

Anand and Chak spent the next one week scouring through Baiganwadi, knee deep in refuse. Asked everyone who would listen to them and hung posters, to no avail. Anand, devastated and heartbroken, wondered if he would break the promise made to Amrit. That night he called Diana and poured his anguish out and his absence of progress. Diana knew he was over his head in this search suggested, "I recommend that you hire a private investigator, if any such exist in the city."

"That's a brilliant idea, thanks for your support, Diana. Next morning, I will make inquiries and locate an investigator."

"How are the medical school enquiries progressing?"

"I had to grease palms to get them to agree to look for Zahina. As of now, there is no success. It is like she disappeared into thin air."

"It is the second largest city in India with over millions of people. Your search is truly for a needle in a haystack. You need professional help to have any chance of success. Just take care of yourself, attempt nothing dangerous. Our thoughts and prayers are with you," advised Diana.

CHAPTER 49

Unintended Consequences

Siva an ex-DSP of police opened his private investigator office in his modest house in the eastern suburbs of Mumbai, two weeks ago. He refused a few who came to him to spy on their spouses or to find missing pets. Befitting his investigative background, he was determined to take only challenging cases. He was in his office, studying 'A Treatise on Criminal Investigation' written by his mentor. After two decades in the criminal justice field, he found that there is much more to learn, and even with his experience and knowledge. A loud knock interrupted his study and a man entered. Siva concluded the man with a two-day stubble on his face and blood shot eyes was a visitor from abroad.

"Mr. Siva, my name is Anand. I am seeking help in locating a person. I saw your ad in Times of India. I would like to hire you."

"Mr. Anand, you are from America, aren't you? Please sit down and tell me about what you are seeking help about. I am picky about the cases I take."

Anand sat down in a chair facing Siva and saw the piercing eyes of the well-built man in late thirties, dressed in clean freshly pressed clothes.

"Mr. Anand who is this person you are trying to locate and why?"

"Mr. Siva, it would be better if I gave you a narrative account and then you can ask me relevant questions. I want to add that expense is of no concern. May I start?"

Siva nodded and Anand spent the next fifteen minutes explaining who he was searching for and why. He told Siva all that he has attempted so far in this search, while Siva took notes.

"This is a challenging case. All that I can work with are your de-old recollections and the words of a five-year-old. You want me to find this lady Zahina, who you believe is in Bombay and is working as a doctor. No medical colleges according to you have any record of her being a student. Please give me her full name, some physical attributes like age, height and weight, etc."

"Her last name starts with D. I do not know what it stands for, my generation did not bother with surnames, they were a remainder of caste and societal standing, which we did not believe in and wanted abolished." said Anand upset how lame that sounded. "She is five feet four inches about 105 pounds, long black hair, fair complexion and light colored eyes. I have a picture of her from last year," he said, handing a copy of the photo of Zahina and Amrit.

"I agree with you, and also believe in abolishing the caste system. You believe she is hiding from her husband? If that is the case, she may have changed her name. People who change their names usually use their middle and last names and drop their first. Give the address of the college where you both met. My fees for finding her will be between five and ten thousand plus other incidental expenses that I incur. Is that agreeable to you?"

"Yes, thanks for taking my case."

"Please answer the following questions. Where and when did you meet Zahina? Tell me in as much detail as you remember."

Anand told Siva all that he could recollect.

"What about close relatives and friends?"

Anand told him about Shabnam.

"What do you know of Zahina after you left?"

"I know she got married a few months after I left, I do not

know where her husband lives?"

"Do you know her husband's name?"

"Yes, it is on the wedding invitation Zahina mailed me."

"Do you still have it? I would like to look at that."

"I have a copy I will bring it to you soon."

"Let us go in your car right now. We can talk on the way. You can give me the copy and the address of your friend. Also make me a list of all the colleges you contacted here during this investigation. I will proceed with my investigation. Come and see me in two days for an update."

#

Siva took a train back to his office and looked at the decade old wedding invitation. When he read it, he knew the first and last names of the Zahina's parents and where they lived because the marriage was at the residence of the bride. He knew their last name was Durrani and their address. He quickly scrolled through the address book with all his professional contacts in the police force. He came across a police inspector who was working in the town where Zahina lived during her college days. He picked up the phone and dialed.

"Police inspector Rahim, speaking," said the person at the other end said.

"Hello Rahim, this is Siva, if you remember we met at a police convention in Bombay a few years ago."

"Superintendent Siva! How can I forget you gave a brilliant talk on tackling home grown terrorism? It is an honor to be speaking to you."

"Rahim, I am no longer in the police force, I quit a few months ago."

"I am sorry to hear that Siva Ji, it is a loss to the police. I am sure you did not call me about your resignation. What can I do for you?"

"I have a client who is looking for a lady he went to college with. Her name is Zahina Aisha Durrani. They both attended the Christian College in your town from 1962 to 1965. I have her parents' names and address and husband's name. I will be indebted to you if you can send one of your policemen to the college and her parents' home address. I need her current address or a way to contact her. Any information regarding her husband Sayeed will help."

Rahim was silent for a few moments and said, "The name sounds familiar, I had a run in with this guy a few years ago. Please bear with me Siva Ji, give me a few moments to recollect my thoughts." A few minutes later he continued, "I remember now, about six years ago my neighbor, a nice elderly lady called me in the evening and asked my help in getting rid of a man who came to her house demanding to see his wife and his newborn. When she told him to leave, he threatened her with violence. Fortunately, her German Shepherd subdued him. I threatened him with prosecution if he ever came back to this locality and sent him away. Give me two days and I will get the information you requested."

"Thank you, Rahim, this will save me a lot of time and expense for my client. If there is anything, I can do for you please call."

#

Ahmed walked into Sayeed's butcher shop. His boss, the police inspector, asked him to approach the owner of the shop to find out the whereabouts of the owner's wife, Zahina.

"As-salāmu ʿalaykum, Sayeed bhai."

"Aʿalaykumu as-salām, Ahmed bhai," replied Sayeed

"Sayeed, how is business? How are you doing?"

"Doing well, business is excellent. Inshah Allah," replied Sayeed, "And you?"

"By the grace of Allah! I am well."

"What brings you to my humble shop? Would you like to buy some fresh lamb meat, my brother?"

"Where is your wife? What is she doing nowadays?"

"How dare you ask about my wife? Where she is and what she is doing is my business. You are a god-fearing Muslim, are you not? You have trespassed our social norms, Ahmed. If I

259

tell others about this, they will shun or excommunicate you." Sayeed fumed.

"Cool down brother, I am here on police business, be respectful of my position. I am not asking about your current wife, but the one who ran away with your son, Zahina. Do you have her address in Mumbai?"

Hearing the name Zahina, Sayeed's face turned deep red with anger. He grabbed a butcher's knife and shouted, "Address in Mumbai? How do you know she is in Mumbai? If I knew her address, she would be dead by now and my son would be back with me."

"We know she is in Mumbai but where exactly we don't, that is why I am asking you."

"Why do you want to know where that infidel is? What do you care?"

"I don't care where she is, but my inspector does?"

"Why does he want to know where she is?"

"Sayeed, you ask questions to which I have no answers. Why would the inspector tell me why he wants this information? All that I know is that he got a call from a big Sahib in Mumbai and next he calls us in and sends us all over town to find her address."

"Did you say Mumbai?"

"Yes, is there a problem?"

"No brother no problem, you have given me the information I was seeking for the last five years. Here take, this nice leg of lamb as my gift to you," said Sayeed delighted that he knows in which city his sinning ex-wife is. *Allah, the merciful, has shown me the way to avenge this infidel woman for defying his teachings.*

He closed his shop and went home to let his mom and unmarried sister about the recent development. He would not tell his current wife and the mother of his twin daughters, because like Zahina, her duty is to bear his children and serve the rest of the family.

Ahmed appeared again next day in the store to give additional information to Sayeed about his ex-wife, "The inspector told us she is a doctor with a clinic in a slum."

Sayeed gave him a goat's head in appreciation of the information, "Roast this on hot coals my friend, it will be a delicious accompaniment to your evening meal."

#

"I located the infidel who kidnapped my son, stole my dowry and dishonored our family. I know she is in Bombay. I will go to there while Ammi manages the store and you Simi manage the household and keep my wife in line. I will erase the dishonor that scoundrel has brought on our family," said Sayeed.

"Sayeed, you have a hard head and are volatile. You want revenge by slicing her throat. Though I would love to see her die, it would be foolhardy. It will get you in jail or death by hanging. You need me by your side to help you in the search and in retrieving your son."

"All right, I will plan tomorrow with my employees and we both will leave the following day to Mumbai."

"I have a better idea. Let me go to Mumbai and stay with my friend Shakira. You tend to your business while I find the infidel woman. It is easier for me to go to places where women congregate. Once I find her, I will call you. Come and recover your son. If you want to beat her up, go-ahead and do it. No killing her because that will send you to your death. You know that I hate her as much as you do."

"Like I said before, sometimes you have wonderful ideas in that dumb head," said Sayeed.

CHAPTER 50

Slum Dwelling

Anand spent the next two days making rounds to all the slums and poor areas he visited before, asking the same questions and getting nowhere. The same was in Dharavi. All the people he asked had said they did not know anyone in the picture. As he was walking out something seemed odd, and he could not figure out what. Something was nagging in the back of his mind, his subconscious. When they got in the car and Chak was driving back to the hotel Anand said, "Chak we have to go back to Dharavi, there is something I need to check."

Entering the slum, he looked around and could not find any posters of Zahina he posted not even one. It is as if somebody went behind him and pulled all the posters.

"Why would someone remove the posters?" he asked Chak.

"Probably kids, they recycle everything in this slum. I am sure some store is using the paper for wrapping their merchandise."

"Let us hang more posters," said Anand looking around when he saw a small one-story structure with three flowerpots each with blooming red roses on its flat roof, which reminded him of the day he offered a red rose to Zahina. He hoped it was a good omen of things to come.

#

Siva got a call from the inspector Rahim, "Siva Ji, I am sorry no information is available regarding your inquiry. Both Zahina's parents are dead. Her ex-husband does not know where she is. Her boyfriend's mother tells me that the only person who knows is out of reach. If there is anything else you like me to do, please let me know."

"Thank you, inspector Rahim, I am grateful for your effort, as we in the business know, it takes multiple attempts to find leads. We face failure more than success in these cases. Best wishes to you your wife and son," said Siva ending the telephone call, not knowing that his inquiry has lit the fuse on an explosive complication.

Siva met with Anand. He reported about on the meager progress in the investigation, "We know that Zahina's full name is Zahina Aaisha Durrani. Her parents are no longer alive. Her ex-husband does not know where she is. Zahina joined a local medical college under the name of Aaisha Z. Durrani and graduated with honors about a year and a half ago. Her mentor Dr. Khan, a surgeon, knows her well. He is retired and is touring USA."

"Do you know where in USA?" asked Anand elated that some progress is being made in the location of Zahina.

"He is in New York, teaching at the Roosevelt Hospital."

"Great. Tonight, I will call that Hospital and try to get in touch with Dr. Khan and see if he will tell me where Zahina is."

"Have you found out anything through your search?" asked Siva.

"No progress really, I toured the slums many times during the last few weeks. Nobody seen or heard or know Zahina. Most of the posters I put in asking for information on Zahina are still there except in Dharavi. I couldn't find any of the twenty I posted."

"Ha, Dharavi! You drop or throw anything there it will find its way to recycling, in minutes and sometimes even before it hits the ground. All your posters I am sure have become something else."

"I am concerned somebody is deliberately hiding Zahina in Dharavi. They are hiding her for some nefarious reason," said Anand.

"Dr. Anand I will visit Dharavi tomorrow and inquire. Call me if you get any information from Dr. Khan," said Siva.

#

Next morning, Siva went to Dharavi parked his motorbike, entered the slum on foot. Siva was dressed in pants and half sleeve shirt, with a 35mm camera hanging around his neck and a small notepad and a pen conspicuously visible. He roamed the streets and alleys. He took pictures, made some notes and started conversations with anyone he could.

For those who asked what he was doing he replied, "I am writing a report on Dharavi, about its people and their plight for an American magazine."

Siva never directly asked about Zahina or a clinic. He tried to probe their difficulties in obtaining services like water, sewer and electricity; crime; and how they handle sickness. He got answers, but nobody said anything about a clinic or a lady doctor who provides medical care. Most responses were vague as if rehearsed. Why would a group of people be reluctant to talk about the clinic, if one exists here? Can close to a million people be conspiring to hide the truth? Siva never had such an experience in all his investigative years. After a futile search Siva went home.

Siva returned next day and resumed his search. As Siva was wandering around two husky men approached and one said, "Come with us. Dada Tommy wants to talk with you."

Siva was about to refuse them but changed his mind, hoping this Dada Tommy may provide additional information. The two men led him through a maze of streets and pathways. They entered a rundown shed with a metal roof and gravel floor. In the windowless gloomy space, he saw a man on a chair, the single electric light behind him obscuring the man's features.

"What do you want to talk to me about?" asked Siva.

"First let us get acquainted, I am Dada Tommy. What is your name and what brings you here, sir?"

"My name is Siva. I am writing an article for an American

magazine about Dharavi, the largest slum in India," replied Siva, "And what do you do, Dada Tommy?"

"I am the guy who keeps unwanted people from bothering the hard workers of Dharavi. I am a peacekeeper for Dharavi," replied Dada Tommy standing up and turning to one side bringing his face into the light.

"Ha!" exclaimed Siva, "I knew you from a long time ago, if my memory serves me right, I believe your name was Tomar then."

"How do you know me from then? Why are you here?" said a surprised Dada Tommy.

"How do I know you? I know you because you were a petty thief who got caught stealing a six-year-old's bike and received a good thrashing? Do you remember the police inspector that saved you from that punishment and set you free? It is I who saved your skin that day."

"I thank you if you say you were the one who intervened that day. Inspector, you were in control that day, not here, not now. I control this place with my people."

"I am no longer an inspector or with the police force. I am a freelance writer roaming in Dharavi. I assume there is no law against that," said Siva.

"Only if what you say is true. I have learned that before befriending or antagonizing anyone, I should know what I am dealing with. You are a private investigator and are here on false pretenses. Please come and sit-down inspector, let us have a frank discussion about what brings you here. I may help if it fits with my objectives. If not, I can make it uncomfortable for you. Can you tell me who you are looking for? Maybe I can help you. If that person is in Dharavi, I am likely to know or someone who knows." Dada Tommy suspected the client was Kudi doctor's ex-husband looking for her. Dada wanted to sidetrack the inspector. He also knew that he cannot threaten or scare Siva to drop his investigation.

"I am not at liberty to disclose my client's name without his permission, but the person I am looking for is a lady doctor who we know works in a slum," said Siva, confirming Dada's suspicions.

"What lady doctor would come and work in this hellhole, inspector? If there is a doctor here, I would know about it. But as a favor, I will ask my men to scout the poor areas and slums and if they come across a lady doctor, I will convey the information to you. I already have your address and telephone number," said Dada Tommy escorting Siva out.

Siva was not sure what to make out of this meeting. He knew Dada manipulated him. He could not figure out why an ex-criminal would go through such a masquerade to hide Zahina. He decided to come back here to search without alerting Dada Tommy.

CHAPTER 51

Sayeed Advances

While Siva was doing his investigation, Simi was searching for Zahina in Bombay. For the last few days, she was canvassing the slums, with a photo of Zahina. Simi's search like Anand's and Siva's was frustrating and fruitless. She visited various Mosques in the rundown areas of the city, looking for Zahina.

#

Friday as usual, I bathed, dressed, donned my burkha and went to the mosque. I was about two hundred yards from the mosque's entrance when I felt a sudden dread. I did not know what spooked me, but as I drew closer, a person standing by the entrance in the shadows, looking around, drew my attention. With the sun shining in my eyes, I could not recognize the person, yet my heart was galloping. I got a little closer, the dress the woman had on looked familiar; like the one I owned. A little closer I recognized Simi. I was terrorized with the thought Sayeed would not be faraway. Any sudden moves were likely to draw Simi's attention, grateful for my burkha, I walked into the Mosque like any other woman. I held my head high and walked in front of Simi, giving her a brief glance and a nod of my head. Once inside my poise disappeared and I sat down behind a pillar and rested my head on my knees wondering what to do. To control my rising panic, wandering thoughts and racing heart, I took a few breaths and focused my thoughts on Amrit, Vidya and Anand. In a few minutes I had my emotions under control and focused on the sermon.

#

Many women with burkhas obscuring their faces, bothered Simi who was staring at the women entering the mosque. A Burkha clad woman walking toward the entrance drew Simi's attention. A single step faltered as the woman looked in her direction. *Is that Zahina?* The woman walked confidently toward the entrance, looked into her eyes and gave a nod in greeting. *If it was Zahina, she would have turned and retreated.* Simi dismissed the woman and continued her surveillance. After two hours, she gave up, walked towards the bus stop. Waiting for the bus she came across a poster of Zahina's face offering a reward for information. She pulled off the poster and put it in her handbag. Once on the bus she looked at the poster and saw Gateway of India in the background. *If Zahina visited there once, she might return.* She headed there.

On the fifth day of her persistent vigil at the Gateway of India, Simi discovered the clue that will lead her to Zahina and eventually bring success to Sayeed's quest. That day she treated herself to lunch at the Taj, a short distance from her location. While eating lunch, she saw a man entering the lobby. He looked familiar. *Where do I know him from?* Recognition dawned him as the one in the photo in Zahina's trunk, Anand. His presence was a sign, Zahina was close by.

Simi moved towards Anand with the picture of Zahina in her hand, thrust the picture in front of Anand and said, "Excuse me, do you know this lady? Her name is Zahina and she worked with me here in Mumbai. I am trying to locate her."

"Yes, I know her and am also searching for her? Why are you searching for her?"

"I have one of her expensive necklaces, she loaned me when I went to visit my family. When I came back, she was gone. My name is Simi."

"I am Anand, and I knew Zahina from college days."

"Great, maybe we can join forces and find her."

"Sorry, I prefer to work alone. When I find Zahina, I will ask her and if she agrees I will take you to her."

"Okay. I will give you my telephone number. Please leave a message."

"I am staying in this hotel you may also call me."

Simi was disappointed by the refusal of partnering. *I will follow Anand.* She called Sayeed with her progress and asked him to be ready to come to Mumbai at a moment's notice. Sayeed felt his prayers were answered. Elated that his multiyear quest in seeking revenge on Zahina was coming to fruition. Unlike then, he wanted to inflict pain on Zahina as payment for making him a laughingstock in his neighborhood. He handed over the shop to his mother and caught a train to Mumbai. By the end of the week, he hoped to get his son back and fulfil his revenge.

After waiting for two hours in the Mosque, I left the Mosque looking around to see if Simi was still around, hired a taxi and headed to Ravi's home.

I decided to seek Vidya's help. I called Hari Ji and found out Vidya was out in the forest. The only way to reach him was through Ravi, who has the resources to deliver messages to Vidya.

#

Anand's attempts to get in touch with Dr. Khan were unsuccessful. He called the medical center in USA, going through multiple routings, found out Dr. Khan went on a camping trip to Banff and Jasper National Parks.

He was surprised at the chance meeting with Simi, who was also looking for Zahina. Somehow her approach, mannerisms and her story, he felt were deceptive. *Why would someone else be looking for Zahina, the same time he is?*

CHAPTER 52

Premonition

Vidya was roaming Dandakaranya, the sacred Indian forest located in the middle of India. He saw twice Rudra previously, and in both instances the tiger stopped in its tracks and stared at Vidya, with no sign of aggression, let out a snarl disappeared into the forest. Vidya was working with the forest rangers to locate a suitable another mate for Rudra. The plan was to relocate it to the southeastern portion of the forest on Amma's property and introduce other tigers slowly to promote genetic diversity.

Rudra stepped out of the tall grasses about a hundred yards away, and unlike the previous times, advanced toward him with a loud snarl with its long gleaming canines exposed. Vidya stood his ground, noticed the tiger was not limping. Rudra stopped and stared into his eyes, snarling and growling. *Was Rudra was trying to communicate with me?* He stood still as the tiger jumped forward and let out a mighty roar. Vidya slowly backed out and Rudra stood there watching him.

Vidya arrived back in the village where he was staying with Kalu. As he settled in the loft with the buzzing bees, his thoughts turned to the strange encounter with Rudra and the tiger forcing him out of the forests. As he was about to fall asleep, he had a premonition of evil closing on someone he loves. Vidya intuitively felt he must get to Mumbai and that Zahina was in danger.

Next morning, he asked a villager with a motorbike to take him over to the nearby town. He went to the post office and booked a telephone call to Ravi.

#

"Welcome, Zahina, haven't seen you in ages. How are you doing? What can I do for you?" said Ravi.

"Ravi Ji Namaskar, I am in trouble. I need Vidya to come and help me."

"I will send a message to Prakash Khan right away to contact Vidya and ask him to come here. What is the message?"

Zahina told him about seeing Simi, her ex-sister-in-law and how this might turn into a catastrophe for her wellbeing, if Simi and Sayeed find her.

"Zahina, why don't you stay with us for a week or two. Simi may go home by then."

"Ravi Ji, I have to be there for my patients. I cannot abandon them."

"I will try to get hold of Vidya, he has become one with the forest, I hear. Let me ..."

The ringing telephone interrupted Ravi. He picked up the telephone, listened for a second and said, "Speak of the devil, Vidya, Zahina and I were just talking about contacting you. Good you called at the right moment."

"How is Zahina? I am concerned about her safety," said Vidya on the other end.

"Zahina saw her ex-sister-in-law today at the Mosque. She is very perturbed. There are posters of Zahina all over town, asking for her location promising a monetary reward. I asked her to stay with me, but she wouldn't. You know how committed she is to her work."

"I am coming to Mumbai and stay with her until this is fixed this once for all. Expect me there in two days, I will catch the express train to Mumbai from Nagpur. Please, Ravi Ji, watch over Zahina until I get there."

As Vidya got on the train to Bombay, Sayeed disembarked in Bombay Central Railway Station.

#

Anand finally got in touch with Dr. Khan. Hearing Anand's request, Dr. Khan said, "I hold Zahina's location a secret. I know her history, she talked about you and her husband. I will help you if you can prove your identity, no offense, but you are only a voice on the phone claiming to be Anand. I must be certain before I tell you where she is."

Anand thought for a minute and said, "Dr. Khan, have you met Amrit, Zahina's son?"

"Yes, I met him a few times since his birth and last time was about eighteen months ago. He calls me Nana Ji."

"Sir, I will give you a telephone number in USA will you talk to him? I adopted Amrit a few months ago and Dr. Chen and his wife Diana are taking care of him. They can vouch for me."

"Give me their telephone number. I will call in the morning, it is too late to call now. Call me same time tomorrow."

#

Simi was following Anand, waiting nearby the Taj, until he exited. The first day she tried following, Anand got into a waiting taxi and took off. Next day she had a taxi ready for her and followed him all over town, stopping at slums where he stopped and followed discretely at a distance. She was tired of following him with no results and concerned about the money she was spending on taxi fares. Sayeed will not be happy with how much she wasted on blindly following Anand. She desperately needed a break. One evening Anand stopped at a residence, with a sign on the front door, 'Siva Private Investigator'. *Anand hired a detective to locate Zahina.* Simi thought of following the detective next few days but gave up on the idea knowing it would be much more difficult to follow a detective. She noted the address of the residence, just in case.

#

Anand called Dr. Khan the next day. "I confirmed your identity Dr. Anand from Amrit and Dr. Chen. I tried calling Zahina to alert her of your presence in Mumbai and your efforts to get in touch with her but failed. Promise me you will not barge into her unannounced. Zahina is a strong woman.

But knowing the history between you two, Your sudden appearance may shock her. I insist that you be conscious of this in your approach. Do I have your promise?"

"Dr. Khan, I give you my word that I will not cause any trouble or distress for Zahina. I will approach her through an intermediary, Mr. Siva, a private investigator. Now please tell me where Zahina is?"

"She is in Dharavi. She is the sole healthcare provider for close to a million people, who she believes are her responsibility. How she manages there is beyond my comprehension. I was the one who sent Zahina there as a nurse, about six years ago to work a few hours a day. She made it her full-time job and lives there in the clinic. In return the people of Dharavi protect her, and see to her wellbeing bringing her food, clothing, and necessities. So be careful how you approach her. The people in the slum will do anything and everything to protect their Kudi Doctor."

"I almost forgot to tell you Dr. Khan, there is a nurse looking for Zahina, to return a valuable jewelry. I thought the woman was a phony."

"As far as I know Zahina does not have any valuable stuff with her. Whatever she had, she left with Vidya. Do you know the name of this nurse?"

"She told me her name is Simi."

Anand heard a sharp intake of breath on the other end, "This changes everything. Simi is not a nurse she is Zahina's sister-in-law. That she is in Mumbai is a disaster. Sayeed her ex-husband cannot be far behind. You must protect her. The last person she needs to encounter is her ex. Ask your detective to arrange protection for Zahina until Sayeed leaves. Get going before they find her."

"Thank you, Dr. Khan. I will lay my life for Zahina. I owe her. You have my promise."

#

Anand, perturbed and troubled by the turn of events, went looking for Siva, did not find him anywhere. He headed towards Dharavi, in the Chak's taxi but got off about 2 miles from Dharavi.

"Chak wait for me here. I need to go by foot the rest of the way."

Anand walked over to a roadside stall selling tea and snacks, ordered a cup of tea and looked in the direction he came and saw Simi emerge from a taxi that just arrived. It confirmed his suspicions, Simi was following him, he needs to be extra vigilant and lose her. Anand immediately paid for the tea and started hurrying away, knowing that Simi would follow him. He pulled out a piece of paper from his pocket as if checking an address, looked at the street signs, made a right-hand turn and continued to lead Simi on a worthless journey. He stopped, asked for directions a few times with people nearby. He left the paper with the last man he asked for directions. He stopped at another stall to buy a cup of tea and watched as Simi stopped the same person who he talked to and gave the paper with the address to.

#

Simi followed Anand on foot, convinced he was leading her to Zahina. She saw him refer to a paper from his wallet, look at the road signs, building numbers as he walked. She saw him talk to a few people, probably asking for directions. She wanted to talk to the same people, but the thought of losing him in the crowded streets dissuaded her. When he stopped to get a cup of tea, she talked to the same person.

"Bhai Saab, please help me. My brother is looking for someone we believe is trying to steal his money. I saw you talking to him. Can you tell me where he is going?"

"If you give me two rupees, I will not only tell but give you the address that fool left with me."

Thinking this is the best two rupees she ever spent, Simi gave him the money. As he handed her the paper, the guy said, "That brother of yours, is a fool. The address is for a building one mile in the other direction, but he insists on searching for it in this neighborhood. Good luck! Walk in that direction for fifteen minutes and ask around, you will find it in no time."

Simi was ecstatic that she got Zahina's address and can get there first. Anand returned to the Taj, checked out and moved to a hotel closer to Dharavi.

#

Simi went about looking for the address and found a multistory building housing about 30 families. She knocked on doors asking about a lady doctor named Zahina who worked in the slums. Nobody ever heard of her. After spending two hours canvassing, she gave up confused about what happened. She went back to the place where she saw Anand and found him gone. She fumed and cursed herself, the guy who duped her, and her brother. As she was cursing, remembered she was to pick up Sayeed from the railway station two hours ago, knew she was in for a tongue lashing, got on an auto-rickshaw to the station.

#

Sayeed got off the train and looked for Simi but could not find her. The Central Station was vast with many platforms, packed with travelers, porters lugging enormous pieces of baggage, vendors peddling snacks, drinks, toys and religious objects. He stayed on the platform like Simi asked him. Impatient, he started cursing Simi for being late, sat in a corner and dozed off, tired and hungry. Simi came in three hours later carrying pav bhaji and a glass of hot sweet tea. Seeing the offering of food Sayeed stopped cursing, consumed the food and followed Simi to the home she was staying. On the way she told him all about her previous successes and failure that day.

"In the morning we will go to the Taj and pick up the trail again," said Sayeed.

"As you wish, brother."

#

Their early morning surveillance operation watching the hotel Taj was a bust. They spent hours in the hot muggy weather; did not see Anand and had no leads. Simi called the hotel and found that Anand had checked out the previous evening. Sayeed started cursing, mad at Simi for letting the lead to Zahina give them the slip.

"I have one more lead, the detective Anand hired, I know where he is. Let us focus on him and he will lead us to Zahina," said Simi.

"Praise Allah the merciful. You have escaped a beating from me with those words. Let us go find the detective."

"It is already dusk. By the time we get there it will be dark. Let us get there early tomorrow and follow him. We need a vehicle to follow him. My friend's husband has a motorbike. He will let us use it," said Simi.

CHAPTER 53

Glimpse

Anand met Siva's the day he moved out of the Taj and gave an update. "I know where Zahina is. Dr. Khan confirmed my identity before divulging the information. He was also concerned how Zahina would react to my sudden appearance. Please locate the clinic where she is working and confirm her presence. Approach her carefully and tell her I am here and would like to meet her; and Amrit is missing his mom. If she is willing to meet, set up a meeting between us. If she refuses, act as an intermediary and plan a reunion of mother and son. Thank her on my behalf for sharing her son with me. I promise to provide all resources and funds for their wellbeing and comfort. Also apologize to her on my behalf for my neglect and indifference all these years."

"Today is Friday, we are going on a family trip and will return Sunday night. I will go and locate Zahina on Monday."

#

Saturday morning Anand dressed in a cotton kurta and pajama, went to visit Dharavi to find the clinic and get a glimpse of Zahina. He wrapped a thin cotton shawl around his head covering his face. Nobody paid any attention to him, dressed in the local garb. He roamed the slum with its dusty atmosphere. After an hour of roaming, he came across a small building with about dozen people, mostly older men and women standing in front. He walked closer to see what they were all waiting for and realized it was the clinic he was searching for all these days. He had a fit of coughing, his insides irritated by the dust and smoke. *This smoke and dust will kill me or ruin my lungs.*

An elderly lady who was watching him said, "You are lucky to be at the clinic. Kudi Doctor will take care of you. Go sit there and wait your turn."

"Shukria Mata ji, I have a few errands to run and will be back." replied Anand, his heart thumping and elated with the success of his long arduous quest.

He restrained himself from barging in. *I will hang around and when Zahina steps out, I will see her from a distance giving solace to my soul.* He waited the entire day until all the patients left. Half an hour later a woman walked out, and his heart thumped in anticipation. As she came closer, to his disappointment it was not Zahina. He waited around the clinic until nightfall, all the lights were off, and the clinic went dark. Nobody else came out and he left disappointed but determined to return next morning.

#

At 6AM he saw the slum bustling with activity. He found a tea shack with a view of the clinic, purchased a newspaper, a cup of tea and settled down on a rickety chair continuing his watch. After about four hours he was getting fidgety, not knowing if this was another futile attempt. The clinic door opened and a burkha clad woman stepped out, looked around and briskly walked away. His heart missed a beat. *This must be Zahina. Why is she wearing a burkha? Has she become a devout Muslim?* He followed her, keeping a suitable distance. Every few minutes she would suddenly stop, look around and proceed. The first time it happened, he froze in his tracks. It was a crowded and her eyes never set on him. He knew if he suddenly stopped when she turned around, she would notice him. He continued his stroll, stop here and there without getting too close. She stopped at a dhaba empty except for a turbaned Sikh cooking. As he got a little closer, he heard a melodious song emanating from the man. The woman stopped, lifted the burkha off her face. He would have given a

278

million dollars to see the face, but her back was toward him. The woman said something, and the Sikh turned around with a bright smile on his handsome face, the singing got louder; the woman sat down on a bench with her back towards Anand. The Sikh bought her a steaming cup, which she accepted and laid her hand on his forearm. *Maybe I am mistaken. This is not Zahina but the wife or girlfriend of the Sikh.*

Anand walked beyond the dhaba and turned around. The woman's face became clear. It was Zahina. She was sitting and drinking tea and the Sikh was serenading her with his vibrant voice. He saw the glowing face of Zahina and felt a pang in his heart. *Is this what I came for? Who is this man? What is his hold on Zahina?* Anand saw him handing out a packet to Zahina, who stood up and gave the Sikh a hug and pulled the burkha top over her face. Anand was about twenty feet from her when Zahina raised her eyes to his and held his eyes for a few seconds. He was glad for the shawl obscuring his face. If there was recognition, he did not see it. But there was a change in Zahina's demeanor, the relaxed appearance disappeared, and she appeared tense. She turned on her heel and rushed towards the clinic. *No need to follow her now. Let me stop in this Dhaba and get something to eat.* Anand went into the dhaba and sat on the same bench Zahina sat.

The Sikh alerted by the sound and looked at Anand, "You are just in time my brother, I have saag paneer and tandoori roti, would you care for some. Can I get you a cup of hot tea or a cold lassi to start?"

"Yes, I am starving. I walked by and heard the song you were singing, a favorite from my younger days."

"You are the second one today who said that. Kudi Doctor likes that song, I sing it for her every Sunday. My name is Charan. What is yours?"

"An... Anjan my name is Anjan. What did you mean by Kudi Doctor?"

"Oh! That is the lady doctor who treats all the sick. She came from nowhere and settled here, living here for the last five years. Everyone calls her Kudi Doctor, with love and respect."

"You are very lucky to have someone like her here."

"Do you know her?" Charan's relaxed face turned suspicious.

"I just got here. How can I know her?"

"The word is out that somebody from her past is searching for her to harm her. They will have to go through me first," Charan's face turned fierce.

"I have no intention of harming anybody, especially someone you say is a God's gift," said Anand.

"I haven't seen you before. If you have any such ideas, I will stop you," warned Charan.

CHAPTER 54

Confluence

Monday morning, I woke up unaware of the impending disaster. Dressed in my favorite churidar pajamas I entered the clinic; four patients were waiting. In about an hour I attended to their care. The waiting room was empty. No other patients walked in. Where is my Amrit? How is he? Thoughts of Amrit always dragged my spirits down. The sight of Simi the other day made me very apprehensive. The person who makes my anguish disappear was Charan. I decided to get lunch from his dhaba and spend a few moments listening to his singing. I checked my bag for my only weapon against assault, a paper bag with a fistful of finely ground cayenne pepper, in the outside compartment with no zipper, for easy retrieval. I walked towards the dhaba.

#

Anand went to Charan's dhaba and kept an eye out for Zahina. The interaction between the Sikh and Zahina led him to believe that there was more to their relationship than friendship. Though disappointed, it relieved Anand that Zahina found happiness. *I hope Siva can persuade her to meet with me at least once. If not, so be it!* He sat drinking tea in the dhaba, looking toward the clinic.

#

Vidya's train was delayed by twelve hours and arrived in Bombay on Monday. He wrapped his shawl around his face to avoid the throngs wherever he went and hired a taxi to Dharavi. He felt the danger unfolding and he was late. The traffic was heavy and progress slow. There was more noise, honking, cursing and shouting than movement. He took out the cricket ball from his shoulder bag and looked at Rudra's claw. *You forced me out of the forest and on to this journey, let me succeed Rudra, let no harm befall my sister.*

#

Dada Tommy's strong men were roaming through the slum. Their routes crisscrossed the clinic, watching for unknown and unwanted persons. Dada Tommy having finished his breakfast walked to the clinic to see what the lady doctor was up to.

Siva went to Dharavi on his motorbike to locate the clinic and talk to Zahina. He did not notice a man and a woman who got on their motor bike and followed him. Siva got to the clinic at the same time as Dada Tommy. Both looked at each other with suspicion.

"You lied to me and sent me on a wild goose chase," Siva accused.

"What are you doing here? Please leave now or should I throw you out?" said Dada.

"I am a licensed PI in a lawful search for a person. You have no right to stop me."

"Right or not, I am the protector of these people against all dangers."

"I am not here to cause any harm to the doctor. A client of mine is looking for her."

"You may not know, but I know a man is trying to find and harm to her. Your client is that man. When I find him, I will feed him to the dogs."

"My client is a respectable doctor who knew this lady in college, he wants to rekindle their relationship."

"Inspector, sorry ex-inspector, that guy has fooled you. I know for a fact that he is here to harm her. Kudi Doctor herself told me that."

"I don't believe that. She is mistaken, he is as genuine as can be. I am here to negotiate a meeting between these two, for them to resolve their differences."

"Not while I am alive, he will not meet her. It scared her when this fellow's sister appeared at the mosque."

"I didn't even know my client had a sister."

"Like I said before, this guy has fooled you into working for him. I suggest you leave."

"I never left a case unsolved, and this is no exception. If what you are telling me is true, I will get my client arrested and justice delivered."

"Can I trust you inspector? I still owe you."

"I give you my word I have served the laws of this country for many years. You can trust me."

"I accept. It appears the doctor is not here, let me treat you to a cup of tea at our famous dhaba."

Sayeed and Simi watched from a distance, the detective conversing with a person. "We should be careful, or they will spot us. Let us follow the detective and he might lead us to Zahina or Anand," said Sayeed.

#

Anand saw a woman walking towards the dhaba. When she was got closer, he recognized Zahina, took a quick gulp of the remaining tea and got up and hid behind a vendor's cart piled high with red clay water jugs and a clear view of the dhaba. Seeing her Charan burst into a bhajan from the Sikh Holy Book, gave her a hug, said a few words and went to the bubbling stew on the stove to pack some.

Vidya was still kilometers away from the slum, stuck in traffic moving at a snail's pace. *I am late and at this pace it would be all over before I get there to prevent the impending doom.* He noticed motorcycles zigzagging their way through the congestion. He threw a few rupees at the driver and jumped out of the taxi, stopped a motorcycle rider and asked for help. The driver took off the helmet and he saw the face of a young woman with questioning eyes looking at him.

"It is life and death, please take me to Dharavi."

"Why should I help you? How do I know you are not a

kidnapper or a goonda?"

Vidya removed the shawl covering his face and pulled out the cricket ball with the embedded tiger's claw. The woman looked at him in surprise, awe and recognition.

"Please get on, I will take you where you want to go."

"I am in a hurry can you go faster?"

"For you Tiger Wallah, I can make this fly!" said the young woman revving the bike.

#

Dada and another man reached the dhaba while I was waiting for Charan to pack food for me. Hearing their footsteps, I turned around.

"Kudi Doctor, how are you doing? I have here an ex-police inspector who wants to talk to you."

"Why would a police inspector want to talk to me?" I asked anxiously.

"He is not really an inspector, he was once, now a private detective."

"What does he want from me?"

"He is representing a client who wants to meet with you."

"I am not interested in meeting any of his clients."

"He says his client is searching for a long time and does not mean any harm."

"I know he wants to harm me. His sister was also searching for me and I saw her watching at the mosque. I am ashamed to call them Muslims."

"My client is not a Muslim," interjected Siva.

"Sayeed is a Muslim, his sister is a Muslim, his mother is a Muslim," I was angry and frustrated.

"My client is not Sayeed. It is ..."

A loud crash followed by an even louder scream interrupted Siva.

#

Seeing his ex-wife for the first time in over five years, set Sayeed's blood boiling. *This wretched woman stole my son and made me a laughingstock. This is my opportunity to get*

284

revenge out in public, like a man. He stepped forward, his eyes blazing, face flushed, Simi held his hand restraining him. With a violent motion, he pushed her aside and moved at a fast pace towards the dhaba. He pulled the knife that he used to slaughter goats and lambs and moved towards Zahina from the rear. He saw a tall Sikh standing behind Zahina. If I can get him down with one stab, Zahina will be next. *One swoop I will pull her head back and slice her throat in front of her companions.*

Anand was watching Zahina through the gaps in the clay pots, piled three high. A disturbance about fifty yards behind Zahina drew Anand's attention. He saw a man push a woman to the ground and walk towards the dhaba deliberately. Noticing a knife in the man's hands and his fierce look focused on Zahina, Anand suspected the person was heading to attack Zahina.

Anand jumped out toppling the clay pots hiding him and screamed, "Zahina watch out!"

At the sound of my name, I looked towards the voice and saw a man dressed in traditional Indian garb waving frantically and shouting. When I recognized that it was Anand, I let out a surprised scream of my own.

Charan heard Zahina's scream and a guy shouting and waving his hands. He recognized him as Anjan, the guy he met yesterday. Charan moved in front of Zahina and clenched the kada in his left hand to stop the crazy guy in the front.

Sayeed still about fifty feet away saw the tall Sikh move to the front, opening a straight path to Zahina. *Allah the merciful, you have answered my prayers and moved the obstacle.* Sayeed quickened his pace.

Seeing Zahina exposed and the guy with the knife on a straight path to her, Anand ran towards her screaming, "Zahina, DANGER! Behind you. Man with a knife. Somebody stop him. STOP HIM!"

Sayeed was ten feet from Zahina and the knife raised above his head. Anand knew he was too late and far to help. And the knife will plunge into Zahina in just a moment. He ran towards the assailant, shouting and screaming.

Hearing Anand's words, Charan reached behind with his right arm, grabbed Zahina around her waist. In the same motion, he lifted her up and turned around. He was now facing the man with the knife and Zahina was safely behind him. His left fist moved with surprising speed and force. It connected with the temple of the assailant. Sayeed's arm was already moving. As the fist flew to his head, the knife plunged into the left side of Charan's chest. The big Sikh went down in a spray of blood, and Sayeed fell down dazed.

All I saw was Charan falling with bleeding from his chest. I fell to my knees, rolled up my chunni, and shoved it at the wound to staunch the flow of blood. There was no thought of Anand in my mind. The shock of seeing the injured Charan erased everything else. I wasn't sure who the assailant was. *If I stop the bleeding and get Charan quickly to a hospital, he can be saved.*

I looked for Dada and shouted, "Run and get a taxi or a car. "

I paid no attention to the other guy.

A crowd gathered around the dhaba. Nobody thought of picking up the knife lying a few feet away.

#

Anand reached my side and said, "Let me help you."

I paid him no attention. I focused on saving Charan, who saved me by placing himself in harm's way.

"Anand check Charan's pulse and tell me." In a crisis there is no time for niceties or pleasantries, I heard Dr. Khan say more than once.

A minute later Anand announced, "Pulse 120 per minute, regular but weak."

Charan's blood soaked my chunni. I looked around and found a passerby ordered him,

"Run to the clinic and bring all the sterile bandages you can carry. Tell Punam I asked for them."

The guy took off like a jackrabbit towards the clinic. I finally looked at the assailant and saw Sayeed. There was a big knot on his right temple where Charan's fist landed; he lay on the ground groaning.

I turned my attention back to Charan, who was pale and breathing rapidly. *Hold on my brother for a few more minutes, help is coming.* I sang the song he always sang for me. I knew from my experience that when most of the senses have shut down, hearing persists and is the last to go and first to recover. I wanted him to know that I was nearby, and he was in safe hands.

#

Anand's focus was on Zahina, who took charge of the injured man and ordered everybody around. He remembered an Incident Control workshop where he learned that the first person on the scene is in control until someone more experienced or qualified takes control. Zahina knew instinctively what he had to learn through a workshop. He saw her hands steady and her demeanor calm. *Someone who has gone through the fire and hardened.*

CHAPTER 55

No End

Simi saw the Sikh get stabbed and Sayeed taking a punch. My brother will get up in a minute and finish what he wanted all these years. She had a sudden respect for him and his tenacity. She waited a little distance away, wondering why her brother was not getting up. The thought of him lying on the ground in the god forsaken slum angered her. I must help him. She crept closer and saw the knife on the ground. A plan formed in her mind how to turn the tables on those who hurt her brother. She surreptitiously picked up the knife and moved forward.

Anand was admiring Zahina's coolness and poise when he felt a presence at his back. A moment later he felt the sharp blade of the knife across the front of his neck. He froze, unable to fathom what was happening.

"Nobody move, or I will slit this miserable man's neck," a woman screamed.

Everyone stayed where they were. Zahina raised her eyes and saw Simi, holding a knife at Anand's neck. With an evil grin on her face she said, "You were a dishonorable woman then and now. Your time to answer to Allah is coming soon and you will burn in the fires of hell with your lovers. Now listen. Leave the bearded man to die and go help Sayeed. Move now or I will cut this man's throat right in front of you."

While Simi was talking to Zahina, Anand tried to move out of her grasp. He felt a sharp fiery burning on his neck. True to her word, the woman drew the sharp knife across his throat and broke the skin.

"I will kill him with a thousand cuts if you don't revive my brother immediately."

"Sayeed injuries are not grave. He has a blow to his head and is in daze. He will be up in a few minutes with nothing worse than a headache."

Simi drew the knife across Anand's throat again, inflicting another cut, blood trickling in a stream, staining his kurta red.

"What don't you understand, stupid woman? Help Sayeed, or this lover of yours will be dead with my next move?" *I control Zahina as long as I keep this guy alive!!*

#

The motorcycle rider with Vidya arrived at the clinic in Dharavi.

"I don't even know your name, I hope we meet again and thank you," said Vidya.

"My name is Sivangi, means lioness in my language. My father named me aptly and brought me up as he would a son. It is an honor to serve you Tiger Wallah," said the young lady as she throttled her bike and sped away.

Vidya went into the clinic and saw a lady handing out bandages and supplies to a man.

"I am looking for Zahina. Where is she?"

"Kudi Doctor is at the dhaba, where a man tried to stab her. The dhaba wallah who stepped in front, got stabbed in the chest. She is safe."

"My senses tell me she is in mortal danger, show me the way. Let us run as fast as we can. No time to spare," said Tiger Wallah, wrapping the shawl around his face.

#

I got up and checked on Sayeed. His breathing and heart rate were normal. I picked a jug of water from the dhaba and poured it on him. He mumbled, thrashed around for a minute and slowly opened his eyes. Seeing me, he sat up. I backed away and went back to attend to Charan.

A few minutes later, having regained his faculties

somewhat, Sayeed slowly ambled over and asked Simi. "Who is this guy and why are you holding a knife on him?".

"Don't you recognize him from the photo I showed you, that guy with Zahina, her lover. Should I slice his throat?"

"No, my fight is with the infidel woman, not him. Give me my knife," said Sayeed grabbing the knife out of Simi's hands, pulled Zahina away from the dying Sikh and held the knife to her throat.

Tiger Wallah arrived at the gathering, quietly and silently like a stalking feline. Nobody noticed him. He saw terrified Zahina being held by a man behind her with a knife to her throat. If he did not stop the man, he suspected was her ex-husband, would murder her. He knew from where he was, he had no chance; the crowd shielded the man. Tiger Wallah moved sideways to find an opening.

"This is my wife whom I divorced. I will cut her throat if any of you move. Let us leave and I will hurt no one," screamed Sayeed.

"What are you going to do to her? Leave her alone and we will let you go, no questions asked," said Anand, who was now tending Charan.

Sayeed's eyes of turned toward the source of the voice. Tiger Wallah moved looking for an opening among the now dense crowd.

"My plan is to take this woman to a place away from here, recover my son and slit her throat."

Sayeed was dragging me away from gravely injured Charan. In a few steps I with my assailant will be around a corner and out of sight of the dhaba. I looked at Anand my love and mouthed my last words before a certain death, "I am sorry. Please save Charan. Take care of Amrit."

Anguished Anand looked at me but continued caring for Charan.

Tiger Wallah knew that in a few steps the victim and assailant will turn the corner and disappear. The crowds between him and the man holding the knife, obscured a direct line to the man. He was powerless to save Zahina. *Rudra don't let me down.*

Five more steps and I will be around the corner thought Sayeed. I will take this wretched woman out of the city and cut her until she tells me where my son is. I will then slit her throat and watch her die; recover my son and bring him up as a good Muslim. He took another step backward, dragging Zahina in front of him. Four more steps. Sayeed felt his goal for the last few years, within reach. He took another step. Only three more and it will all end soon.

Anand was in a turmoil. *Should I leave the gravely injured Sikh and try to rescue Zahina? What twist of fate brought me this close to my lost love only to be snatched by a maniac intent on ending her life? As a physician I cannot abandon the person under my care. What will I tell Amrit?* Tears were flowing from his eyes as he mouthed the words, "I loved you always. I am sorry for abandoning you. I promise I will look after Amrit."

I knew my life was about to end. I hoped that Vidya would arrive in time and save me. But I did not see Vidya. I took a deep breath resigned for my fate. Looked at Anand as his lips moved to say, "I loved you always, I am sorry for abandoning you. I promise I will look after Amrit." I did not know how I heard those words with all the commotion in front of me or if it was my imagination. I felt relaxed and peaceful knowing that my son will have a father and is unreachable by the brute who is going to end my life. My thoughts turned to my son Amrit and rest of the world around me faded away.

Sayeed took another step. His heart was beating fast with impending fulfillment of his revenge. Two more steps and I will be out of sight of these people. He took another step.

It is now or never thought Tiger Wallah. The cricket ball appeared in his hand. Tiger Wallah crouched with his muscles tensed and his hands and feet pressed to the ground. His right hand held the ever-present cricket ball with the embedded tiger claw. A vision of the tiger's explosive jump on his prey appeared in his mind.

The apprehensive crowd parted and moved away from the crouched masked man, not knowing who he was and what he was up to.

Tiger Wallah sprang up like a coiled spring; a roar erupted from him loud enough to silence the crowd. His upper body rose above the crowd with an unobstructed view of the assailant. As he shot up his left arm extended pointed at the assailant's head and his right hand with the cricket ball extended backwards. A primal scream erupted from Tiger Wallah and in a blur of arm movement the ball flew from his right hand toward the assailant.

I heard the sound and saw Vidya rising above the crowd. His both arms were extended in opposite directions, one holding an object. I felt the pressure of the knife on my neck disappear as a scream erupted. I took the opportunity to move forward a little and used the ball of my left foot to deliver a blow to Sayeed's knee with all my strength.

The ball with the embedded tiger claw shot forward at lightning speed.

Sayeed felt his knee buckle with a crack as the tiger claw on the ball found it's mark and tore open a four-inch gash on his scalp. He uttered a moan and fell down unconscious the knife slipping from his hands.

Tiger Wallah stealthily moved towards the downed man. The silent crowd was noisy again unable to comprehend what happened in front of their eyes moments ago, the roar, the leaping man and the downed assailant. By the time it dawned them that a man in the crowd threw something at the assailant and disabled him, Tiger Wallah retrieved the ball and disappeared.

I turned around to see where the attack came from. I saw Vidya and I nodded at him. Out of the corner of my eye I saw a slight movement, turned my head and saw Simi bending down to reach for the knife just a few feet away. My anger erupted like Mount Vesuvius; her generous rump was an inviting target. I shot out my leg and delivered a mighty kick to her posterior, like a penalty kick in my soccer playing days. Simi ended face first on the ground and started wailing and slowly extended her hand towards the knife again.

I moved over to Simi and delivered another kick this time to the head, "Take that kuttee, this is for the cuts you inflicted on Anand."

"And this is for asking your brother to break my teeth," I said delivering another powerful kick to the head rendering Simi unconscious.

As I turned to look at Charan, I saw Sayeed laying on the ground moaning, his eyes turned to mine. I knew for Charan to survive I must put Sayeed out of action.

Sayeed hollered, "Help me, Zahina, you owe me that much."

I picked up my bag lying on the ground next to Charan, took a handful of cayenne pepper and threw it on Sayeed's face and bleeding scalp.

"Yes, I owe you. Take that you miserable man. Now we are even," I said to the screaming and crying Sayeed.

"Inspector Saab, please secure these two people while I care of Charan. Immobilize them so they cannot interfere with saving Charan," I told Siva, who promptly tied their hands and feet and with a rope.

"I will call the local police and see they receive what is due to them," said Siva.

CHAPTER 56

Saving the Savior

I got to Charan and saw Anand, bleeding from his neck wounds and in a low voice singing the same song I sang a few minutes ago, holding a large gauze pad over the wound on Charan's chest.

Concern for Charan who was barely alive, replaced the stress of the violence. I suspected his pleural space around the lung was filling with blood collapsing the lung. Without immediate surgery and support, he would not survive long.

Soon the summoned taxi arrived, we put Charan's inert body on the rear seat with his head in my lap and Anand, a bandage around his neck in the front seat, headed for the hospital, where I trained and was on the staff. A nurse and I wheeled Charan into the operating room. I ordered two units of O negative blood, 2 liters of Ringers lactate, a blood type test and six additional units of crossmatched blood. While the anesthesiologist was setting up Charan for surgery, I scrubbed and dressed in surgical garb and entered the OR.

In a few minutes Charan was under anesthesia and the Ringer's lactate and the blood were running into two IVs. I grabbed a trocar and plunged it to the left pleural cavity. The blood collected in his chest cavity gushed out, confirming my diagnosis. I let the blood flow out to relieve the pressure on the lung. I remember assisting Dr. Khan twice when he operated on penetrating chest wounds. *Must stop the bleeding to save my savior.* To stop bleeding the chest must be opened. There was no time to summon an experienced surgeon. If I operate and botch it up, I will be responsible for Charan's death. I let my indecision bother me for a moment, took a deep breath and went ahead with surgery.

"Please maintain the vitals and pump blood as fast as you can. Are you ready doctor?" I asked the anesthesiologist.

"Yes, he is all yours."

I made an incision extending the stab wound and located the bleeding artery and tied it. After tying about a dozen smaller blood vessels, the bleeding stopped. The next hour I worked diligently to clear the pleural sack of blood and clots and rinsed it thoroughly with saline.

"BP 100/56, heart rate 106."

I placed a thoracic drain with a water trap for the partially collapsed lung to expand. Once I sutured the wound and applied bandages, I sat down hands shaking, and body shivering as the adrenaline rush vanished and reality dawned.

"I have seen no one with the vitals so poor survive, Dr. Zahina. Your skill and poise saved this man. If I need surgery, I will ask for you," said the elderly anesthesiologist.

"Please see Charan to the recovery room and ask the intern on call to keep a close watch, with vitals every 15 minutes for the first two hours and every hour thereafter. Notify me if there is any downturn. I will be in the doctor's night room."

"Yes, Dr. Zahina."

#

It was dark by the time I changed and got to the room, lay on the bed exhausted physically and mentally and was asleep in a minute. Past midnight I woke up, looked at the watch and realized I slept for about five hours. After a quick wash I went to check on Charan.

"His BP is 110/60, heart rate 90 and respiratory rate 24," the young intern informed her. "He woke up about an hour ago and wanted to know if you were safe and mumbled sorry for not protecting you Dr. Zahina."

"Thanks for your help. I will take over now. You can go back to your room and get some sleep."

#

I sat by Charan's side, holding his hand in mine. Minutes rolled into hours. I saw him slowly waking up. His fingers moved and gripped my hand and his eyes opened, "Kudi Doctor is that you? I was dying and knew it, I saw Devinder beckoning me. I heard your singing and had to come back. I also heard another voice, a man's voice singing. You both brought me back to life. Thank you."

"I almost got you killed Charan, you took the knife, meant for me. I have to thank you."

"I guess it was not our time yet, thank God we are both alive. Who is the other guy?"

"That is Anand, came all the way from America looking for me."

"It must be that crazy guy, breaking all those pots, shouting and waving his hands," said Charan with a faint smile on his face. "He has a pleasant voice, that friend of yours, congratulations."

"I am not sure he came looking for me for that reason....," I said hesitantly.

#

Apprehensive, I went to check on Anand. *Why is he here? Where is my son? What would you say after a decade of separation? What are my true feelings for him? I used the thoughts of him as a staff to support my sagging self. Is there a future for us? The past intruding on the present in the least expected way and making the future uncertain.*

I went over to the emergency room, but Anand was not there. He was discharged after his neck wounds were sutured. Where he went, I did not know. I was relieved I do not have to face Anand immediately after yesterday's traumatic happenings. I needed time to unwind.

#

Anand went looking for Zahina after his neck wounds were sutured. He started at the OR and found no one there. The day's events caught up with him. And he returned to his hotel. *Will I run into Zahina again or she will disappear from my life again? Do I even have the courage to face her after all these years? During yesterday's unplanned and accidental face to face was under extenuating circumstances, all that I heard from Zahina were professional demands as she took charge of the events and the care of her savior. My last memories of her were a happy woman who loved and wanted to be with me. She is now a mature woman, confident of her abilities and the seriousness and nobility that came with executing her heart's desire to serve the poor. How can one find that resolve, strength and commitment in oneself? How did she manage all that chaos and trauma around her and assume leadership of the event and bring it to a successful ending? I hope Zahina will grant me a chance to confess my wrongs and seek forgiveness.*

#

"Zahina."

"Anand."

Anand walked into the clinic next morning while I was with patients. We were looking at each other, too emotionally charged to say anything else. I knew my face was flushed and eyes shimmering. Anand looked like he had seen a ghost. His face was pale, brow glistening with sweat, downcast eyes, and fists clenched. His lips were quivering, but no sounds came out. The shock of yesterday's events had not worn off. *How often does one come across a lost love more than a decade later; immediately face a life-threatening situation orchestrated by a maniac with a knife and his equally ruthless sister; see a best friend stabbed and incapacitated; a man you trust with your life arriving in the nick of time to save; and the hectic actions needed to save the dying savior. What do you say after a lifetime of separation? How do you express your emotions? Will he reciprocate or have the tides of time destroyed our bonds? Is reconciliation possible? Acceptance of the past without regrets? There was enough blame to go around. Is one of us more culpable? Where do we start? Where do we end? Is the beginning of another chapter in our lives together, or is this a brief interlude in our separate lives, with another gut-wrenching separation?*

Anand's thoughts probably mirrored mine.

Anand slowly lifted his eyes to mine, "I came to reunite Amrit with you, Zahina."

His eyes were downcast again.

The word Amrit cleared my mind of all the conflicting emotions. I wanted to ask him about my son, my Amrit. Looking at Anand, I realized he was struggling to say something more. He hasn't changed. The connection between his brain and vocal cords was out of sync. *Is that all he came for, after all these years, to hand me my son?* The joy of getting my son back did not extinguish the angst in my heart. *He better say something to me about our separation and future, to quench my rising anger and disappointment.*

After a long-drawn silence, he raised his eyes to mine and said, "I came to beg you to forgive me for what I did. I understand if you cannot forgive me. When Amrit said, 'My mom's name is Zahina' I knew I cannot live with myself, taking him away from you. He wants you. He wants to be with you. I promised Amrit I will reunite him with his mom."

Anand came for reuniting me with my son. With this mission accomplished, is he ready to disappear? How many times have I dreamt of this moment when this knight in shining armor comes to sweep me off my feet and make me forget all the indignities I endured? It overjoyed me knowing that Amrit and I will be together. Is that enough? I did not say a word, just looked at a disturbed Anand. I kept quiet, knowing he wants to say something more and I did not want to interrupt his thoughts or change the subject to Amrit, however I much I wanted to.

After what felt like an eternity, he started speaking, "Zahina I have wronged and caused you insufferable pain and misery. There are no words to express how ashamed of myself and my behavior. I want you to know that I have always loved you and still do. I understand that you have every reason to despise me and if you want nothing to do with me, I will accept it as my penance."

Why doesn't he say what he wants directly, instead of beating around the bush? What does he want me to do? Explain to him what I went through when he left me for America? The horrors, mental and physical tortures. Tell him how in depression, I tried to kill myself?

I who always ready with words was tongue tied, unable to vocalize and kept mum.

In that small, cramped room in the clinic, my home, with patients trickling in, Anand fell to his knees, looking up at me with his large brown eyes filled with anguish, and said, "Zahina come with me to America, reunite with your son; stay for a while, or as long as you wish. If you do not want to share my home, I will move out. I will not make any demands on you. You can leave whenever you want to. Take Amrit with you. If you decide to stay you will make me the happiest person on this earth. I will cherish you and take care of you. Please come with me, Zahina."

"Stop being dramatic Anand. I have deep roots here that are difficult to break. Stay here for a week and let us get to know each other again. Neither of us, are what we were then. No promises, let us give it a week and see what is in store for us. Now tell me about my son! Everything he did and said, from the day I let him go. Do not miss a single minute or word."

"I have a better idea why don't you talk to him on the phone, he will be so happy to hear your voice, Zahina. Let us go to my hotel, we will book a call from there. I have a car waiting."

CHAPTER 57

Treading Softly

We talked on the way and waiting for the call, not like two who were close friends and in love once, but as strangers talking awkwardly, both treading carefully not to say something that would blow up this long-sought reunion.

When the call came, Anand answered and briefly talked to Diana, waited a minute and said, "Amrit I have someone who wants talk to you," and handed me the phone.

I picked up the phone, my eyes pouring out tears of happiness and said, "Amri my son, this is Ammi."

"Ammi. AMMI. My AMMI," screams erupted on the other end. "I miss you, Ammi. Come soon, Ammi, come now."

Amrit and I talked, babbled and cried on the phone for a long time. With a heavy heart I handed the phone to Anand. He explained to Amrit, "Your mom is thinking of the trip and it might take a week or more to get her there. If she cannot come, I will bring you here to be with your mom as I promised."

He talked to Diana and handed me the phone, "Diana wants to say hello."

"Hello, I am Diana. I am looking after Amrit while Anand's away. You have a lovely and handsome son. You must be very proud of him," Diana said in a soft, pleasant and American accented voice.

"Yes, he is an exceptional kid, but I did not spend as much time with him as I should have. Thank you very much for the trouble you took to care for my son. I owe you a lot."

"He is no trouble, a gentle soul, likes to play with my daughters who adore their little brother. Please come and visit us when you come here. Anand is like a brother to me. I am sure you will like it here."

"Yes, if I come to America, I will meet with you."

The call ended and I looked at Anand and said, "Thank you for taking my son out of trouble and finding a safe place for him. I am also very grateful to you for coming to find me and unite me with my Amrit."

"There is nothing I can do to correct the wrongs I did to you Zahina."

"I have my share of wrongs to go around. I did not have the courage to defend myself or the strength to control my wandering and depressed mind after we went different ways."

Anand wanting to change the topic said, "Who was that man who came in suddenly and subdued Sayeed yesterday and disappeared? Do you know him?"

I looked at him with a slight smile on my face, "The world knows him as Tiger Wallah, who went after a wild tiger to retrieve a precious object, a cricket ball you gave him when you were kids."

It took Anand a few moments to digest the facts and his eyes opened wide and with a surprised look on his face said, "That can't be Vidya, he was so meek and mild those days."

A few moments later as he connected the dots, "Oh my God! It was you who took care of me in the Naxalite camp. I asked Tiger Wallah many times and he said I was hallucinating. How can I thank you for saving my life? Zahina, please tell me what happened to you."

#

I began from the day he left till yesterday told him my story. "That brings us to the current moment," I said finishing my story.

Anand's face was crestfallen, realizing he was the primary cause of my troubles.

"Come with me, be with your Amrit. Make your home in

301

America. I will be there for you. I cannot undo what my actions have done to you, but I will take care of you and Amrit until my last breath. You both will be safe there," said a distraught Anand.

"Is that all Anand, after all these years, is there nothing else you want to say to me? About us?"

"I want to tell you the same thing I said to you in the park a thousand years ago. But I do not know what your feelings towards me are, after all these years?"

"Whatever you want to say, say it and I will give you an answer. But before you say anything, I want you to talk to Vidya and get his approval. I will not go against his wishes. I trust him with my life. He is the only guardian I have left in this world," I said and noticed the despondent look on Anand's face.

I knowingly brought Vidya into the mix, not only to make Anand face Vidya and explain himself but also to have time to think about what Anand was proposing before accepting. Moving to America and breaking my roots and bonds I developed here during the last five years and all the people who depend on me for their medical care is something I cannot do easily. I need time to sort my priorities and responsibilities and plan if I were to accompany Anand.

"Get me in touch with Vidya, Zahina. Let me try to convince him."

#

"Anand, you broke your promise to the woman you loved, and I respected, made her life miserable and let her spend over a decade in hell. Why would I even speak to you now or when you were a prisoner of the Naxalites? Because of your mom."

"I am not asking you to forgive me or restore our friendship. I messed up Zahina's life and I don't dare ask her for forgiveness. I regret my behavior and abandoning her. I want to at least make it partly right getting her together with Amrit. She asked me to persuade you to let this happen. I am grateful to you for taking care of her. If there is anything I can do to repay you, please let me know. I will be indebted to you for the rest of my life."

"I am not capable of judging or chastising anyone, Anand. Tell me honestly, if I let Zahina go with you, will you keep her and Amrit safe and care for them? I promised you once I will take care of Zahina. Those words are as true today as they were then. Before I let her go with you, I must be sure you will take care of her. Convince me."

"Yes, I will take care of them both, keep them safe and comfortable. Provide for Amrit's education and wellbeing. If they want to stay in America or return here, I will provide for them. I promise I will keep my word."

Vidya grabbed Anand by his shoulders and pulled him close, "Look into my eyes and say you are telling me the truth."

Anand's face was less than a foot from Vidya's, as he stared into the harsh piercing eyes of his friend and said, "Yes, I told you the truth. I will take care of them. Please let her go with me. Your promise is fulfilled. Zahina is now my responsibility."

The fierce look of Vidya softened and he pulled Anand into an embrace, "I knew you would come one day looking for Zahina. I had to test you with fire to be sure. That is why I wouldn't let Zahina reveal herself to you in the forest. She will always be a young girl in my eyes, though she is a mature, capable woman now, and is still madly in love with you. Let her express that in her own way. Be patient with her, love and cherish her, the sister of Tiger Wallah."

"Why don't you come with us to America and stay with us for a while?"

"I have to decline, Anand. Growing up, I moved from a city to a town to a village and then to a forest. That is where I am most comfortable. For me, America is as far from the forest as we are from the moon."

"Thank you Vidya, before I go back to America, can I come to visit you and your family. Maybe we can cook some rice and dal one day."

"Yes, I like that, but now I have to go back to my forest. We have selected a tigress, mate for Rudra. It is time we take the couple home, a forest your mother set aside for them."

#

"Zahina, I talked to Vidya he agreed to my request."

"Request for what Anand?"

"That you accompany me to America."

"For what Anand?"

"To be with your son and be safe?"

"Is that all? Aren't you missing something?"

"I want to be with you. I want to be with you always forever."

"Why?"

"Because I never stopped loving you, Zahina. You are my one and only love, from the day I met you the first time till I die."

"Why did you abandon me, Anand? Is it the way to treat one you love?"

"Someday when I gather enough courage, I will tell you how I strayed, but for now leave it."

"I will hold you to that."

"You haven't given me an answer."

"I loved you always Anand, but we are not the same young hormonally charged kids anymore. That love and the unwavering belief that you will come back kept me alive during my hard times. I waited for you all these years to come and rescue me. But now I have roots and responsibilities here. Let me think through these and plan before I leave with you. There are a few people to talk to and get advice from. One of them Charan, my adopted brother, is in the hospital recovering from a stabbing that was meant for me. The other is Dr. Khan, who guided me like a father through my tough years. I do not know how I can even broach this topic with Dada Tommy and Punam. My love for Amrit is pulling me toward USA, but my feet are grounded here in this slum. Give me time."

#

Anand was ready to return home, I said to "I need two weeks to sort my affairs and decide about going to America."

"While you sort out your affairs here, I will return to America to be with Amrit. I will call you every day. Tell me your decision and I will abide by it," said Anand.

Two weeks of talks and discussions which involved finding a replacement doctor for the clinic, convincing Dada Tommy and Punam that I must leave to be safe with my son and finally get the blessings from Charan my adopted brother who has recovered enough to be out of the hospital to be back at his dhaba. I was ready to decide.

"Anand, I made up my mind. I will go to USA to be with my son. After I spend a few weeks or months, I will decide if I can stay there or not. I don't have the courage or clarity of thought to make a binding decision. I am sorry, but my thoughts are wandering, and I am indecisive. Not that I don't trust you, I don't trust myself to make the right decision. Are you ok with that?"

"Yes, Zahina. I will facilitate and support any decision you make. I promise you."

"Can I trust you with all travel arrangements? I don't know where to start."

"Yes, I will make all the arrangements," replied Anand.

CHAPTER 58

Reunion

Anand returned with an approved visa and tickets. We landed in his hometown a week later. Amrit was waiting with a Chinese man, an American woman and their twin daughters, for me when we arrived.

Amrit came running towards me, screaming, "Ammi. Ammi. I missed you."

I picked him in my arms, my tears flowing. We hugged and cried and laughed while others stayed aside, letting mother and son get reacquainted. Anand introduced his friend Sun, his lovely wife Diana and their twin daughters. My new support group and my family in America.

#

We went from the airport to their home, where Amrit was staying with his adopted sisters. USA was an unfamiliar experience, the openness of the people and their acceptance of strangers into their homes. I remembered the first letter Anand wrote from USA more than a decade ago, 'sticklers for rules but generous in heart.'

My heart was overflowing with conflicting emotions, happy for reuniting with my son, concerned about leaving my country, my acquaintances and the people of Dharavi dependent on me behind, the unsettled issue of Anand and my relationship, what my future holds for me in this society and a myriad others. I resolved to take things as they come and not worry too much. Time to enjoy my son, meet people and learn about this society.

Diana was a blessing, taking me out when Amrit was at school and helping me get used to America and its people. Most days when the kids were at school we got together and talked about our lives and aspirations. She was my source for Anand's life since she met him.

"He is a quiet and hardworking doctor, according to my husband. I have never seen him go out with any woman. I knew his past troubled him. Anand never admitted or explained to us what it was. Now hearing from you, I understand his sorrow at losing you. I do not know what caused him to break communication with you, and all his friends," said Diana.

"If he still loves me, he has never expressed it to me. I really do not know what my future holds or what I should do. I cannot stay here if he does not want me."

"I know that Anand has difficulty expressing his feelings, give him time and do not make any hasty decisions. If you want my unsolicited advice, take the initiative. I know he has great love for you and is sorry that he caused all your problems, including taking Amrit from you."

I left the meeting still unsure of my future with Anand and what I should do next.

#

Three weeks passed and Anand and I were not any closer, we were still two individuals sharing a roof. One day after supper, I retreated with my son to our bedroom. I read 'Green Eggs and Ham' to Amrit, who fell asleep before I finished. I brushed and changed and slid into my bed. I tossed around unable to sleep, my insecurities playing havoc with my mind. I decided to have a cup of tea and forget about sleeping. I settled down on the kitchen table with tea. My thoughts were swirling in my mind like clouds before an impending storm. *Does Anand truly love me? If he does, what should I do? Leave all in Dharavi and India behind? What if he doesn't? Should I move out with my son and resettle in America or return to India? Does the move back to Dharavi, endanger my safety and Amrit's?* Caught between conflicting priorities and indecisiveness, immersed in my thoughts, I was startled by a sudden cry. I went upstairs to check Amrit who was asleep. Another cry. I quickly went down and knocked on Anand's door. Another cry, and I pushed open the door and went in; saw Anand thrashing on the bed and moaning.

Concerned that he was unwell, I shook him by his shoulders, and said, "Anand are you ok?"

Anand opened his eyes with a lost look on his face. His eyes roamed around unfocussed and confused until they settled on mine. The tense look on his face disappeared.

He grabbed my hands and said, "Zahina, thank god you are still here."

"I have been here all these three weeks. Where would I go?"

"I dreamt that you took Amrit and left me. It seemed so real. I could not survive if I lose you again."

"It was you who left me Anand, WHY?"

Still holding my hands, he stood up and sat me down on his bed, knelt on the floor. In the soft glow of the night lamp his eyes were shiny with tears. He was struggling to vocalize, and I knew I must stay quiet.

After a few minutes, he found his voice, "Zahina I loved you then, never stopped loving you. I cannot forgive myself for my indiscretion. I strayed Zahina, in a moment of weakness and doomed you to misery and unmentionable indignities. I then erroneously decided that you would be happy without me in your life, and it would be best if you forgot me."

"You should have at least let me know why you stopped all communications and disappeared, Anand."

After an interminable silence Anand started talking and there was no stopping him; about his arrival in USA; the meeting an American woman; the Christmas party; the drive around town; the visit to her apartment; the short affair; the breakup; the guilt of breaking his promise to his real love; the decision to withdraw from all further relationships.

My mind was in a turmoil learning of the events that sealed

my fate. *If I knew this, would I have forgiven Anand and escaped all the indignities of an unwanted marriage?* I raised my eyes to his and saw tears flowing down Anand's eyes and my heart melted at that sight of this boy/man, my only love. I placed my hands on his head, gently running my fingers through his and pulled him forward. Anand rested his head on my knees, and I waited for him to regain his composure.

"Anand you should have told me, we could have prevented all the turmoil and unpleasantness. In love we share, understand and accept besides love and lust, our desires, aspirations, failures, shortcomings, disagreements and wrongs. Only then we can nurture our love and make it everlasting. Can you promise me that, that you will from now on Anand?"

"Zahina, I am humbled by your strength and wisdom. I promise you all that you ask. Please tell me you forgive me."

"I loved you then and always. Only the thought this day would come one day, gave me hope and strength to survive the last decade. There is no need for asking or forgiving," I said, stood up and pulled Anand up, embraced him and rested my head on his shoulder, with a feeling of fulfillment and content that I have not had all these years.

"Be gentle Anand," I said as we went to bed together that night. His gentle ministrations lessened my anxiety. We had a blissful consummation of our love that night.

#

"By the powers granted by the State of Louisiana, I hereby pronounce you husband and wife. You may kiss the bride now!" pronounced the Judge.

With those words Anand and I were married, witnessed by my beaming son Amrit, Diana, Sun and their twin daughters.

The same week after more legal proceedings, Anand became Amrit's legal father.

My quest has ended, and I fulfilled my lifelong dream.

#

Six months passed and I realized I was pregnant, "Anand

you are about to become a father," I announced one morning.

"I couldn't be happier. You already gave me one son and the second will complete our family. Thank you, my love Zahina," said Anand embracing me and showering me with kisses.

#

My second son Arjun is 6 months old, and I am content with my life. I have settled into a routine in America and was preparing to take the tests to join a residency program. I wrote a letter to Dr. Khan of my decision and profusely thanked him for all the encouragement and support I received from him. Two weeks later I received his reply, which I anxiously opened.

My dear Beti Zahina,

I am very happy for you and Anand with whom you share your life. He is a very fortunate fellow to have you as his wife and life's companion. I am convinced you will succeed in all your endeavors, knowing your skills, unshakable determination and selflessness.

When I asked you to go to Dharavi, it was because I wasn't prepared to go there myself. Your service there and the respect and admiration you earned from the people was the hallmark of your character. I too learned a lot from you during those years; your absolute commitment to the destitute has taught me the most important lesson of my life. There is no better cause than serving the poor and neglected. I could not and would not let all the work you did go to waste. I am now running the Municipal Health Clinic, which the people of Dharavi renamed "Kudi Clinic" in your honor. I will try my best to follow your footsteps, but alas I can never match your degree of commitment.

You are like a daughter to me, and I will greatly miss your presence. When you come to India, please pay me a visit.

Yours Sincerely,
Ahmed Khan

The letter brought to surface emotions and thoughts, if

unchecked, could disrupt my family life.

EPILOGUE

3 Years Later

I came home from the hospital that Saturday evening having spent the last two days on call as a second-year surgical resident. Nobody was home, I knew Anand would be out with the kids at the park; a few minutes to wash up, change and rest after the grueling on call for 36 hours. In the bedroom, I found a letter from Dr. Khan waiting for me on my dresser. I quickly showered, changed, settled on the bed and opened the letter.

My dear Beti Zahina,

I am glad to hear of your experiences as a surgical resident. I know in my heart that you will succeed and excel in your chosen field. I am honored to be a part of your early training. Inshah Allah, maybe I will learn some new techniques from you.

Though I wish it to come true, alas it will not. I was diagnosed with acute myeloid leukemia and am undergoing chemotherapy for the last two months. Until today, I was working at your clinic. Progression of the leukemia forces me to quit in the next few days. Inshah Allah, I will succeed in my effort to find a replacement doctor.

Everything, good or bad, has its own lifespan, Zahina. However, much we try, nature takes its own unalterable course. You and I provided a necessary service to our brothers and sisters in Dharavi, but I am afraid it is ending.

As you know, I have no children and my wife of forty-seven years has left me for her heavenly abode years ago. I always considered you my daughter. I am leaving all my earthly possessions to you and your children. My lawyer will contact and send you all the important papers.

Next time you go to the Mosque, say a prayer for me. Reply soon because I have little time left in this world.

Yours Sincerely,

Ahmed Khan

#

Anand and kids came home after playing in the park, eager to see Zahina after a two-day hiatus. Anand was surprised to find the house dark and the always smiling Zahina not in the hallway, waiting for them. He went looking for her and found her in the bedroom, sitting motionless and staring into space. Anand went to her and gently turned her face towards him and looked into her eyes. The same look that pierced his heart many years ago adorned Zahina's face. He did not know what calamity brought it on but suspected the life Zahina and he built together was in trouble.

GLOSSARY

Amma (Telugu): Mother, respectful way to address of any
  woman
Anapakaya (Telugu): A large green gourd.
Apasmara (Sanskrit): An evil being, a demon.
As-salāmu ʿalaykum (Arabic): Muslim greeting.
Aʿalaykumu as-salām (Muslim response to greeting)
Baiganwadi: Slum in Bombay.
Bandi (Telugu): Cart, usually drawn by ox or horse
Bandi Wallah: One who drives the bandi
Beti: Daughter.
Bhai (Hindi): Brother.
Bhajan (Hindi): A musical religious recital.
Birbal (Name): A Minister in Emperor Akbar's court
Chacha (Hindi): Paternal Uncle.
Chappals (English): Footwear similar to flip-flops.
Chotu (Hindi, Punjabi): Affectionate address to a
  youngster or younger brother.
Chulla (Hindi): A metal or earthen stove fired with wood
  or coals or other soil fuel, for cooking.
Chunni (Hindi): A woman's long colorful scarf worn over
  shoulders and sometimes over the head.
Churidar (Hindi): Woman's trousers/pajamas.
Dandakaranya (Hindi, Telugu): The great forest that

occupies middle of India.

Dhaba (Hindi): Roadside restaurant usually a shack.

Dharmsala (Hindi, Sanskrit): Free or low cost, short stay housing for travelers.

Dholak (Hindi): Small Indian drum.

Divali (Hindi): The festival of lights celebrating victory of good over evil with fireworks.

Dupatta (Hindi): A shawl like covering used mostly by women.

Dura (English): Thick fibrous membrane that covers the brain

Frozen Section (English): A slide preparation technique using quick frozen tissue for rapid diagnosis.

Goonda (Telugu): Ruffian, thug.

Granthi (Punjabi): Head priest of Gurudwara (Sikh Place of worship).

Hajj: Annual Muslim pilgrimage to Mecca.

Hanuman (Telugu, Hindi): The monkey god who accompanied Rama with his army of monkeys, to fight Ravana who kidnapped, Rama's wife Sita.

HMB45 (English): A cell protein used for diagnosis of melanoma

Indra: Indian God.

Jaggery (English): Solidified cane juice used in lieu of sugar.

Jatka (Telugu): A horse drawn carriage.

Juuta (Hindi): Shoe / Chappal.

Kali: (Telugu, Hindi): Demon slaying Goddess.

Kameez (Urdu, Hindi): See Kurta.

Karivepaku (Telugu): A green curry leaf.

Keertan / kirtan/ (Hindi): A religious recital.

Khadi (Hindi, Telugu): A home spun cotton fabric.

Kheer (Hindi): A pudding made with milk, sugar and nuts with broken rice / wheat / vermicelli etc.

Kheer (Hindi): A sweet rice or noodle dish cooked in milk with raisins and nuts.

Kumkum (Telugu): A red powder used in religious
ceremonies and on foreheads of married women.

Kurta (Hindi): A long dress tops worn over churidar.

Kutti: Female dog. Does not have the same implication of
the American word 'Bitch'.

La illaha illa-Allah ...(Arabic): ...there is no God but
Allāh... Muslim prayer.

Laddu (Telugu): A sweet commonly served during festive
meals.

Lathi: A wooden stave used by police in crowd control.

Lungi (Telugu, Tamil): a traditional dress in the southern
state of Madras, consisting of a long cloth that
extends from the waist to the toes that is worn
wrapped around the waist.

Masala Dosa (Telugu): A savory pancake made with
fermented rice flour and lentils served with spicy
potatoes.

Mela (Hindi): A large group celebration.

Mirch Masala (Hindi): Green Peppers cooked with spices.

Moksha (Telugu, Sanskrit): Liberation of soul from the
cycle of life and death, the highest goal to achieve
for Hindus; a transcendental stage, reached by
renouncement of earthly ties and possessions, that
frees one from the cycle of rebirth.

Naan (Hindi, Punjabi): Unleavened flat bread cooked in a
tandoor.

Namaste, Namaskar: (Telugu, Hindi): The traditional
greeting in India with hands folded together and
head bowed

Nil Gai (Hindi): Blue deer, Indian antelope.

Pakora: A spicy savory deep fried fritter usually made
with chickpea flour.

Pallu: The part of sari, that goes around the shoulders
covering the chest.

Panchayat (Hindi, Telugu): Traditional village council
made of five elders.

Pandavas (Telugu, Sanskrit): Five just brothers in the great Indian epic Mahabharata who fought the unjust Kauravas.

Pappu (Telugu): A dish made with lentils.

Paramannam (Telugu): A sweet rice based desert made with jaggery and milk, enhanced with raisins and nuts; may be flavored with saffron; served on auspicious occasions.

Pavbhaji (Gujrati, Hindi): A street side spicy snack of cooked vegetables on a bun.

Phool Wallah (Hindi): Flower (phool) vendor.

Poori Aloo (Hindi): A deep fried puffed bread served with spicy potatoes.

Ras am (Telugu): Peppery thin watery soup made using tamarind and spices.

Rupee: Indian currency (1 USD = 5 Rupees approximately in 1960's).

Sadhu (Telugu): A Holy person who has renounced worldly possessions and connections.

Sahib (Urdu): Respectful addressing of someone of higher stature, akin to sir.

Salwar (Urdu, Hindi): A full length trousers worn by women.

Sambar: A savory spicy lentil based soup with vegetables and tamarind.

Sahib: A respectful way of addressing.

Shabad (Punjabi, Hindi): A musical religious recital.

Shehnai (Hindi): Musical instrument.

Shiva (Telugu, Hindi): One of the trinities of Hinduism, the protector and slayer of evil.

Shukria (Hindi, Urdu): Thanks.

Sindhur (Syn. Sindhoor, Sindoor) (Hindi): A red powder or paste used to mark the forehead during religious ceremonies; also used to mark the forehead of married Hindu women.

Tahsildar, Tehsildar (Telugu, Urdu, Hindi): Tax collector

and record keeper.

Tirupathi: Place in Andhra Pradesh where the Lord Venkateshwara's temple is located.

Tulsi, Tulasi (Telugu): Holy Basil, used in religious ceremonies.

Vaisakhi: Indian festival of spring; the new year day for Sikhs.

Venkateshwara (Telugu): One of the incarnations of Vishnu, one of the Trinities of Hinduism.

Yard Coffee: The coffee is brought in a glass with another empty glass. The waiter while pouring the coffee from the top glass to the bottom and rapidly pulls the glasses apart as much as his arms allow and as swiftly brings the glasses together without spilling a drop.

Wallah (Arabic, Urdu): Someone from-Delhi wallah or someone of a profession-Taxi Wallah.

AFTERWORD

Zahina's story is a dark one, a darkness that consumes about ten years of her life. It depicts the life of some Indian women's fate of oppression and domination, due to cultural and religious beliefs, societal constraints, lack of judicial support and poor administration of existing laws. In trying not to make the story too melodramatic, many of the dark years of Zahina's experiences are condensed; a sample of day to day abuses Zahina bore give the reader an insight into her life. I tried to avoid a prosecutorial detail of the abuses she endured

Zahina's experiences are not because of her Muslim faith. Abuse happens to Indian women of all faiths, Hindus, Sikhs, and Christians and others, crosses economic, class and educational boundaries. Fortunately, it is not rampant but does occur with a fair regularity. *Readers would agree that even once is too many.*

The abusers are not the only evil. Those who prey on uneducated, uninformed, and gullible public to purvey and preach their misguided and misinterpreted societal and religious dogmas, for their personal gains are the promoters of this abuse. Thi is not restricted to the Indian subcontinent. I know of three young Indian women who were abused and escaped their husbands and their in-laws, each from highly educated upper middle-class families, in my small town in America.

Readers will note that though early Zahina chapters are dark, they will see the light trickling through at the far end. As I write this story, I did not know how far it is or if there are other dark areas beyond. I hope this young lady finds true happiness in the end.

ACKNOWLEDGEMENTS

First and foremost, my wife Amarjit for her support and encouragement.

My sister in law Late Sita Devi for the oil painting of Tiger -- cover picture.

Michael D. Wynne for help and support in formatting.

Many who previewed the manuscript and told their stories that helped in creating the current work.

Made in the USA
Middletown, DE
10 October 2022

12417313R00186